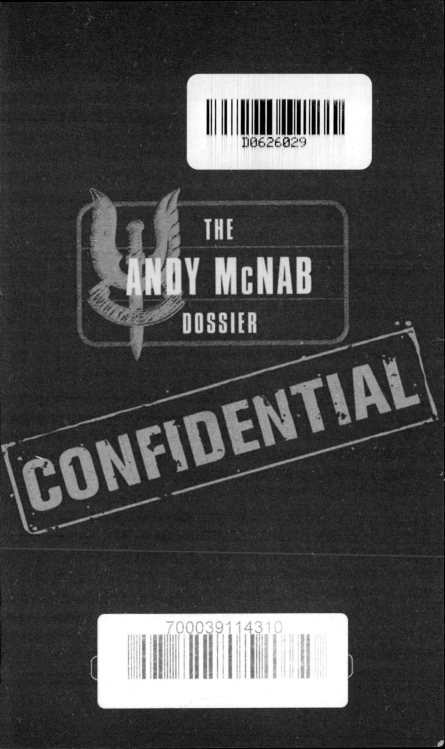

D0626029

THE
ANDY McNAB
DOSSIER

CONFIDENTIAL

700039114310

ANDY McNAB

➲ In 1984 he was 'badged' as a member of 22 SAS Regiment.

➲ Over the course of the next nine years he was at the centre of covert operations on five continents.

➲ During the first Gulf War he commanded Bravo Two Zero, a patrol that, in the words of his commanding officer, 'will remain in regimental history for ever'.

➲ Awarded both the Distinguished Conduct Medal (DCM) and Military Medal (MM) during his military career.

➲ McNab was the British Army's most highly decorated serving soldier when he finally left the SAS in February 1993.

➲ He is a patron of the *Help for Heroes* campaign.

➲ He is now the author of twelve bestselling thrillers, as well as two Quick Read novels, *The Grey Man* and *Last Night Another Soldier*.

'A richly detailed picture of life in the SAS'
Sunday Telegraph

BRAVO TWO ZERO

In January 1991, eight members of the SAS regiment,
under the command of Sergeant Andy McNab, embarked
upon a top secret mission in Iraq to infiltrate them deep behind enemy lines. Their call sign: 'Bravo Two Zero'.

IMMEDIATE ACTION

The no–holds–barred account of an extraordinary life,
from the day McNab as a baby was found in a carrier bag
on the steps of Guy's Hospital to the day he went to fight in
the Gulf War. As a delinquent youth he kicked against
society. As a young soldier he waged war against the IRA
in the streets and fields of South Armagh.

SEVEN TROOP

Andy McNab's gripping account of the time he served in
the company of a remarkable band of brothers. The things
they saw and did during that time would take them all
to breaking point - and some beyond - in the years that
followed. He who dares doesn't always win . . .

SPOKEN
FROM
THE FRONT

Real Voices from the Battlefields
of Afghanistan

Edited by
Andy McNab

CORGI BOOKS

TRANSWORLD PUBLISHERS
61–63 Uxbridge Road, London W5 5SA
A Random House Group Company
www.rbooks.co.uk

**SPOKEN FROM THE FRONT
A CORGI BOOK: 9780552160803**

First published in Great Britain
in 2009 by Bantam Press
an imprint of Transworld Publishers
Corgi edition published 2010

Addresses for Random House Group Ltd companies outside the UK
can be found at: www.randomhouse.co.uk
The Random House Group Ltd Reg. No. 954009

The Random House Group Limited supports The Forest Stewardship
Council (FSC), the leading international forest certification organisation.
All our titles that are printed on Greenpeace approved FSC certified
paper carry the FSC logo. Our paper procurement policy can be found at
www.rbooks.co.uk/environment

Mixed Sources
Product group from well-managed
forests and other controlled sources
www.fsc.org Cert no. TT-COC-2139
© 1996 Forest Stewardship Council

Typeset in 11.5/15pt Palatino by
Falcon Oast Graphic Art Ltd.
Printed in the UK by CPI Cox & Wyman, Reading, RG1 8EX.

2 4 6 8 10 9 7 5 3 1

SPOKEN FROM THE FRONT

Prologue

April 2008

Ranger Jordan Armstrong, The Royal Irish Regiment

I joined up to go to Afghanistan – just as our boys were starting to go to Helmand province. I wanted to experience the fighting. I saw it as a challenge. I knew before signing papers in the careers office that I would go to Afghanistan. I had seen videos of the boys in Afghanistan. It definitely looked mad but I still wanted to try it. I always got a nervous feeling just thinking about it.

We flew to Afghanistan for my first tour on 25 March 2008. I had been abroad once before – to the South of France for holidays and that was it. We flew out from [RAF] Brize Norton [in Oxfordshire] to Kandahar. I was thinking: This is it. I'm going to do whatever I have to do and hopefully I will come back. I had butterflies when we were on the runway at Brize Norton. I thought: I have a long six months ahead of me. My first impression when I arrived in Afghanistan was of the heat and dust – and how flat it was. It was flat in Camp Bastion. I'm an LMG [light machine-gun] gunner. That is my weapon. I'm trained to fire it. I was in Corporal Harwood's section. There were eight of us in it.

April 7 was a bad day. The ANP [Afghan National Police] came back from a patrol to Sangin DC [District Centre]. We were supposed to go out at the same time that they came back in – around three [a.m.]. But the FSG [fire support group] boys were firing off Javelins [anti-tank missiles]. One got fired and instead of going off into the distance it actually landed in the camp [Sangin DC]. But it didn't explode so they cordoned it off. This meant our patrol was delayed. It was good for us because we were then still at the base to deal with a major incident.

An RPG [rocket-propelled grenade] being carried in a bag by the ANP went off inside the camp. I think it was dropped by mistake. They had been carrying the RPGs in a bag on their backs. It blew up seven of them. Two of the men were killed, others lost limbs. It had gone off at the back of the base – Sangar [small fortified position] Two. It was an ND – negative discharge. I don't know if it was bad drills or bad luck.

We were nearby unloading. I ran over with the others. I saw a lot of boys with their guts hanging out. There was one being carried away with both legs blown off above the knees. He wasn't screaming. He was quiet. We got them [the injured] on stretchers and took them over to the med centre. I had to pick up one of the dead boys. His back was blown out and I had to throw him up in the truck. It sounds a bit rough to throw him in the back of a Land Rover but that was what I was told to do.

I hadn't seen anything like that before [Armstrong was then just nineteen and only two weeks into his first tour]. I was actually all right when I saw them [dead and maimed bodies]. I wasn't sure whether I was going to be sick but as soon as I saw them I was all right. I thought I would have been faintish, but I wasn't. We had a good platoon sergeant. He took control and said: 'Get a grip, boys. Just get the job done.' Some boys were sick, though – they couldn't handle it. You don't know how it's going to affect you until you see it.

Acknowledgements by Andy McNab

It's easy to know where to begin my thank-you list. I'm grateful to all those servicemen and women who have contributed to this book. Without their offerings – and their time and patience – there would have been no book. I am indebted to those who provided the outstanding raw material that I have simply had to edit.

More than twenty people have contributed three or more stories to this book. Each has a potted biography detailing his or her life and career before the first story they tell. In addition to these servicemen and women, I would like to thank two soldiers for their single, but nevertheless significant, contributions.

The first is Captain Kate Philp, whom I met and interviewed during my visit to Afghanistan late last summer. She was charming and fun and I would have interviewed her again, but on 15 November 2008, the Warrior armoured vehicle she was

ACKNOWLEDGEMENTS

travelling in was blasted by an improvised
explosive device. Her left foot was so severely
shattered that it had to be amputated. I salute her
courage as she recovers from her injuries and I
thank her for allowing me to publish her interview
from last year. The second soldier I would like to
thank is Fusilier Daniel Wright, from 1 Battalion The
Royal Welsh, who has allowed me to publish
the poem he wrote while serving in Afghanistan.

A big debt of gratitude is owed to the Ministry of
Defence (MoD) for the way it has embraced this
project so fully. The MoD provided me with un-
paralleled access to servicemen and women in
Afghanistan. In particular, I would like to thank
Captain Dave Rigg MC for his commitment to the
book. Before leaving the Army last year, Dave
helped gather together those who were willing to
contribute their stories. He is one of the 'voices' in
the book and he also sat in on several of the interviews. Sam Harrison, from the MoD's press office,
also helped me greatly in the later stages. Many
other senior military personnel have assisted in
numerous ways, and I thank them all.

This book highlights the courage of those on the
front line. My thanks go to Mark Lucas, my literary
agent at LAW, and Bill Scott-Kerr, the publisher at
Transworld, for being so enthusiastic about the
project from the start and, more importantly, for
bringing it to fruition so quickly.

Last but not least, I would like to thank Tony

ACKNOWLEDGEMENTS

Lynch, my business partner in our media company Spoken Group, who accompanied me to Afghanistan last year. Tony kept me 'on message'; otherwise I would have sat about with a brew, waffling on to the troops and going on patrol without asking them a single question.

Introduction by Andy McNab

Real Voices

This is a book about modern-day heroes fighting a modern-day war: a conflict in Afghanistan that has so far claimed the lives of over 250 British service-men and women. *Spoken from the Front* shows the courage of British servicemen and support staff as they faced the unique difficulties posed by ongoing conflict in a country ravaged by war.

Last year I had the idea of producing a book based on the stories of our men and women who have served on the front line in Afghanistan. I didn't want to tell their stories for them: I wanted them to give their own accounts in their own words. I was fortunate: the MoD liked my proposal and gave me access to soldiers (of all ranks), pilots, reservists, engineers, medics, Royal Military Police and a host of support staff. Their action-packed, moving and, at times, humorous testimonies are told here through interviews and diaries, along with letters and emails written to family, friends and loved ones. These men and women come from different backgrounds and have various motives for telling their stories, but they have one thing in common: they have risked their lives serving their Queen and country on the front line.

Spoken from the Front is not a definitive history of the war in Afghanistan. I will leave that to the historians. What I think and hope this book provides is a fascinating snapshot of life in the most dangerous war zone in the world. I believe the strength of this book is its simplicity: some accounts are raw and horrific, others more matter-of-fact and reflective. But they are all told by people who were there and witnessed incidents with their own eyes. *Spoken from the Front* captures the preparation for battle, the battle itself and its consequences. The horrors, cruelties, drudgery, excitement and 'banter' of modern warfare become apparent from eye-witness accounts.

Rather than tell the story of the war through hundreds of largely anonymous characters, I decided to tell it through the voices of around twenty servicemen and women, who appear several times throughout the narrative. This, I hope, will give you a real feel for what their lives are truly like in this deadliest of war zones, and will enable you to follow their adventures – with their trials and tribulations – as they unfold. The first-person accounts are told chronologically, starting in the spring of 2006 and going to the end of 2008. The date given is when the incident took place – rather than when the interview was carried out. When the interview was conducted some time after an event, every effort has been made to pinpoint the date of the incident as accurately as possible.

As I write, some of the men and women featured in this book are back in Afghanistan to embark on new tours of duty.

The War in Afghanistan

In early 2006, the 'war on terror' took on a vital new phase, particularly for Britain. The level of commitment required and the difficulty of the tasks taken on by the UK government were significantly 'upped' from previous years. As part of the West's determination to confront the Taliban after 9/11, Britain had joined the US-led Operation Enduring Freedom in October 2001. With the help of the Northern Alliance, an organization of mostly mujahideen fighters from northern Afghanistan, the Taliban was quickly defeated.

The first UK troops were deployed in November 2001, when Royal Marines from 40 Commando helped to secure the airfield at Bagram. A 1,700-strong battle group based around 45 Commando was subsequently deployed as Task Force Jacana.

For the next four years, Britain maintained a force in Afghanistan but, with the Taliban having seemingly melted away, the extent of the fighting was limited. The West was determined that Afghanistan would not return to being an ungoverned space that could be exploited by the likes of al-Qaeda and where the Taliban could regroup.

On 7 December 2004, Hamid Karzai became the first democratically elected president of Afghanistan. The National Assembly was inaugurated on 19 December 2005 and, in contrast to the days of the Taliban, women were given a prominent role with a quarter of the seats held by females. However, the government's remit did not extend across the country, much of which was still detached from Kabul and in danger of falling back into Taliban hands. It was imperative to persuade the Afghan people that the new government was a power for good and that, with the help of the people, Afghanistan could become peaceful and prosperous. The reconstruction of the country was a vital step in that process. After more than twenty-five years of conflict much of the civil infrastructure was barely identifiable. The people lived in squalor, many without clean drinking water, and sanitation systems were reserved for only the most affluent. Afghanistan had plunged beyond third world: in large parts of the country, it was medieval.

On 26 January 2006, John Reid, the defence secretary, announced that 3,300 British forces would be deployed to southern Afghanistan in support of Karzai's new government. It was left to 16 Air Assault Brigade to form the backbone of the task force and they were to be deployed to Helmand province. Reid expressed optimism that 'we would be perfectly happy to leave in three years and without firing one shot'. But history, the terrain, the climate and the possibility of a Taliban resurgence meant that it was unlikely to be so straightforward. The British mission was to act as a stabilizing force and to assist with the reconstruction process, which had failed to make any real impact in the south.

The first troops to deploy to Helmand were Royal Engineers from 39 Engineer Regiment, with a security force provided by 42 Commando Royal Marines. Their task was to construct a camp for the incoming troops. Camp Bastion was built in the desert of central Helmand, the biggest military base built by Royal Engineers since the Second World War. In May, the troops of 16 Air Assault Brigade began to arrive.

If, on paper, a 3,300-strong force seemed substantial, the reality was that it was wholly inadequate to enforce any sort of law and order in Helmand. The British commanders had just 700 infantry soldiers to play with. Dispersing the force across the province, as the Afghans wanted, would have resulted in a precarious dilution of the brigade's combat power. But keeping the servicemen in the relative safety of Camp Bastion would achieve nothing. A middle way had to be found.

The scale of the task was truly daunting. Helmand province is some 275 miles long and 100 miles wide – a total of about 23,000 square miles. The majority of the country is flat desert but there are vast mountain ranges too. Then there is the Green Zone: a thin strip of irrigated land no more than five miles across at its widest point, which provided a perfect hiding place for the Taliban. The Green Zone stretches along each bank of the Helmand river, which snakes its way the entire length of the province. Helmand province shares a southern border with the unruly tribal region of north-west Pakistan.

The climate is not for the faint-hearted. At the height of summer, it is unbearably hot with temperatures soaring to 55°C. In the depths of winter, temperatures in the mountains plunge as low as –20°C and the area is prone to some of the loudest and most terrifying thunderstorms in the world. Previously dry wadis (riverbeds) become raging torrents in a matter of minutes.

The terrain and the climate had proved too much for many over the years. In 1842, General Elphinstone's 16,000 troops had been largely wiped out during the retreat from Kabul. More than a century on, after the Russian invasion of Afghanistan, the Red Army had failed to hold Helmand with an entire division of 25,000 troops – the sort of figure that British commanders could only dream of having in the region.

By June 2006, the task force had deployed troops to a number of Helmand's towns: Musa Qa'leh, Now Zad, Sangin, Kajaki and Gereshk. The provincial reconstruction team was located in Lashkar Gah, Helmand's capital. Often these remote positions were sited in old police stations in the town centre. The task force's engineers were kept busy making them defensible and providing basic sanitation. Before long the platoon houses were attracting Taliban activity and by midsummer many were under constant attack. The forces that occupied them were too small to dominate the surrounding ground so they were forced to sit tight and weather the storm of rocket-propelled grenades (RPGs), small arms and Chinese 107 rockets. Maintaining the logistics supply line with the platoon houses was particularly difficult, with the terrain making resupply by road often impossible, and the limited landing sites making helicopter resupply fraught with danger. As the fighting intensified, troops ran precariously low on ammunition, and extracting casualties often meant Chinook helicopters having to risk landing in the midst of ongoing fire-fights.

By the end of August, the brigade had suffered twelve fatalities through enemy action. Perhaps even more concerning was that the towns to which it had intended to bring security and reassurance had become devastated war zones. Many local people had moved out. Day by day, the situation in

Helmand became more difficult but the British were determined to pursue their objective despite the odds being stacked against them. One thing was certain: the challenges facing servicemen and women going to Afghanistan were formidable. But from early on all the signs were that they were determined to meet them.

1

Introduction: Operation Herrick 4

In April 2006, the troops of 16 Air Assault Brigade started to arrive in Helmand province as part of Operation Herrick 4. The entire force totalled around 3,300 troops. This was a journey into the unknown for British soldiers because they were taking over from US forces. However, it soon became clear that the hope of John Reid, the defence secretary, that we would be able to leave within three years without a shot being fired was unrealistic.

The main combat power was provided by 3 Battalion The Parachute Regiment supported by 1 Battalion The Royal Irish, the Apache attack helicopters of 9 Regiment Army Air Corp, Chinooks from 27 Squadron RAF, 7 Parachute Regiment Royal Horse Artillery, a battery of Desert Hawk unmanned aerial vehicles from 32 Regiment Royal

Artillery and Royal Engineers from 51 Parachute Squadron. Other support roles were assumed by 13 Air Assault Regiment RLC (Royal Logistic Corps), 7 Air Assault Battalion REME (Royal Electrical and Mechanical Engineers) and 16 Air Assault Medical Regiment. Harriers from the Joint Force Harrier detachment, which had been operating from Kandahar since September 2004, provided troops with vital close air support; 34 Squadron of the RAF Regiment offered Force Protection.

April 2006

Colour Sergeant Richie Whitehead, Royal Marines

Colour Sergeant Richie Whitehead, of 42 Commando The Royal Marines, is thirty-five. The son of a civil engineer, he was born in Ipswich, Suffolk, and has a brother. His family moved to Chatham, Kent, when he was eleven. Whitehead joined the Army Cadets aged twelve and the Royal Marines at seventeen, a year after leaving school. He has been on operational tours to Northern Ireland, Bosnia, Iraq, and Afghanistan twice, the first in 2002, in the wake of the 9/11 attacks on the US, and the second to Helmand province in 2006. Whitehead left the Royal Marines in September 2008 with a medical discharge to work as a regional director for a specialist asbestos company. He lives near Dartmoor, Devon.

We arrived in Lashkar Gah at the end of March. But it wasn't my first tour to Afghanistan. I had been one of the few to be there in 2002 when the Marines were sent there as part of Op Jacana. On that occasion, we ended up staying for five months. It was seen as the big search [for Osama bin Laden], the show of force, and to support the Americans in the hunt for terrorists. It was all very new for us as a brigade. It was a steep learning curve, which we took in our stride. There wasn't anything really in and around Bagram [air base] but there were a lot of operations going out into numerous cave complexes and to the far south to places like Khowst. Back then no one went that far south. It was eventful in that we met a lot of people.

There were local villages around us. There were always incidents. There were two villages near our little perimeter track that we made through the minefields around the outside of Bagram: in one village our track went through it and so, obviously, the Americans gave them a briefcase of money and said, 'Thank you very much for letting us use your field.' So, those villagers were happy with us. But the other village, which was approximately 500 metres away, hated them because they [the first village] got the money but they themselves didn't. So they used to mortar each other every night and set traps for each other's kids and stuff like that. We had to take charge of that and try to sort it out. But the locals in Kabul, where the Taliban had fallen the year before, during Op Anaconda, were generally very pleased to see us. It was very quick how you saw a Western approach to everything: the women started wearing jeans under their burkas and things like that.

So it was strange being back in Afghanistan four years later. Before we got out there, the advance party was caught in a suicide bombing. The first multiple out there had to deal with it. They got hit by a suicide bombing at the front gate at Lashkar Gah camp, which shocked them massively. There were a couple of injuries, nothing serious, just walking wounded. Of course, the suicide bomber died. And the vehicle was written off. So we were sat around on our bergens [rucksacks] delayed, waiting to get out there and obviously we heard about it.

It was a weird time because we had a lot of young lads in the Army, and a lot in my multiple. They had never been operational. They gave them to me because apparently with my experience I could take care of them. So the anxiety was quite noticeable, to say the least. Before we got there, everyone was like, 'What are we going into?' Very anxious.

As soon as we got out there, we took over from the Americans. The Americans had a very forceful, aggressive way of handling the local fraternity. They would suit up, heavily armoured in their SUVs, and drive around Lashkar Gah as fast as possible to get from A to B and back again. Our battery commander had his head screwed on. He had discussions with all the multiple commanders and we wanted to go out there with our arms open. But from day one it was 'Suck it and see.' We thought: Are we going to wear berets or are we going to go too soft? Are we going to always have our weapons like this [he raises his arms] or are they going to be down by our sides? These debates were going on from the start, while we were out on patrol. No one knew what our approach should be because we did not have any information to tell us how to do this or that. So it was another steep learning curve. But we got to grips with it well. The population loved us.

This time round [Operation Herrick 4 and into Operation Herrick 5] I was a multiple commander. When we originally turned up in Lashkar Gah, there were only 250 people [today there are more than 1,500]. There was a nice fountain in the middle and a volleyball court, all designed and made by the Americans. There was a perimeter fence and inside there were little pieces of hardened accommodation that the Americans had built. I was lucky enough to have one of these. It was a six-man room with three bunk beds but you had your portable TV and your Xbox.

1 May 2006

McNab: *This was a significant day. The Union flag replaced the Stars and Stripes at Lashkar Gah as America* *formally handed over the 'watch' of Helmand province to Britain. The first members of 16 Air Assault Brigade had been arriving there throughout April. The military task was to keep the peace and to support development projects organized by the Foreign and Commonwealth Office and the Department for International Development. The aim was to bring Helmand into the ambit of the central Afghan government. British efforts were to centre on bolstering the authority of the governor and reforming the province's parlous police, judiciary and penal system. But it was privately acknowledged that the Taliban had been steeled by America pulling its forces from Helmand, which produces most of Afghanistan's £1.6 billion-worth of drugs.*

May 2006

Captain Nick Barton, DFC, Army Air Corps

Captain Nick Barton, DFC, is an Apache helicopter pilot with the Army Air Corps. Aged thirty-two, he grew up in West Sussex and, after leaving school, took a gap year in New Zealand teaching sport, and travelled the world. He graduated with a master's degree in mechanical engineering with French. In 2001, he went to Sandhurst for officer training, sponsored by the Royal Engineers. After he had passed flying aptitude courses, he joined the Army Air Corps. Following his eighteen-month helicopter pilots' course, which started in January 2002, he joined 656 Squadron as an Apache pilot. He has completed four

tours in Afghanistan, serving with 656, 662 and 664 Squadrons, and has since been posted to instruct at Sandhurst.

The Apache is a clever aircraft. It has amazing technology. It's robust, very durable and very capable. And it has awesome fire-power. It can fly at 140 knots max. We – there is a crew of two – can cruise at 120 knots. In Afghanistan, we have an extra fuel tank. We carry twenty-four rockets, and a standard load is two Hellfire missiles, although we can adjust the weapons' load according to the mission. We sit one pilot in front of the other. You can fly from each seat. The more experienced person is usually the mission commander. Ideally, he should be in the front seat, since it's the only one from which you can operate the laser and control the sights. For weapons' guidance, range, etc., that is a front-seat job. Ultimately the Apache is an attack helicopter. The optics are amazing – on a very clear day, at midday, you will be able to break out a guy at about twelve Ks [kilometres], depending on haze. A new sighting system is becoming operational at the moment, which will greatly improve the night-time capability.

Ideally, you want to get target rounds on your first burst from your 30mm, probably your initial weapon for a point target. There is always going to be some slight error in the gun of, say, ten to fifteen metres when you're firing from two K in a moving aircraft. Flying straight at the target is more accurate. You then want to be able to adjust straight away so you're looking for perfect second rounds hit.

Most of the time you fly as a pair [of Apaches] so you have four pairs of eyes looking out – and you have mutual support if you develop a fault or problem. The patrol commander will be mission lead and he will do the majority of the radio work, and your wing aircraft will be the lower aircraft. The higher aircraft is going to get a better line-of-sight comms, leaving the wing to focus more on the targeting. However, some patrol commanders do it differently. Our main role is attack: providing close-fire support for the ground troops. Our other role is providing escort protection to other aircraft, which are going in to the tastier [more dangerous] landing sites.

I first went out to Afghanistan on 1 May 2006. We flew into Kabul, over-nighted there, then went down to Kandahar. Initially we operated out of Kandahar for the first month and a bit – we used to deploy for the day and operate out of [Camp] Bastion when it was a shell compared to what it is now. So we were operating off a gravel pad – quite sporty [challenging/dangerous] – and it was austere in comparison to the runways and air-traffic control that we have now.

Afghanistan was pretty desolate. You were never quite sure what you were going into. There's a certain amount of tension about anyone's first tour. I certainly had a few questions as to why we were there. But you can console yourself by thinking: My job is to be as good as I can be, to provide the best support to whichever call sign needs us.

18 May 2006

McNab: *Our troops in Afghanistan received an early indication of the scale of the Taliban resistance. More than a hundred people died as Taliban fighters and Afghan forces clashed in the fiercest fighting since Britain had arrived in the province. A wave of attacks left some eighty-seven Taliban fighters and suicide bombers dead. The battles also left about fifteen Afghan police, a Canadian soldier, an American civilian and an Afghan civilian dead. Nine hours of fighting had begun after reports that Taliban fighters had massed in Musa Qa'leh a day earlier.*

19 May 2006

Flight Lieutenant Christopher 'Has' Hasler, DFC, RAC

Flight Lieutenant Christopher 'Has' Hasler, DFC, is a Chinook helicopter pilot with the RAF. Aged twenty-nine, he is Canadian and was born in Jasper, a town in the Rockies. He was brought up in Nova Scotia and went to New Brunswick University to do a degree in

international relations. However, he decided not to complete his course because he joined the RAF. Initially he questioned the value of his six-month training at RAF Cranwell in Lincolnshire, but he knuckled down and fulfilled his ambition to fly military helicopters. After a relatively quiet tour of Iraq, he served in the Falkland Islands, Northern Ireland and Europe. He arrived in Afghanistan, as a flying officer, in May 2006 for a two-month tour. He has since been promoted to flight lieutenant and has done a further five tours to Afghanistan. Hasler, who is single, is based at RAF Odiham in Hampshire.

The Chinook is essentially a troop-carrying helicopter, used to drop off and collect troops [including injured soldiers]. It is about 100 feet long, 20 feet tall, and it can fly at up to 160 knots. It is armed with two mini-guns and an M60D machine-gun. It is flown by two pilots who sit side by side. We also have two crewmen, who do everything the pilots don't do: loading and unloading and also firing the guns if needed. The crewmen work the aircraft – we just fly it. If we're dropping off light-ordered troops, just with their weapons and ammunition, then we could carry thirty to forty max in Afghanistan. But it also depends on the conditions – how hot it is, how high we are. Thirty to thirty-five troops would be a good, safe number. Flying helicopters for me is a schoolboy dream that I've never grown out of.

20 May

Departed the Sqn at 2100L [local time] to pick up a few crewmen, and headed to Brize [Norton] to catch our Tristar. For once, the movers at Brize didn't fuck us around too much and we were on the plane in quite good time.

I was pleasantly surprised when a girl from my Initial Officer Training course [at RAF Cranwell] sat beside me. Besides being a Harrier pilot, extremely pleasant and quite clever, she is also very attractive. This had the benefit of making the trip to Kabul seem much shorter.

As we approached Kabul, we were instructed to don our Kevlar helmets and CBA [body armour]. This is a very peculiar sight; being in a white airliner wearing combat gear . . . funny maybe only to me.

Upon arriving at 1500L, we were received by the movers and told that our onward flight to Kandahar wouldn't be leaving until 0500L the following morning. It almost felt good being fucked around again by the movers, like some sort of global balance was restored.

Finally, we arrived at KAF [Kandahar airfield] at 2300L on the 19th. KAF runs on Zulu time [a military time zone the same as Greenwich Mean Time], though, so it was actually 0300Z. It would have been great to get our heads down at that point, as we were all exhausted, but instead we were thrust immediately into theatre briefs . . . very long briefs.

We awoke today with the sun and were subjected to more briefs and familiarized ourselves with the running of the ops. The latter took the majority of the day.

Upon initial assessment, it is quite clear to me that 'Afghan' is going to be much busier than Iraq. Just today a large US, French and ANA (Afghan National Army) convoy left Camp Kajaki down in the north of Helmand and headed for Camp Robinson in the south. They were ambushed by approx 15 TB (Taliban) and suffered heavy casualties (35–40 dead), including 2–3 French and 2 US. The Chinook IRT [incident-response team] was ordered to pick up the casualties and provide top cover (aided by Harrier and Apache). Later, the 3 Chinooks were tasked with landing the Paras in and around the TIC [troops in contact] in order to provide a defensive line.

Yesterday a Canadian FAC [forward air controller] was killed by an RPG whilst directing A-10s [planes] and Apaches onto an enemy position. She was the first female cas [casualty, fatality] suffered since the Second World War. This place is definitely dangerous and we are right in the middle of it.

May 2006

Major Maria Holliday, QGM, Royal Military Police (RMP)

Major Maria Holliday, QGM, of the Royal Military Police (RMP) is forty-nine. She was born and brought up in Chorley, Lancashire. An only child, her father was an armaments inspector. She attended Holy Cross High School in Chorley before joining the Army in 1978. Her father had served in the Army during the Second World War and Holliday was just four when she announced she intended to follow in his footsteps. She joined as a private in the Women's Royal Army Corps (WRAC), but later transferred to the RMP. Holliday served in Northern Ireland for more than seven years, during which she was awarded the Queen's Gallantry Medal (QGM). She was commissioned as a late-entry officer in 1999. She served in Iraq in 2005 and Afghanistan in 2006. Holliday is based at the Army's Bulford camp in Wiltshire.

I arrived in Afghanistan in early April 2007 as the company commander for 174 Provost Company 3 RMP and as the force provost marshal [FPM] for the UK task force. We deployed on 6 April after completing a six-month training period in the UK. When we first deployed, although my company headquarters was in Kandahar, I also had a detachment in Kabul and the majority of my troops were in Helmand province. I spent an awful lot of time on the road, so to speak, but actually in helicopters. If I had been collecting air miles I would have been doing very well! I was spending quite a lot of time in Helmand but about seven weeks into the tour I was also appointed as the SO2 ANP in addition to my company command and FPM role – this meant I was a staff officer responsible for the Afghan National Police, as part of a newly formed Security Sector reform cell.

I had never been to Afghanistan before. When you land on an RAF flight somewhere like that, all the lights get turned off and you have to put your helmet and all your body armour on whilst sitting in your seat on the plane; I think people who have never experienced that before feel a bit of trepidation landing like that – it all goes very quiet. When you arrive in Kandahar it's a huge, multinational camp. It was only half built at the time. A lot of things were still going on in terms of building but it had all the normal facilities that you get on a large army base whilst on a deployment, like little shops and cafés and stuff like that. Because it's an air base, it's a huge camp but you don't get to see anything of Kandahar itself, unless it's your job to patrol there.

Throughout May, I spent my time going between Kandahar, Kabul, Camp Bastion and Lashkar Gah. As company commander, I had to make sure that the brigade commander was getting the RMP support he needed, in the right places and at the right time, to support his operations. So it was just ensuring any planned operation was given RMP support at the right level and choosing the right characters for it, depending on what the operation was. One of our main roles out there was getting involved in detention issues, giving advice and guidance to commanders on the ground when they took an Afghan detainee. We had to ensure that that detainee was handled correctly and that the evidence to support the arrest was gathered in the right way. We would guide them [British soldiers] on how best to produce that evidence and what evidence would be needed to support the detainee being handed over to the Afghans.

It was a very difficult situation, bearing in mind that we were there to support the Afghans. We were not at war with them so any arrested locals were designated as detainees – they were not prisoners of war. Quite often during operations in Helmand – which involved other nationalities [such as the Americans] – if somebody was injured, they might be flown to the British medical facility in Camp Bastion, even if they were suspected to be Taliban. Then, by virtue of the fact that the British medical services were looking after them, they became a British detainee. So trying to gather the evidence against them was difficult because we were going up different military chains, different national chains.

But that was not our only role. We also acted as first responders where we could in the case of a UK death. Our Special Investigation Branch [SIB] colleagues are appointed coroners' officers: they gather evidence and investigate the death. Every UK death is treated as an alleged murder; the SIB gather evidence for the UK coroner on his behalf. So, as first responders to any UK death, we had to gather any evidence we could from the scene in terms of forensic evidence and witness statements. That is part of the RMP role, which can be difficult depending on where the incident has occurred and what the tactical situation is on the ground. There were some scenes [scenes of crime] that you simply couldn't get anywhere near because it was too dangerous.

We also police the [British military] force. As part of our traditional military-police role, we would investigate fights or thefts just as we would anywhere else.

In normal policing terms, it was relatively quiet because the troops were so busy and Afghanistan is 'dry': they weren't allowed to drink alcohol, and alcohol always fuels fights and the like, so, in terms of traditional policing, there was very little to do. The main thrust of our work, and certainly that of the SIB, was investigating the deaths of British soldiers but also supporting operations. We had thirty deaths throughout our six-month tour. The SIB were the prime investigators but we worked alongside them.

21 May 2006 [diary]

Flight Lieutenant Christopher 'Has' Hasler, DFC, RAF

A frustrating day. I've been here for a few days now and still haven't flown yet. I was a half-hour from getting airborne today, with all of my kit at the ready, when the aircraft I was taking over went U/S [unserviceable]. This seems to be a recurring problem, due perhaps to the amount of flying that we are demanding from the cabs.

With any luck, I will complete my TQ (theatre qualification) tomorrow. In any normal theatre [such as Iraq], a TQ would involve a rather sedate trip, including a local area familiarization and some dust-landing practice. In Afghanistan, however, the op tempo is such that there are no spare cabs or training hours available. Therefore, my TQ tomorrow will be six hours of operational training, flying the Paras into the very spot where the convoy was hit yesterday.

May

We did an op – Op Mutay. It was the Paras' first air-borne assault. It was to the eastern village of Now Zad. We knew there were enemy forces there and we just wanted to kick the nest a bit and see what happened. It was broad daylight when we flew in a five-ship assault.

I prefer flying in daylight. You can't see the tracer

[firing from the ground] and you can't hear it because the Chinook is so loud. If you're getting engaged, you don't know about it, and that's sometimes a bit better. And you can see where you're landing so there's less chance of a crash.

I was a flying officer at the time and therefore the co-pilot in charge of navigation. I was trying not to get us lost or land in the wrong place. We had decided to assault three compounds. When you're about half to three-quarters of a K away, you try to identify the landing spot. But if there's a shitload of compounds it's hard to ID the right one. It works sometimes but it's not an exact science. You have an aiming spot and you have to make sure your buddy [the other Chinook] can get in too. But for the last twenty feet or so, there's so much dust that you're blind. It's like flying in clouds. You just have to trust your techniques and hope you don't hit a big boulder or go into a ditch you hadn't seen, or something else goes wrong.

We were engaged before we landed but we didn't know about it. Then, as soon as the troops got off, there was incoming [fire]. We landed two aircraft in the back garden quite close to the compound to shock the hell out of them. The downdraught kicked up a huge amount of dust. It was my first real dust landing in anger with guys shooting at me. Everything was moving so quickly. You're aware straight away that you're under fire because you're on the same net [radio network] as the boys.

Contacts were being called in but there was nothing we could do. Our ramp was down, offloading troops, but you just have to stay there until all the boys are out. At least the guys in the back [the two crew] have a mini-gun [a six-barrelled Gatling-style weapon] and two M60s [machine-guns] that they can hide behind and shoot back.

We could see the fire too but we had no idea where it was coming from. There were moments where I thought, Please hurry the fuck up, but you can't rush the boys because they're going as quick as they can. They don't want to stay on the helicopter any longer than they have to because they're vulnerable as well. The helicopter is a big, noisy target. It's no secret: we're most vulnerable to RPGs and small-arms fire when we're on our approach and when we're on the ground.

Once everyone was out, we took off. It was tense – maybe we're just pansies – but we were up again after just a few seconds. We went airborne and we held in pattern waiting for a pick-up call, or if there was any injury we'd go and get them. We listened on the nets for the call to come and get the injured but it never came. Once we were clear, the two Apaches went in and covered the boys [on the ground]. It was the first real helicopter assault on the enemy. We also had stacks of fast jet up above us too . . .

Once all was quiet – after maybe twelve hours – and everyone [the estimated thirty Taliban] was dead, we went to pick up the boys. And that's the way it should be. It was a really good day. Nobody got so much as a paper cut that day and they killed a lot of their boys [Taliban], so spirits were up. There had been a couple of really close calls, though. One of the troops took a round through his chest plate – through the magazines that were on his chest – and out the other side. Another guy took an RPG through his Land Rover – they weren't armoured then. And another guy got kicked by a cow – they killed the cow obviously! The dits [stories] afterwards were pretty fucking hilarious. It was great. There had been a large scope for things to go wrong, but it was great. We felt very good about things. It was a good eye-opener.

May 2006

Captain Nick Barton, DFC, Army Air Corps

My first ever contact was during Op Mutay. I was the wing aircraft [of two Apache helicopters] on my first tour. I was still a captain but only the flight 2IC [second in command]. For the first six weeks it seemed that, operating as a pair, one of the flights had been in the right place at the right time, had fired quite a lot, and had had all of the contacts. Not that you ever want to engage but that's what you're trained to do. For Op Mutay, we were the high-readiness pair and were only due to support the op if there was a problem with the deliberate tasking flight or if it endured past their crew duty.

As was customary we had read into the op: in outline a daytime op for a 3 Para air assault into Now Zad to target Taliban forces in a few known compounds. We launched 250 [men] in two waves of Chinooks, a fire-support group and all the rest of it into the badlands of Now Zad. At the time, we didn't know how bad they were. The op was starting to sound quite busy with reports of quite a few contacts and the supporting Apaches had been firing again. Since we were not dedicated to support specifically, it was likely that the same flight was going to have another busy day. We got stepped up. One of the aircraft had taken a couple of rounds and had to be shut down for servicing. Our pair complete, we replaced them and went up making best speed departing from the gravel pad at Bastion at approximately 10 a.m. There were various platoons on the ground in two rough groups and we split our pair up accordingly, one aircraft working to each of the two forward platoons. Ideally you are speaking directly to the JTAC [joint terminal air controller] of the lead company that wants your support.

As they [the Paras] were pushing up to this particular building, I thought: Shit, that's someone firing at them – just as they called, 'Contact' [over the radio]. I was seeing the muzzle flash from the guys [Taliban] behind a wall. Fortunately, I was visual with the firing point, something I now realize is a luxury as the firing point is often very hard to see. We were a bit too close to engage straight away and, it being my first contact, I took a bit of time to get in position, get clearance from the JTAC to fire 30mm and get accurate rounds on. We would have been at between two and two and half thousand feet, about one K from the target. Without a shadow of a doubt, there were two of them firing over a wall. They were firing an AK-47 [assault rifle], and possibly one had a PKM [machine-gun] with a slightly longer barrel. We were still operating every-thing under self-defence [Rules of Engagement]. They were probably 150 metres closing to 100 metres of where the friendlies [British forces] were. I was the aircraft commander in the front seat where you operate the sights and do most of the firing. You make sure the sight, TADS [targeting acquisition designating sight], is pointing accurately at the target; it's compensated for motion so it's nice and steady. You're zoomed in on the day TV camera as much as you can be. You lase [laser] for range, action the gun, check the range and, provided there are no other weaponeering messages, you fire. You watch for the fall of shot, adjust accordingly, and fire again.

Our first burst was perhaps fifteen to twenty metres from the target and we got cleared to fire again with a good rounds call from the JTAC. We could see the muzzle flashes so we put 120 rounds in and around the wall. They stopped firing but there was an orchard on the west side so we couldn't see any bodies or if we actually got them. We know that they no longer fired so it achieved its aim and the Para platoon swept through the area. Knowing what I know now, I could have paused a little bit more so that my initial burst was as accurate as it could have been rather than firing off axis. If you're running straight at them it's going to be more accurate and, hopefully, you can hit them before they start running. The best approach is to track them, then ambush them with 30mm rounds at the point of your choosing.

But it was good. We had four different radios going: an Ops Room radio, an inter-aircraft radio and two different frequencies speaking to the controller of two different company groups. So the divvying up of tasks within the cockpit can be tricky.

The contact went on for five or ten minutes. When it went quiet, we came back for fuel. But the Paras had done pretty well to clear through a pretty dodgy area. It was an eye-opener for everyone at that time. Later in the day, our pair [of Apache] went back up to co-ordinate the pick-up and recovery. The recovery was done with one or two Chinooks less than the drop-off to squeeze it in before we lost the light. Our role was to provide the continued cover as well as confirming the pick-up grid for the Chinooks. It was hot and the Chinooks were [each] picking up forty-four guys plus all their kit. By all accounts it was pretty sporty lifting out of the landing site with extremely limited power. Fortunately everyone got back [safely] and it was mission accomplished.

The temperature and the altitude make a real difference to how thin the air is and how hard the engines have to work to produce the same power. In the UK, lifting the same aircraft load, we would have been lifting with approximately 82 per cent power. In Afghanistan, in 45°C at 3,000 feet, we would probably be lifting at 93 per cent power. But that was our first big op and it felt good to be a part of it.

23 May 2006 [diary]

Flight Lieutenant Christopher 'Has' Hasler, DFC, RAF

It's been a long day. Into work for 0300 to start learning the ropes of DA [duty aviator]. I also had to do myriad jobs for the boss. Not that I minded, of course: the poor guy has shitloads on his plate at the moment and it probably helps him a great deal if someone reads his emails for him (although I'm sure he will reread them anyway).

We were all told there is a rescue op going on. A number of ANP [Afghan National Police] had been driven out of their town by the TB [Taliban] (10 kilometres west of Kajaki Dam). They are holing up in a safe-house, which is located in the middle of a steep valley. They do not have comms and it is unknown how many of them are still alive or if they have been overrun completely. The last report, which was received 4–5 hours ago, said they were down to 20 rounds apiece. We all know that the TB do not take PoWs.

Our mission is to take two Chinooks, supported by two AH [attack helicopters / Apaches], one with two Paras and one empty. The Chinny with the Paras (my aircraft) will land and offload the troops top cover. The Paras will move forward and recce the safe-house. It will be filled with either ANA [Afghan National Army] or with TB. If things run smoothly, the second CH [Chinook] will be called in to pick up the ANA, or bodies of. If things go badly and the Paras run into a contact, we will try to recover them while the Paras rain down as much lead as poss.

It is now 1640Z and I am supposed to be up at 2200Z for a 0002 lift. As I was leaving the HQ a new piece of int [intelligence] came in. There are RPG-armed troops amassing in the hilltops, apparently with the aim of shooting down a Chinook. I'd better get my head down. I don't want to fall asleep when the bullets start coming!

24 May

It wasn't long after I finished writing the last entry that I was awoken and told that the op was still on. With time only to clean our teeth, we grabbed our kit and made for the HQ. After a quick brief, we got ourselves to the aircraft, flashed them and flew to Camp Bastion, all while it was still dark. The sun started to rise halfway over the red desert; five minutes later it was 32°C at 200 ft.

At Bastion, all the players gathered for a mission brief given by Maj Will Pike, OC [officer commanding] A Cy [Company]. The mission had changed slightly in that both CHs [Chinooks] will now be carrying troops and landing simultaneously. Int also hadn't nailed down a specific location for the police chief and his men. Instead we had three 'probable' grids which would be confirmed by the overhead Apaches.

The Apaches would be looking for a building in a compound with a blue and white gate, flying a blue and white flag. Also, upon hearing the approaching helo, the chief was meant to start a fire with tyres on it, thus creating a highly visible black smoke.

Before we were even meant to arrive on the scene, a predator UAV [unmanned aerial vehicle] would be high above the TGT [target] Loc [location], providing a real-time picture and threat assessment. With all these assets at our disposal, we had a fairly good, warm, fuzzy feeling ... notwithstanding the brief TB threat, which was significant.

After a cup of tea and a bacon sandwich, provided generously by the Paras, we lifted and departed the TGT. We lifted exactly on time 0315Z and with our predicted 45 min transit we would be on scene at 0400Z (0830L).

I was in the lead aircraft and in the left-hand seat. My job was to navigate the formation to the TGT, control comms between the HQ JTAC [joint terminal air controller], FST [fire-support team] and all of the air assets and run the mission as we were the command aircraft.

The captain (Squadron Leader Lamb) would fly over the right and generally free himself of further workload in order to maintain capacity. Another task of mine was to manage the fuel for the 2 a/c [second aircraft]. The op was planned in such a way we would be arriving back at the base with only 15 mins fuel remaining.

Things started to go badly when HQ called to say that the UAV was late and would not be arriving until after we were on TGT. We were instructed to press on regardless. The situation grew more tense when the Apaches reported that they were high above the TGT, 5 mins in front of us, but none of the grids matched the description of the safe-house. We opted to remain high and south of the TGT and throw in a few orbits while the Apaches had another look about.

We were growing quite twitchy as we were orbiting over known enemy territory, thinking the TGT was looking more and more like a trap. I was also very aware that while we waited, our fuel gauge was continuing to fall.

Fuel was coming to a critical stage when an

Apache piped up saying he had spotted black smoke. We immediately dived down to 50 feet and made best speed to the general area, while I frantically punched the new grid into the computer.

As we approached, the AH [attack helicopters] were giving a further picture of the TGT. It seemed to match the given description accurately. With less than a mile to go, we still weren't visual with the safe-house. We rounded the corner of a hill, still doing 130 knots when we came visual. Andy Lamb threw out the anchors and we landed just shy of the compound with the other a/c in our 5 o'clock. Our wingman's troops ran off and set up an all-round defence, while our troops went into the house to escort the ANP out. Meanwhile we scanned our arcs of fire, while the Apaches provided us with a local-area int picture.

We lifted all the call signs aboard in little more than 9 mins. Unfortunately, without firing a shot. The TB, it seems, either weren't up for a scrap or they were miles away. Who knows?

One final thing of note: one of the ANP, a boy really, was so scared of flying in a Chinook that he pissed himself. One would have thought that being left to the TB would be more frightening . . . Each to their own, I suppose.

25 May
What started as a very quiet, sedate day became suddenly very interesting. A Pinz [Pinzgauer 2½-ton

truck] had broken down in the middle of the Sangin Valley (über bandit country). Our job was to go in and pick it up before the enemy got to it first. My cab would go in first and drop in a platoon to secure the site and rig up the Pinz for underslinging. The second cab would come in after us and lift the lorry out. Meanwhile, two Apaches would provide top cover.

We were airborne at 1530Z. This, however, was after a massive comms faff: we lifted but had to return because we didn't have the right troops on board. Also, via the poor comm we had many reiterations to the plan, which had the effect of the crews involved not really knowing what the final plan was.

We passed on to the TGT site, which was forty miles east. The AH were already overhead and were starting to give very good int ... or very bad, depending on your perspective. They had spotted several ground groups of suspicious locals on motorbikes and [in] four-wheel drives. Furthermore, a JTAC (C/S widow) [call sign 'Widow'] was reporting sustained enemy fire very close to his position, which in turn was very close to our LS (landing site).

We established ourselves in the overhead and began a recce of the area. After locating the wagon, we awaited the green light from the AH. He soon said that the area 1,000m around the Pinz was cold and we were clear to approach. We dropped the lever and descended through the threat band as quickly as possible. The Pinz was abandoned on a track, 50m up from a dried-out riverbed. We were over the riverbed at 50 feet and the dust levels were very light. Once over the bank and on the track, the aircraft blew up a huge cloud of dust, which completely enveloped us and caused total brown-out. We still had 25 feet below us and 15 knots ground-speed and continued the rest of the way down totally blind. We landed with a firm thud and waited for the dust to settle while the troops ran out of the back. The first thing I saw when the dust settled was a set of wires not 5 feet in front of the disc [rotor blades].

With the troops gone, we lifted vertically to escape the dust and wires and proceeded low level to the west to gain air speed before climbing up as hard as the aircraft could go to a safe level. Before we could do that, however, the Apaches said that a group of men on 4x4s were advancing 400m in our 12 o'clock. We banked hard left in the opposite direction and then proceeded 'upstairs'.

Now it was our playmate's time to do the same and pick up the load. He executed this perfectly, despite very trying conditions due to the near zero visibility when in the hover while overhead. He departed and we went back to pick up the troops. After lifting the platoon, we were told they had to be dropped off at Camp Robinson, 7 kilometres to the north.

At the same time, we were getting more and more reports from colleagues on the ground of incoming enemy fire. Most of this fire was coming from [Forward Operating Base] Robinson itself. With the light levels fading rapidly and the Apaches above us, we decided to land anyway. This was done without incident. We took off again, transited home and made an approach to the right in darkness.

30 May 2006

Major Maria Holliday, QCM, Royal Military Police (RMP)

We had an RMP lad killed on a helicopter that went down. He was working for RC [Regional Command] South. Of course, that hits home when it's one of your own [RMP] cap badge and a number of lads in my company knew him well. There are only about 2,000 of us in the Army.

It happened during an operation. It was a US helicopter. He was part of a combat media team: Corporal Mike Gilyeat, aged twenty-eight – 'Gilly' to his friends. I had met him for the first time in Kandahar, only two weeks prior to the incident. Because of our distinctive red hats, I noticed him at the repatriation service of another UK soldier who had been killed; he was with a young Canadian colleague. If you see another red hat, you automatically talk to them because there aren't that many of us around. I just said, 'Hello,' and that if he needed any RMP support while he was there, we were always there as the company to assist. He was in theatre on his own because he was sent out from Northern Ireland for a special photographer role; therefore he was not part of an RMP company.

I was actually at the Brigade Headquarters in Lashkar Gah when the helicopter went down. At first, we just had some initial information coming in. We didn't know what nationality the helicopter was. On that particular operation Dutch, US and British helicopters were taking part, so to start with there was some confusion as to what had happened. It then transpired that we'd been lucky to a certain degree. I believe that a platoon of British soldiers had just been dropped off and it was as the helicopter was taking off again that it went down. We were trying to identify who was on it. The crew was US so at first we had no idea there had been a British person on it [the helicopter went down in an isolated area near Kajaki in Helmand province, when it was apparently under fire].

The incident happened quite late at night and people were up into the early hours of the morning trying to establish the full details. It was first thing the next morning that I heard that there was a RMP NCO [non-commissioned officer] on board. I knew that it wasn't any of my own unit because I would have known if they'd been there so the only other military policeman in theatre was that young lad,

Corporal Gilyeat. Some of the guys in my unit had worked with him in Iraq.

Every time a UK soldier is killed in theatre, there will be a repatriation service to put that soldier on the plane to send him back home to the UK. Our brigade – 12 Mechanized Brigade, which we were supporting – was doing its own thing at the same time that the repatriation service was taking place at the airport in Kandahar. We were in Lashkar Gah, the Brigade Headquarters, having our own little ceremony. It was outside in an open area of ground. A warrant officer called everyone to attention. Everybody stood in various ranks and files and a padre said a few prayers. A member of the soldier's unit gave a eulogy about him and then we had a two-minute silence. Because he [Corporal Gilyeat] was RMP, we formed the coffin-bearer party at the main repatriation [in Kandahar]. We did as much as we could to help repatriate the body. For our guys, the sad thing was that we were also the ones who investigated the death: the SIB took on that investigation too.

My greatest concern is when I am putting our people out on the ground to support deliberate operations and to support the infantry. I know the characters in my unit and I probably know their wives and families too. You are putting young people on the ground when lines of communication in Afghanistan, for small units such as mine, are quite difficult. Obviously the battle groups could communicate with the brigade but trying to have communications with a particular individual was nigh on impossible. If there was any likelihood that they [the infantry] would take detainees, then generally there would be an RMP presence on the op. If they went out on an operation, we generally didn't get to speak to them again until they got back. We also had an RMP presence in some of the isolated detachments, such as Kajaki, because if there was an incident up there, such as a UK death, it could be very difficult to get to. So you had someone on the ground who could instantly respond. We would put these guys up there and they would embed with the infantry lads.

Including the RMP GPD [general police duties], SIB and MPS [Military Provost Service, like prison officers] there were seventy-three of us [Provost] all told in Afghanistan at the time. We were lucky that we all came back safely [except Corporal Gilyeat]. Sadly, the Royal Anglians lost nine and had something like fifty-seven injured. The tempo of operations during that summer was quite high so it was a constant planning process. We were always planning the next operation. As one unfolded, you were already into the planning phase for the next.

Some of the Afghans found it strange dealing with a woman. Most were OK with it, but there was one incident which amused me: the OC of the SIB, who was male, was reading the paper one day in Kandahar and there was an article all about girls out-performing boys in exams in Britain. He mentioned this to the interpreter, a young Afghan man in his twenties, who said: 'How can that possibly happen?' And the OC said: 'Well, it does.' And the interpreter said: 'This would not be allowed to happen in Afghanistan. We would manipulate the results – it would not be allowed in our country.' That made me laugh.

June 2006

Lieutenant Colonel Duncan Parkhouse, 16 Medical Regiment

Lieutenant Colonel Duncan Parkhouse, of 16 Medical Regiment (part of 16 Air Assault Brigade), is a senior member of a medical emergency response team (MERT). Aged forty-two, he was born and brought up in Exeter, Devon. His father was a civil servant, his mother a teacher, and he has an elder sister. After attending Exeter School, he went to University College Hospital as a medical student. At twenty-one, he signed on as a military cadet because he wanted to combine medicine with a career in the Army. Married to a former nursing officer, he is based at Colchester, Essex. His tours of Afghanistan last, on average, two months, and he is a veteran of no less than six between 2006 and 2008, which means he has spent an entire twelve months there during just three years.

After a major trauma, a certain percentage of victims will die within the first ten to fifteen minutes. There is another peak at around the hour mark. Then there is a third peak at the two-to-three-day mark that is due to complications. With the best will in the world, we [the MERT team] are not going to be able to do a huge amount about the ones that are going to die within the first ten to fifteen minutes, particularly in a military environment.

So instead what we are doing is looking to keep people alive during what we call the 'golden hour'. We have always had in place a medical evacuation system from the point of view of the wounded. But when we first came out [in early 2006], we looked at the med plan and we knew it was going to be difficult to evacuate soldiers who were wounded on the ground back to us within the golden hour. We estimated that it would probably take – with the problems of extraction and the hostile environment – up to two hours to get them back to surgery. So we wanted to mitigate that by pushing out on our evacuation teams – senior doctors who have specialist skills in resuscitation. We are basically your emergency-department doctors, your intensive-care doctors and anaesthetic doctors. The aim is to help the small number of soldiers who may succumb – who may die in transit – because of the potential delay. And that's what the concept of the MERT is all about. It is bolting a small, specialist medical team on to an RAF evacuation team to produce a link from the medic or young doctor on the ground, and the all-singing-and-dancing hospital where a patient will eventually end up.

MERT dates back to the Balkans conflict, if not before. At that stage we had an incident response team [IRT]. An IRT was a way of getting specialist agencies to the site of an incident. That was not only medical, also engineers, bomb disposal, Military Police. That was when we were first putting medical teams on helicopters to go forward and pick casualties up. That was very much a local organiz-ational structure: it was not doctrine. That was when people first had the idea of putting medics or any specialty on a helicopter and maybe leap-frogging other medical nodes along the way to speed up the casualty evacuation. In Iraq this was continued in the early days of 2003–4. We would have specialist RAF teams usually involving a para-medic and a nurse, sometimes backed up by a doctor, depending on the nature of the incident. The thing is those doctors were not necessarily pre-hospital-care-trained to the standard of what we have now in Afghanistan. It was a different war, different situation. It worked reasonably well and they worked very hard.

Coming back to 2006, when we – 16 Medical Regiment – deployed with 16 Air Assault Brigade, we had a lot of experienced critical-care doctors including anaesthetists and emergency medical care practitioners, A-and-E docs. Also, they had the ethos that they really wanted to support 16 Air Assault Brigade as much as possible in-field. 16 Medical Regiment took this idea of a medical IRT and formalized it into a medical emergency response team [MERT]. It was actually breaking new ground and, like all things when you break new ground, there was a certain amount of resistance to it. I would suggest that the one person who had the most input in starting it was a chap called Lieutenant Colonel Andy Griffiths – in the early spring of 2006. As well as Andy, the other man who really pushed it was the commanding officer of 16 Medical Regiment, Lieutenant Colonel Martin Nadin – now a full colonel. They simply wanted to support the troops on the ground as much as possible.

The MERT is a concept. It is purely about getting the care that the soldier requires to him or her as early as possible. And that is really making sure that these critical interventions, which can be life-saving, are done as quickly as possible by having a team on the helicopter that mitigates the extra length of time it takes. You can carry on doing the treatments while evacuating them and see how they should be treated when they get to the base hospital. The [MERT] team make-up will vary depending on your resources and what is going on on the ground. In the spring of 2006 in Afghanistan, we had a four-person team and that was based around an RAF paramedic, an RAF flight nurse, a senior clinician with critical-care experience – probably an anaesthetist or emergency medicine doctor – and the fourth member of the team was an Operating Department practitioner [ODP]. In 2006, we were averaging three shouts [medical call-outs] a day, but sometimes we would do as many as five.

One of the reasons why I do this job, and one of the reasons other people do this job, is that in the military medical system there is a huge duty of care for the soldiers on the ground. Personally I think the NHS has lost that. The NHS does not have that link with the general public any more and there are lots of reasons for that. But we certainly still have that very strong ethos of supporting the guys on the ground.

June 2006

Colour Sergeant Richie Whitehead, Royal Marines

We had a couple of attacks on the camp [Lashkar Gah] as they [the Taliban] started to get a little bit braver. Or we were perhaps setting one too many patterns – they started to learn what our routine was. The first ever RPG attack was in the early hours of the morning – one or two a.m. It was pitch dark and I was doing my rounds, walking around the base. And a guy with an RPG had literally just walked up to the fence and fired it at a sangar. It missed the sangar and the RPG just went on, like a rocket, straight over the camp and outside again. He had completely missed us from twenty-five metres. How that happened I don't know. I rushed into the sangar, where there was one of my lads, a young Scot named Ted. He had only just come out of training and he was just sat there in amazement saying: 'Did you just see that?'

I said: 'Yes, but are you all right?'

He said: 'Yes, but did you just see that?'

I said: 'Yes, I did. It's OK. It's fine. There's no point dwelling on it.' It was just like a bang and a rocket, like a firework, going off. The RPG just hit some derelict ground on the outside and that was that. But from that point we realized we needed better torches – dragon lights in the sangars – because what we were issued with was not good enough. You could not see out, which meant this guy had just walked up to the fence and fired at us.

11 June 2006

McNab: *A British soldier was killed and two were seriously wounded in a fire-fight. Captain James Philippson, aged twenty-nine, of 7 Parachute Regiment Royal Horse Artillery, was the first British serviceman to die after the deployment to Helmand province: his patrol was ambushed by Taliban fighters outside Sangin. The servicemen were in Land Rovers when the attack happened. Anthony Philippson, the victim's father, said his only consolation was that his son had died in 'the job he lived* *for'. Apache attack helicopters were called in to support the troops following the ambush. Several Taliban fighters were killed.*

July 2006

Flight Sergeant Paul 'Gunny' Phillips, RAF

Flight Sergeant Paul 'Gunny' Phillips, RAF, is forty. He was born and brought up in Dundee, Scotland, and is the eldest of three siblings. He left school at sixteen and began on a Youth Training Scheme (YTS), rebuilding car engines. He joined the Royal Marines in 1985, but left in 1990 and worked in various jobs on 'Civvy Street'. In 1993, he joined the RAF and spent seven years as a storeman, serving three years at RAF Lossiemouth and four years on Tactical Supply Wing at RAF Stafford. In 2000, he began retraining to become a member of the air crew and joined 27 Squadron in 2003. He did tours of Northern Ireland and Bosnia as ground crew and later, as air crew, two tours of Iraq and four two-month tours of Afghanistan. He is based at RAF Odiham in Hampshire.

I hate to use the term but I am a jack-of-all-trades, really. My role is probably the most multi-skilled job in the air-crew world. To run down my duties: I am responsible for the on- and unloading of passengers and cargo, responsible for voice-marshalling the aircraft by day and night in confined spaces, voice-marshalling the aircraft for underslung pick-up and drop-off, air navigation assistance, radio work, limited search and rescue capability, and air-to-ground gunnery. I can field service the aircraft but not in nearly as much detail as engineers.

My tours of Iraq were an absolute breeze compared with Afghanistan. Iraq was just a bimble around the desert enjoying the view. I didn't fire one round in anger. But Afghanistan was a massively different kettle of fish. My first detachment to Afghanistan was with the Dutch Air Force from February 2006 to May 2006 [where Phillips received a general's commendation for his work]. I wasn't involved in any enemy contacts whilst with the Dutch. Then I went back out with the RAF in July [2006]. I had been in theatre for three to four days and there was a big op on called Op Augustus. We were trying to grab some high-value [Taliban] targets in Sangin. It was planned as a five-ship [aircraft] insert with 3 Para. It was intended as a dawn raid but it started to slip and all the timings went out of the window. They couldn't get a definite on the [main] target: they were still trying to work out whether this guy [Taliban] was there or not. But the second objective was to land on the HLS [helicopter landing site] and start clearing the area anyway, then sweep through these two compounds where they thought some relatively high-value targets would be. We were out to the east of Sangin holding for a good thirty or forty minutes for the

Predator [unmanned aircraft] to clear us in. And everyone was thinking: It'll get knocked off [postponed]. They [the Taliban] will have scarpered. Then somebody, somewhere, decided we were going to go. So we pootled off to the HLS.

I was in the third cab of the first wave because there was going to be a three-ship to drop off three platoons. There were two ships coming behind us to drop off another two platoons. We must have been a couple of hundred metres from the HLS on the approach and somebody said: 'There's a group of people on the HLS.' I was on the left-hand – the port – gun and I stuck my head out of the window and there was this big group of [Afghan] civvies just stood in the middle of the HLS with these three honking-great twenty-ton Chinooks heading towards them. They got the message and started to leg it. As we went over the top of them, they were still running under the aircraft. They were running across the HLS and I thought: I don't know whether they've got weapons or not but I'm not going to give them the opportunity to use them if they have. So as we went across [the HLS], I waited until the aircraft was about twenty feet beyond them and I put a burst of fire down as warning shots. And I've never seen so many people cover a hundred metres so quickly. They got the message and they got out of there pretty sharpish.

Just prior to that happening, the number-one cab had got opened up on quite heavily. It turns out that this HLS was fairly well defended and it went from being fairly benign to being like *Star Wars* in nano-seconds. I was in Has's [Flying Officer Christopher 'Has' Hasler's] cab. There was tracer going every-where – both outgoing and incoming. It turned into a two-way range fairly rapidly. We had just touched down by this point and we were being fired at from two positions. Ginge [Flight Sergeant Dale Folkard] was on the right-hand side, but he couldn't really fire at anybody because the number-two cab was in his way. On the left-hand side, I saw a couple of muzzle flashes from about eleven o'clock. It was from like a small ditch with a tree-line just behind it. I never felt any rounds coming in but I certainly saw the muzzle flashes so they got the good news [fired upon]. And then I could see silhouettes running from one compound to another.

I thought: I've just been opened up on from about fifteen metres from where they are now. So they got the good news as well. But we managed to get the guys [the Paras] off and shortly after that the aircraft departed rather rapidly. We must have been on the ground for thirty or forty seconds. So there were two definite firing points there and there must have been four or five individuals moving from one compound to another. I was firing an M60 [machine-gun]. Sometimes you can tell if you've hit people and sometimes you can't. That time I couldn't because it was that dark. We had all the tracer going off and I was firing a weapon with my [night-vision] goggles on, which had backed down slightly. So you really are firing at a muzzle flash. But once I started firing at the muzzle flashes they stopped firing so, at the end of the day, I achieved my aim because I either suppressed them – or killed them.

That was the first time in my life that I had been in a contact. It was memorable. Frisky: massively so. You can feel the adrenalin pumping. The minute you know something's happening you can almost hear your heart pounding in your ears. You don't really notice it at the time but [you do] once you have a breather and take stock. Once we'd lifted out, we had a quick check: everyone was OK, no holes in the aircraft. I must have looked like a startled rabbit. I said [to Ginge]: 'Fuck me, that was sporty.' I was bouncing around in the back of the cab like a little boy, all excited. I looked over at Ginge and he was just sitting there going, 'Fucking hell.' I said: 'I can't believe we just got away with that,' because I thought someone somewhere was going to get whacked badly. But we managed to get three cabs in and three cabs out and nobody got a pasting.

1 July 2006

McNab: *Lance Corporal Jabron Hashmi, aged twenty-four, of the Intelligence Corps, became the first British Muslim soldier to be killed in the 'war on terror'. He died* *in an attack by the Taliban on the British base at Sangin. Hashmi's family spoke movingly about how, as a devout Muslim, he had been committed to bringing peace to Afghanistan. Zeehan Hashmi said of his brother: 'He was a very happy young man but very cheeky and mischievous. He was very daring – he had no fear of anything. He was a bit of a joker who could really make you laugh, but also make you cry if he wanted to.' He was the fifth British soldier to die in the past three weeks. Corporal Peter Thorpe, aged twenty-seven, of the Royal Signals, was killed during the same attack, which injured four other servicemen.*

7 July 2006

Flight Lieutenant Christopher 'Has' Hasler, DFC, RAF

We had to go into Sangin because the boys on the ground were out of water and ammo. As we came in, the aircraft were engaged but, sadly, a guy was killed as he was trying to secure the HLS. So we were called off by the troops. We went back to Bastion. We still needed to get in there and we needed a new plan. Satellite imagery of the area showed us there was just enough space between two buildings where I could put the aircraft down. We had a roller conveyor in the back – pallets on wheels – that we had to get off. But the aircraft on the ground has to move forward as you push on these crates to get them off.

We got there, landed, and there wasn't much room. It was daylight. I was moving forward and the disc was getting quite close to the building, which was higher than the disc. I was out of ideas. I can hardly take the credit but the boss just said: 'You've got to do something here.' So I sort of did a 'wheelie' on the back two wheels. It's a skill we all practise – two-wheel taxiing – but I had never had to do it with a building six inches under the disc. I had to go on the back two wheels and move the heli forward with the building just underneath. So that was interesting. I managed to hold it on the back wheels while they got the crates out and loaded the body on and some of the wounded.

Because it was so hot [swarming with enemy], it was decided the Apaches would light up with their guns an area where we thought the enemy would be. It was a bit odd. As I was doing my thing, just outside the left-hand side, they were lighting it up. To start with I thought it was incoming but later I learnt they were rifling the enemy. It was a bit disconcerting, though, to see these big red balls next to me. But they were just missing us. There was a bit of incoming too, but not much because the Apaches were doing their thing. We were there for quite a few minutes . . .

July 2006

Lieutenant Colonel Duncan Parkhouse, 16 Medical Regiment

I first came under fire on one of the earliest jobs I did. We were going in to pick up some seriously injured casualties and the locals – the Taliban – decided to put on a fireworks' display for us. It was the first time I realized that somebody was actually shooting at me – well, nah, I prefer to think they were shooting at the helicopter that I just happened to be in. I got over it by saying to myself: 'Let's not personalize this. They don't know me from Adam. They're just trying to shoot the vehicle I'm in and, actually, the pilots here are exceptional so I'm probably going to be okay.'

But it was easy after that incident because now I just don't look out of the windows: problem solved! Sometimes you don't even know when you've been fired upon although, with the ballistic protection, you can sometimes hear the bullet hissing. At the time [of coming under fire], it's often not scary because you're so focused on what you're doing.

But on this occasion [when he was first under fire] we were going into Musa Qa'leh, which was always notoriously difficult to get into for lots of different reasons. You could see the green tracer fire coming up towards the Chinook, and just as it started to flare in, you could also see the smoke from the RPGs going across and it was very obvious at that point that they were waiting for the helicopters to come in. We were going to pick up casualties that had suffered mortar injuries. We had a four-strong MERT on board and anything up to ten or twelve soldiers with us. We were landing on an unsecured HLS. It was around eleven at night. Pitch black as you go in. You could see some of the lights from the buildings but at that time most of the town centre of Musa Qa'leh was fairly uninhabited. The only locals in Musa Qa'leh then were ones who were trying to do you harm. And everything was pitch black in the back. Basically, they used to use two ways of getting in to an HLS: either flying very high and then diving down very quickly or low-level flying sometimes down at fifty feet and there would be a lot of jinking around. This landing was the latter: flying low and jinking around. But the problem with Musa Qa'leh was electricity pylons, which kept the pilots very busy. The air-crews were fantastic; how they got us in and out, I don't know. And they didn't have the luxury of not looking out of the windows! They had the tracers coming straight at them.

As we prepared to land, one of the [MERT] team had comms with the pilots using a helmet system, getting updates on the casualties, and the rest of us were scurrying round the cab getting kit out and preparing, putting drips up, making sure the oxygen was switched on, getting out extra equipment we might need depending on what we thought the injuries were going to be. And it was extremely noisy. You can't use normal radios in the back of the helicopter because there's too much ambient noise. So most of it's done by sign language, or standing beside somebody and yelling in their ear. And this is where the team approach is very important.

Retrospectively, it's all quite exciting stuff. In Musa Qa'leh, you want to be on the ground for as little time as possible. The back ramp goes down, the guard force – ten or twelve strong – pile out to their perimeter. They are, basically, maybe twenty or thirty metres away from the aircraft, because as soon as you move about ten metres away, you lose a visibility because of the fine dust. And it was pitch black. So they did that and then the medical team came on with the casualties – because there's no way you can have a verbal handover under the rotor blades. So, they had written something down about the casualties and their treatment. Then they brought the casualties into the cab on stretchers and put them in the designated space on the aircraft where we felt was appropriate. Where you put anyone depends on the type of injury because you may want to put him head first or feet first because helicopters don't fly flat, they fly nose down. So it may be more important to have them head up if they have head injuries, or if you're worried about them bleeding out then it's feet up. But they are usually positioned in stretchers on the floor – often strapped down on the floor.

You have to work out with the pilots their plan of evacuation. Were they going to do a few minutes of low flying or were they going to, as soon as they could, go up to fifteen hundred feet? Nine times out of ten we would like them to go up because, as soon as they get up there, there's a more stable platform for us to work on, and as soon as they get up high, they can put some ambient light on in the back. But sometimes that's not possible – once again it comes down to communication with the air-crews.

On this occasion, we were on the ground for no more than sixty seconds. It felt a lot longer. There were three casualties and then we just had to make sure the order was right for us to do interventions. With multi-casualties, the team would break down and the paramedic would often sort out those who, on the face of it, were the less seriously injured. Paramedics are used to working by themselves. The senior clinician and the ODP [Operations Department practitioner] usually work as a team on the worst casualty, and often the RAF flight nurse would have a roving role. She had the comms with the air-crew. She was our link, as well as helping out when we required a third pair of hands.

On this occasion, the three casualties had mortar injuries. Basically, they were on guard duty in a sangar on a perimeter wall and a mortar or RPG had got lucky, struck it and penetrated the sangar.

One guy had serious head injuries with a broken right leg and he was unconscious. We knew he was going to be the worst one because the other two were conscious, which is always a good sign. If they're able to talk, by definition they have a good airway and enough blood pumping around them to keep them conscious. It's very basic signs you're looking for, though it doesn't mean they don't need help.

The ODP and I started working on the guy with the serious head injury and at the back we left the paramedic to assess the two who were conscious. He very quickly did an assessment and he basically gave me the thumbs-up, which meant their injuries were nothing too serious – and we could concentrate on dealing with the casualty in front of us, as he was the most seriously hurt. He was there on a stretcher. At the same time, we told the flight nurse, who was in comms with the pilots, that, as soon as we could, we'd get the pilots to send a message back to the hospital confirming how serious it was. We were also letting them know how serious it was. We can categorize our injuries in various ways. At that stage, we were using the T1, T2, T3 system. T1 was critical, T2 was serious, T3 was minor, walking wounded. This guy was T1 – and the other two were T2s. If someone is requiring a stretcher to move, they are a T2. The flight time from Musa Qa'leh to Bastion is approximately twenty-five minutes. As soon as the pilots have done their stuff and got us up there to fifteen hundred feet – which is usually within twenty seconds – we get some basic light on.

During the flight back, this guy was unconscious, or had a significantly reduced level of consciousness. I was concerned that he had a major head injury. You can't do anything about the original injury: if there is any brain damage it has been done by the bang on the head. But what you want to do in serious head injuries is to prevent further damage. And the best way of doing that is to be sure the patient has enough oxygen, enough blood flowing around his system. And the best way to ensure that is to anaesthetize him and ventilate him in the back of the cab. These are techniques that normally take place in hospital but we're finding that they help an awful lot to reduce morbidity and disability at the end of the day.

A ventilator is essentially a life-support system. You have to give the patient drugs to render him completely unconscious and 'paralyse' him. This patient had a drip in already [when the MERT took him over] so we gave him his drugs through the drip. The paralysing agent worked: it takes about thirty seconds. All the time we were giving him oxygen and 'bagging' him by hand. The ODP did a manoeuvre to stop him regurgitating while he was unconscious. Then we tried to intubate. This is quite a delicate procedure, even in a hospital with good light and with a patient not moving around. Although the patient was paralysed, we had a whole helicopter moving around and juddering.

And you have actually got to put a tube the diameter of your finger, and about a foot long, through the vocal cords of the patient. So my target was probably about 10mm and the tube diameter was about 8 mm: you have got to be accurate and it's a relatively skilled procedure. But it's a potentially life-saving procedure – the guys who need it wouldn't survive the twenty-five minutes back [to Bastion] without it.

Then the ODP assessed the patient for further bleeding, external bleeding. He couldn't find much but the patient had a broken right leg – it was point-ing in the wrong direction. There was no bone sticking out but the leg had an extra 'joint', which it shouldn't have had. The patient was covered in crap – mud, stuff like that. Everything was happening simultaneously. Once we had secured the airway, we didn't want to lose it. Then we used blades to slit his clothes off to expose his chest, making sure there were no injuries to it. We use blades with a curved bottom so you can't stab the patient by accident: they're childproof, basically. I was concerned because there was no obvious injury to his chest but we were not ventilating very well. One side of his chest was not moving and I thought, because he had been in a blast situation, that he might have blast lung, caused by the pressure wave of an explosion. An explosion can burst a lung. His abdomen had no obvious injury. It was soft, it was not expanding and there was no bleeding into it. It was just his leg.

You can lose a lot of blood from a broken femur and he was quite shocked so I was assuming he was losing blood from his leg internally. And once we had checked there was no reason why the ventilation was not working – i.e. the tube was in the right place – I decided, technically, to operate. Basically, that meant making two holes in the side of his chest.

He was unconscious, he was sedated, he couldn't feel anything. So I put two holes with a big scalpel blade mid-way down both sides [of his chest]. Then I could stick my finger into his chest, making sure there was no obstruction and making sure that the lung was up. And the lung was down on one side because I couldn't feel it. As soon as I stuck my finger in, the next thing I could feel was a 'sponge' and that was the lung. The right lung had collapsed. I was releasing any trapped air that had caused the lung to collapse. And gradually it came up and the ventilation became easier. He was obviously responding to that treatment. Only a senior clinician could have done that. And that is the sort of intervention that putting a senior clinician on the MERT can achieve. Probably only five per cent of all casualties require that intervention so the argument [from critics of the MERTs] is: why are we endangering the life of a senior clinician, a valuable asset, to help such a small number of people?

I would say a valuable asset is only valuable if it is used appropriately. Otherwise it becomes an expensive ornament. So unless you're going to put them out there, they can't help. And each patient saved is a British soldier who is now back with his family at home. His injuries may be severe, but he's back with his family. Anyway, we did all this [treatment] in twenty-five minutes because, after that, we landed in Bastion.

The hospital HLS in Camp Bastion is approximately five hundred metres from the front door. When the Chinook arrives, bringing in casualties, military ambulances are already waiting to ferry the injured to the emergency department. Everyone knows how many casualties are on board because of the number of ambulances waiting: one per casualty. The next few minutes can be the most dangerous for the casualties, moving them quickly from the back of the Chinook into the ambulances without causing them further harm. Usually there's no time for the Chinook to shut down, which means the rotors are still turning and the engines are still pushing out the super-heated exhaust fumes. Add to this mixture the darkness and the adrenalin that's running high, and it's easy for mistakes to happen: intravenous lines can be pulled out, airway tubes become dislodged, even stretchers dropped.

In most cases, the casualties are loaded into the ambulances without too much delay. The ambulance crews are well practised by now. On the first few occasions, when the crews sometimes drove up too close to the Chinook, the hot exhaust would melt the blue lights on top of the vehicles! I accompanied the most seriously injured casualty in the back of the ambulance with the ODP; the other members of the MERT escorted the remaining casualties. Within a few seconds, we were at the emergency department. The trauma teams were awaiting our arrival. They had been waiting a while, and were already aware of the number of casualties and their injuries. The last link in the chain for the MERT is to hand over the casualties to the awaiting trauma teams, one team for each casualty. Clinical information is handed over quickly and succinctly. We use a recognized system, which takes thirty seconds, and as soon as it's complete, the trauma team descends on the casualty simultaneously assessing and treating the injuries. This is a well-practised drill.

The role of the MERT is now complete; it has provided that link from the medic on the ground to the emergency department in the field hospital. It has handed over live casualties.

The trauma teams quickly confirmed the serious nature of the casualty we had handed over. The head injury was the most serious, and required emergency neurosurgery. At this time, in 2006, there was no neurosurgery in Afghanistan. This casualty needed to be evacuated to Oman. The transfer was the responsibility of the embedded RAF critical-care transfer team. These teams are constantly on standby at Camp Bastion to transfer the critically injured from the hospital to other locations around the globe, if required.

The transfer went according to plan and the casualty arrived in Oman within three hours. He underwent neurosurgery within six hours of wounding. Six hours may sound like a long time, but even back in the UK this time line is often not possible. The fact that this is achievable in Afghanistan, in the middle of a war zone, is a testament to the medical system and the people who run it. No one part is more important than another: from the medic on the ground to the MERT, the hospital at Bastion and finally the transfer team of the RAF, it's a chain. And any chain is only as strong as its weakest link.

In this instance, the casualty survived, despite very severe injuries, and he is now back with his family. The two other soldiers injured with him underwent immediate surgery at Bastion and were evacuated back to the UK, where eventually they made a full recovery.

July 2006

Colour Sergeant Richie Whitehead, Royal Marines

I had to take a last-minute visit to Garmsir, down south. They needed a forward air controller – JTAC [joint terminal air controller], as they call it. And there was none available because 3 Para, in their wisdom, had taken everything and everyone with them for their ops. I was in the Ops Room and they were short [of an air controller]. I said: 'Everyone should be able to do this. We've all had basic training of being able to call in air if needed.'

And someone said: 'Can you do it?'

I said: 'Of course, I can.'

He said: 'You've got half an hour.'

I went and packed my kit. We drove down through Nad Ali and via western desert in WMIKs [armed Land Rovers]. It was a big patrol and it was with an OMLT [operational mentor liaison team]. The chief of police [Afghan National Police] from Garmsir had rung up the colonel, the head of the provincial reconstruction team and said: 'Look, there are a thousand Taliban down here about to attack us.' We knew early on that whatever number you were given, you divide it by three at least, because the Afghans do exaggerate just a touch. The colonel wanted to know the true picture – the lie of the land – so he sent some people down to see what was actually going on. This was at the peak [of the 2006 Taliban resistance] because the summer was a lot busier than the winter months. It was hot, 60°C plus on some days. It was horrendous. There was a captain in charge of us. Fourteen headed down in four wagons, all WMIKs. Off we went for what was supposed to be twenty-four to forty-eight hours.

But we came back ten days later because of different things that were happening. We had to have resupplies down there. We got mortared, shot at. We called in Apaches on different targets that we had. We were literally one of the first patrols to Garmsir. We were the 'Dirty Dozen', as we called ourselves. We were there to sneak about and have a look and see what was going on.

We were all senior men. There were a few warrant officers, one colour sergeant, a couple of sergeants, two corporals, and there were a couple of officers and we were just like: 'We're too old for this. What are we doing?' We were just thrown together.

During the drive down across the desert, we were trying to keep out of the way of different villages. The drive took six to eight hours. We took four vehicles from the Afghan National Army with us. We were mentoring these people as well, so we said we'd take them with us. So at night I would put them in a harbour position, a good old-fashioned triangle harbour position. We would be in a small triangle in the middle and then we would stick them on the outside. One, for protection, and two, to mentor them on what a harbour position was all about. We slept in the wagons, or next to the wagons in sleeping-bags.

On one of the very first nights, these lads came running up to us with the interpreters, saying they'd seen someone in the dead ground. And they wanted to go and investigate. We used to take turns to stay up just for questions like this. So, me and my mate said: 'Take five of you and don't go out any further than you can still see us, and then come back.' And this one bloke was notorious for being quite a switched-on kiddie. He was younger. Whereas the others used to group in the evenings and smoke, just like a Cub Scout evening, this bloke actually did want to learn and he wanted to go places. He disappeared and went a little bit further, then he went out of sight. We were watching him through our night goggles and he just disappeared. And I looked at my mate, Tommy, and I was like: 'This is a mistake.' He'd gone. We'd lost him. Then half an hour later he appeared about a K to the left – we'd got our thermal imagery out – and walked back in. A perfect patrol. I said: 'Where have you been?'

He said: 'I saw them [the Taliban]. I just wanted to follow them: they scattered off this way. There were eight of them. They were watching us.'

I said: 'You only went with five men.' So we gave him a bit of a telling-off, and we said: 'Where was your map? Where's your compass?'

He replied: 'I haven't used it.' And he had just walked out a good two K in the desert, turned left, done a big box around with no compass. His local knowledge and his whole background of tribal warfare were amazing. So he came back in and that was that.

Because we knew we were being probed and looked at, we called in air. He [one of the pilots] said there were about eight Taliban and we could see vehicles out on the horizon. There was a B1 bomber in our area. We decided, for a show of force, to ask him to drop a few flares. A show of force, that's all we wanted. We gave them our grid so that they didn't accidentally drop anything on it. But he dropped the flares all over our harbour position. So now we were lit up at three in the morning, like a circus. He'd got the grids back to front. So we had to get up and move quickly because we had completely given our position away.

And the rest of the day went just as badly. We were trying to assess the western side of Garmsir. Every time we stopped, we'd get mortared. They had us pinpointed every time. A nightmare. That's why it took so long. The colonel said: 'Stay there and we will get you some more resupplies.' And the Chinooks came down and dropped stuff, water and food, and we carried on. The mortar positions were dug in. They [the Taliban] would just appear and disappear and that was when we started to learn about the tunnel complex that they had. They were hiding vehicles because we were getting reports of vehicles one minute – we could see brand new Toyota 4x4s – and they would just disappear. In daytime. They weren't scared. Some of them had black turbans and red bands around their turbans. Anything with a black turban and you knew you were against more of a trained force – rather than something just thrown together. Anyway, we concluded there were large pockets of enemy down there. Nowhere near a thousand. But they were fast and well trained: very movable from one day to the next.

10 July 2006

McNab: *The government announced that 900 extra troops would be sent to fight the Taliban. The move came at the request of military commanders because fighting had intensified in Helmand. The first of the reinforcements were due to arrive within two days, and the number of British troops would then be bolstered from 3,600 to 4,500. Senior defence sources denied, however, that the move was the direct result of the death of six British troops in a month. The announcement of more troops was made by Des Browne, who had taken over from John Reid as defence secretary. He denied that British forces had underestimated the Taliban threat and said it had been expected that insurgents would put up a 'violent resistance'.*

14 July 2006

Flight Lieutenant Christopher 'Has' Hasler, DFC, RAF

It was at night and we were making a five-ship [Chinook helicopters] assault on two compounds in Sangin. We thought we had the element of surprise but somehow they knew we were coming. We were low on fuel too but we had support: three or four Apaches, Harriers, B1Bs [US B1 bombers], F15s or F18s, a Predator and more [all aircraft or unmanned aircraft]. We had aircraft stacked up from ground level to space supporting this one op. But we were holding so long – the commander was an Apache guy. I was the third Chinook in to land. But the two aircraft behind me had to peel off because of [a lack of] fuel. This made the troops very vulnerable – they did not have quite enough men on the ground to defend themselves.

So I was tail-end Charlie going in. By the time the heli in front of me was about fifteen feet off the ground, I was still at about a hundred feet and maybe a half K or a K behind him. The landing site was a dry riverbed. And then suddenly it opened up. There were three or four firing positions on each side [of the riverbed]. I saw an RPG go under and over the heli in front of me. He had landed now so I knew I had to go on. It was a long approach knowing you had to fly through this shit. You can't manoeuvre at all otherwise you'll fuck the landing. So it was just a question of 'slow, straight, steady'. The amount of fire was such that it backed down our night-vision goggles. I couldn't see much at all. It was so bright that the goggles weren't giving much [assistance]. I was mostly flying in on instruments. The aircraft flares were popping up as well and they really backed down the goggles too. There was a second of clearness where my goggles came back in and I saw we were about to land in some water. I managed to pitch up and over that but then I got into the dust cloud. I couldn't see anything. It was a bit of a rough landing and the guys were knocked off balance. We said before that the max we wanted to be on the ground was thirty seconds but we ended up being there for a few minutes while getting engaged. I was sitting there thinking, Oh, fuck, without much to do except look at the view. There were other places I wanted to be at that time. But we got the boys off.

We were on the deck and tensions were running high. Then I started to take off but there were two troops still on who hadn't had time to get off. So we lifted off, but then someone shouted we still had two guys on so I held it there. But the guys had already decided they were going to go for it – leave, jump. I was going to put it back down but they just jumped, not knowing how high we were. We were probably twenty feet off the deck but we could have been 200 and they were going to go for it anyway. They just jumped – that was real balls. The radio-ops guy broke his foot landing. It was a communications problem [in the back of the helicopter], but these things happen.

Then another heavy-machine-gun post opened up behind us. I looked at my co-pilot and these big balls of green tracer were passing close to his head. We were very lucky. But we got out of it. I've never seen that amount of fire before or since. It was good fun. We then got engaged all the way up till we were out of the threat band. But we were lucky. I still don't know how it happened but my aircraft didn't take any rounds. The other two aircraft took quite a few.

We were just close to the bank and the fire was coming within inches of the aircraft all around us. We didn't lose any guys, but a guy on one of the other aircraft got shot in the arm.

1 August 2006

McNab: *Three Paras were killed in a carefully set ambush as they went to resupply comrades at a remote outpost in Helmand province. The men were in a convoy of twelve armoured vehicles. The ambush was launched by more than fifty Taliban using machine-guns and RPGs. The men who died, along with another soldier who was seriously wounded, had leapt out of their Spartan armoured personnel carriers to engage the insurgents with their rifles. Air support was called in and an Apache attack helicopter killed at least one Taliban fighter. The dead men were named as Second Lieutenant Ralph Johnson, twenty-four, a member of D Squadron, Captain Alex Eida, twenty-nine, of 7 Parachute Regiment Royal Horse Artillery, and Lance Corporal Ross Nicholls, twenty-seven, also of D Squadron.*

August 2006

Corporal Tara Rankin, 16 Medical Regiment

Corporal Tara Rankin, a combat medical technician currently serving with 16 Medical Regiment, is twenty-nine. She was born in Fiji, the daughter of a teacher, and

is an only child. Her uncle, Trooper Talaiasi Labalaba, served in the SAS and was killed during the heroic battle of Mirbat, Oman, in 1972 when nine soldiers from the Regiment fought off a 250-strong enemy force. She was brought up mainly in Britain, and left school at sixteen, in 1996, to return with her parents to Fiji. Rankin had long considered a military and medical career, partly to follow in her uncle's footsteps, so in 2000 she returned to Britain and joined up the next year as a medic. In 2003 she did a tour in Iraq and went to Afghanistan three years later. In March 2007, she married Corporal Simon Rankin, who serves with the Royal Signals. She is based in Colchester, Essex.

I love my job. I've always liked the medical side of things but I thought the Army would be a challenge so I might as well go for it. I like seeing people getting better, being there for sick people, sick relatives or friends. It's the satisfaction you get out of helping them to get better. I do feel I'm a front-line soldier just as much as the men, but sometimes I have to remind myself that I'm female. It's all about how a female member of the armed forces fits into the environment. If she feels at ease amongst her male colleagues, then she'll fit in well and the men will work well with her.

On 6 August, I was a 7 Para RHA [Royal Horse Artillery] medic, part of a patrol that deployed out on a three-hour ground ops known as Op Snakebite with 3 Para. I was involved as A1 Echelon and RAP

Rear [3 Para] alongside our Canadian med team. The main aim was to resupply Musa Qa'leh and relieve Pathfinder Platoon. We carried out patrolling and route clearance. We were reassuring the local population and, at the same time, looking out for enemy forces or any enemy activities around the area.

We had to treat a guy who got shot. He had been in a small convoy helping deliver supplies to Danish troops based near Musa Qa'leh. He was doing top cover in a WMIK [armed Land Rover]. It was one of those unexpected events but anything can happen out here. A young soldier had apparently got shot by a sniper, just after three p.m. The bullet went straight through his head and chest. I was sad because he was only young – nineteen years old – and it was his first tour as well. When he was shot, I was in a Pinzgauer. We were only a few hundred yards from him: first we heard an echo [from a shot] and then a lot of shouting in the distance. The casualty was brought to us in the back of a Pinz. Then he was put on a stretcher. We had expected more than one but in the end he was the only one. There were four of us waiting for him when he arrived: a doctor, who is in charge, a med senior, who was a sergeant, and two other medics, including me.

We knew from the start that he was very badly injured. But we tried to do what we could for him for as long as possible. We got information on his condition from those who had accompanied him.

But there was no sign of breathing from the chest and no pulse. Eventually, the doctor had to call it a day after about twenty minutes. It was very sad, but there was nothing more that we could do. I had met him before – he was a funny character, with a great sense of humour. I used to see him in the cookhouse with his colleagues at Camp Bastion to say, 'Hi,' and ''Bye,' or to have a cup of tea.

His comrades were in a bad way too. The shock of losing a colleague, a friend, really got to them. Some were in a state of shock, feelings of mixed emotions, as well as being apprehensive for an hour. We had to treat them in the same way as if they were suffering from battle shock.

August 2006

Major Maria Holliday, QGM, Royal Military Police (RMP)

In the middle of the tour, the brigade set up the Security Sector Reform Cell at the Brigade Headquarters in Lashkar Gah. This basically meant that we were helping the Afghan institutions, like the army and the police, get back on their feet. We had already been helping the army for quite some time, but there was a recognition that the police play a vital role in security too and they desperately needed help with training and mentoring. Although the Foreign Office employed some ex-civil policemen to mentor the civil police, they were mentoring at a higher level, the heads of department, and there was nobody really to mentor the police on the ground. So this partly became our role. We set up a cell and formed a team of mentors to go and help them. There was some training going on that the US provided, but this was us setting up the British effort to assist the process. This unit was formed in Lashkar Gah but the boys were going out on the ground starting in Lashkar Gah and then also in Gereshk, Sangin and Garmsir.

I sent a young officer down there to Garmsir: a young lieutenant and a sergeant too. In terms of learning experience, they certainly learnt a great deal because that was a very difficult area to work in. It was full of insurgents, and the only people on the ground in Garmsir were British soldiers, Taliban and Afghan police. All the civilians had long gone: it was far too dangerous. Lieutenant Paul Armstrong and the sergeant did what they could to mentor the police but it was hard work. They had quite a nasty incident where a lot of the guys they had been mentoring were blown up by a roadside bomb. Some died, and others had horrendous injuries. After the incident, the police brought their injured to the British camp. The lieutenant was giving first aid to the guys he had been mentoring and that was quite hard for him because he was only a young guy and, of course, he had formed a bond with them. They had been working together for a few weeks.

The Afghan police are under-funded, under-manned and in a very difficult position. No doubt some may have family ties to elements of the Taliban, but the one feeling I did get was that we were all on the same side, that there was a common enemy. In fact, they were constantly being targeted – and they were losing more police than we were [losing] soldiers. They were targeted on a regular basis, occasionally in their homes but mainly at check-points, small police stations and in their patrol cars. Of course, they didn't have the fire-power that the British had, or the fire-power of the Afghan National Army. They were limited in what weapons they could hold and they were quite vulnerable in a lot of respects.

We started off with just three of us at the head-quarters in this new cell. I then detached an RMP section to it and there was also an infantry platoon dedicated to it. There were no Afghans as part of the cell; our team would go out to Afghans. We formed two teams and they would go to the check-points and to the police stations and initially we were trying to establish exactly what was in Helmand province because it was quite difficult to discover how many police actually existed there. Having the chance as a late-entry officer to command a company on an operation such as Op Herrick was fantastic. That sort of opportunity doesn't come along all the time and I just found the whole experience very rewarding.

There were times when we had some near misses. Seeing the boys come back safely off the ground when they had been near to an incident was always a relief. I liked the Afghans, very tough, resilient people. They were generous. They didn't appear underhand or out for themselves as individuals. They were a united entity.

August 2006

Lieutenant Colonel Duncan Parkhouse, 16 Medical Regiment

We treat a lot of civilians out here and it was this that led to the most surreal situation I've been involved in. We had a call, first thing in the morning, from a mobile operating group out on the ground. We were just finishing a shift at about six o'clock in the morning. The call said that a local villager had brought in a severely burnt child. At that time we were trying to unload civilians back into their own [civilian] system rather than have them clogging up the military hospitals but we went to pick up the child. There was no danger to the HLS and we weren't fired upon. The child had quite significant burns. There was no way the local hospital could deal with that so we brought her back [to Camp Bastion]. By the time we had arrived, we had a call from the same call sign saying that the father had brought in another six burnt children for us to pick up.

What had happened was, this villager had had a fire in his house during the night. At first light, he went to the call sign to chance his luck with a burnt child – to see what the Brits would do. Because we went to pick her up, he obviously thought, Right, fine. I'll go back to my village to pick up the rest of them. So he brought the rest of his burnt family to the call sign. Then we decided we'd go back but try to offload them to the local hospitals because civilians are a huge drain on our resources. Now, one of the things we have noticed in Afghanistan is that the locals use gentian violet as a type of antiseptic. You mix it with water and it goes bright purple. They paint it on everything.

But on this occasion, the Chinook landed on its marker, nose first. So when we came out of the back, we were quite disoriented. We didn't know which way the casualties were going to be. So we walked round the back, and suddenly it was like a scene out of *Apocalypse Now*. You had these huge Household Cavalry men – six foot four all of them – walking towards us in a line with these children. Some of the children were walking, despite quite serious burns. And they were all covered in this gentian violet. From head to toe they were blue. They had big blisters on the heads and whatever. There were about six, most of them under twelve, but there were a couple of about eighteen months and a baby too.

I felt I was dreaming. It was absolutely bizarre. We actually got them back to Camp Bastion. We'd had to resuscitate a couple back on the aircraft. We had to intubate this small baby, which is difficult at the best of times, but especially when you are in a Chinook. In the end, those with minor burns we sent out to local hospitals but we kept two on intensive care for – well, they outlived my time there. I think they stayed for about six weeks. Once or twice they were almost switched off [their life-support machines] because they were unlikely to make it and they were reducing our capability for our guys. But we continued to treat them and, in the end, they got better. They were actually discharged – amazing.

29 August 2006

Corporal Tara Rankin, 16 Medical Regiment

On this one occasion, we had deployed out to Sangin on one of the typical twenty-four-hour ops [Op Bhagi]. We usually go out from [Camp] Bastion. It was the early hours of the morning – about three o'clock. I was still a 7 Para RHA medic now attached to C Company [from 3 Para]. We had been doing what normally happens on ops – patrolling, carrying out route clearance, reassuring the local population and, at the same time, looking out for enemy forces or any enemy activities around the area.

One of our guys [3 Para B Company] was shot as

he was out on top of a building with his company near Sangin. It was about lunchtime and he had been shot in the neck-shoulder by a Taliban bullet. There was a doctor and medics in the area and we worked as a team. It was my medic colleagues from the Household Cavalry and 3 Para who did most of the treatment. By the time I got to the scene he was already 'packaged' and ready to be flown out. He was drifting in and out of consciousness. Shortly afterwards he was evacuated in a Chinook.

I knew the guy who had been shot quite well. He was Sergeant Paddy Caldwell and he was married to a friend of mine, who is also a medic. I had known him since 2001, when I was doing my basic training. I first heard when he was identified by his call sign over the radio and I thought, Oh, no. He's one of the last people I'd thought would get hurt. He's a lovely man – very family oriented, down to earth and someone who really cares for other people regardless of who they are and what profession they belong to.

I saw him again the next day in the main hospital at Camp Bastion. He was still in a bad way – he was about to be flown back to Selly Oak Hospital in Birmingham to be treated and to have an operation. I felt very worried for him and his wife and I just hoped he was going to be all right.

We were heading back into Sangin via these wadis, which were filled with water. As we were peeling back into the compound, we came under heavy enemy contact. Normally you have a contact left, right or centre, but this was from all sorts of directions. I realized there was a guy behind me who was taking time to catch up, as you normally do on your first manoeuvre. But I think it was the shock of being in that situation first time round as a young soldier – he had just come out of training – that got to him [and made him freeze].

He was the GPMG [general purpose machine-gun] gunner. But he was in shock. As much as I tried to reassure him and keep him going, it didn't work. I had to take his weapon and told him that we had to do something about it [the situation] because my normal A2 weapon wouldn't do much. Everyone was trying to locate where the enemy firing position was. So the guy holding the GPMG just went: 'Go ahead. Have it.' I set it up [to fire] applying the principles of usual marksmanship, principles that we have been trained in to use the GPMG. It was a quick target identification. I had seen who was firing at us from a compound. After notifying the platoon commander, I saw the guy fire out of the window. He was a [Taliban] sniper.

So I set the GPMG up on a tripod while under fire. Rounds were actually coming from all sorts of directions, left, right. There were so many things that were going on but all I cared about was getting the guys – all of us – back safe and sound. I wanted to make sure that we had actually pin-pointed where the enemy firing was coming from –

especially the sniper we needed to concentrate on.

From 300 metres, I identified the shooter. I saw his head popping out of the window. He was shooting from a double-storey building. It was the pharmacy building. I shouted to the platoon commander: 'Look out for that second-storey window in the pharmacy.' He looked for about five seconds and he still couldn't see it. At this stage, I thought: Right, something's got to be done about this because otherwise the whole platoon will be wiped out. There was nowhere to take cover.

I did the usual target indication as I used the clock-ray method. I was saying: 'Right, twelve o'clock facing, enemy on second window, double-storey window. Target seen,' and they [her comrades] said: 'No.' So I gave it a bit of time and did it again. I said, 'Target seen.' The reply was the same: 'No.' I said: 'Right, everyone, hold your fire. I'm about to fire to indicate the target.' Then I fired. I don't know whether I was excited or in shock. But the guy came out of the window. I saw him drop out of the window and I held my breath. But he was dead.

We have to abide by the Geneva Convention. As a medic, you're only supposed to carry a weapon to defend yourself and your casualty if need be. But at any given time and place, I have to adjust myself to the situation and the environment. I think for me, at the time when that incident happened, being a soldier came first – before my work as a medic.

Women can take a full combat role. There are some
out there who do. Not all females can do it, but there
are some. Anyway, then we retreated back to the
Sangin compound. On ripping back into the compound [still under fire], I thought: I can't run as fast
as the bullets are going past me. But by now, the guy
next to me had recovered from his little shock
period. I handed the gun to him. I said: 'Thanks, you
can have it back now.'

30 August 2006 [email home]

Captain Charlotte Cross, Territorial Army

Captain Charlotte Cross, of 3 Military Intelligence
Battalion (Volunteers), in the Territorial Army (TA), is thirty-
six. She was born in south-east London. She is the
daughter of an advertising consultant and a schools
administrator and has an elder brother. She has combined
a non-forces career with service in the TA for more than a
decade. A biology graduate from Bristol University, she
worked in publishing, then at the BBC's Natural History
Unit before becoming a journalist. She joined the TA in
1997 because she was looking for a new challenge, and
opted to work in the Intelligence Corps. After TA officer
training at Sandhurst, she was commissioned as a
second lieutenant. She deployed to Afghanistan in 2006
as part of the PsyOps (Psychological Operations) team.
Cross is single, and now works as a television reporter for
the British Forces Broadcasting Service.

As you can imagine, the work is pretty full on and tiring. It's literally non-stop from 0630, when I get up, until 2030 or later when we have our final briefing – and no days off. On Fridays the morning briefing is later, at 0930, to give everyone a lie-in. I've already been out on two patrols in Lash [Lashkar Gah] – yesterday we went out to visit the women's centre and girls' school. Nobody's really visited those places before because it's difficult for male soldiers to interact with the women. We also took the Danish CIMIC [Civil Military Co-operation] team because they do reconstruction work and want to carry out some projects at the women's centre and school. So we've decided I'll be the point of contact for the women now, for both CIMIC and PsyOps. We're hoping the women will be more comfortable talking to me.

We went to the girls' school first, a big single-storey building in the middle of a huge open space in the town. But it's incredibly derelict, just grey concrete rooms really, no windows, just holes, and the surrounding area is just rocky, sandy dust. It's guarded by armed ANP [Afghan National Police], but they're corrupt and useless. None of the people trust them – most of them work for the Taliban in their spare time. They pay them more and give them motorbikes. We spoke to the headmistress for about twenty minutes – she's been threatened by phone and by 'night letters' for running the school. They threatened to shoot her or cut her fingers off. She asked for a safe-house, but we can't give her that. It's very sad, really. There are 125 teachers at the school, teaching hundreds of girls in shifts, and they have literally nothing, so we give them radios, school packs, things like that, and CIMIC build them wells and improve the buildings. But we're not supposed to be creating a reliance on us, just facilitating them helping themselves.

The women's centre was equally inspiring – it's run by a woman who arranges English language, computer and cooking classes for about fifty. They get threatened on their way there – two I spoke to were in the back of a car when a man emptied an AK-47 into their driver. Yet they still turn up – they told me all they want to do is learn office skills and be allowed to work. But, again, their facilities are rubbish and they have to put their own guard on the gate. Nobody provides one for them. We gave them a huge supply of sanitary towels and hygiene kits (just things like soap and toothpaste), and they were so grateful. It's amazing what you take for granted.

This morning I was out on a familiarization patrol. We were taken all over Lashkar Gah to see the various buildings of interest, and the shoddily policed check-points, and we drove through the market and waved at the little children who run behind the vehicles. A lot of them stare and point, then collapse in giggles, when they realize I'm a girl . . .

On that note, an Afghan gentleman came into the office today. He looked utterly shocked when I told him I'm the new boss! He pointed at me and said, 'YOU?' He runs a school and wants computers for the kids. He did smile and shake my hand, though, so I reckon he sees me as some sort of strange foreign alien from another world. Not quite a woman, not quite a man, but something in between . . . That's what my interpreter said. It's gonna be so weird here.

3 September 2006

McNab: *The RAF's ageing fleet of Nimrod reconnaissance aircraft was grounded after a crash in Afghanistan claimed the lives of all fourteen on board. It was the worst single military loss of life since the Falklands War of 1982. The end for the twenty-nine-year-old Nimrod MR2, near Kandahar, came during the most intensive period of fighting in Afghanistan since the fall of the Taliban in 2001. It was carrying twelve airmen from 120 Squadron, one Royal Marine and one soldier from the Parachute Regiment. The aircraft was flying at about 10,000 feet when flames started coming from the tail as it fell to the ground. The accident meant British troops had now suffered thirty-six deaths in Afghanistan since 2001.*

September 2006

Major Maria Holliday, QGM, Royal Military Police (RMP)

Sometimes we would escort high-value targets [Taliban suspects] to Kabul on behalf of the Afghans because they didn't really have the resources to do it. Quite often, if we couldn't get the evidence, the detainees would have to be released. But when there was sufficient evidence to support an allegation that they were a member of the Taliban, they would be handed over to the Afghan authorities. They might have been arrested if they were in possession of a firearm or if they were seen to be firing at UK troops, or perhaps if they were in possession of documentation that would suggest they were a member of the Taliban. It was exactly the same sort of evidence that would be required in the UK. But once we had handed them over, we would have to monitor how they were being treated. We would visit the Afghan jails and speak to the detainees to make sure they were being treated correctly. We had a moral duty of care, if you like. There were no examples of mistreatment during our tour. The [RMP] boys, when they first went down there [to Lashkar Gah], expected to find really bad conditions, but they were OK. The jails were very, very basic but the cells were kept clean. Sometimes the Afghans did surprise us – they were better organized than we expected.

One particular incident springs to mind. The chief of police for Helmand province in Lashkar Gah asked me to go and visit a young girl called Leila. She was sixteen and had been put into the prison in Lashkar Gah. The reason she had been jailed was that she had run away from her family and had gone to Kandahar. She was hoping to get married to a young lad there but she had been found in Kandahar, arrested and taken back to Helmand province. The chief of police was concerned that if she was released back to her brother – who was the head of the family because she did not have a mum or dad – she might be subjected to an honour killing because she was said to have brought shame on her family by running away.

I did chat with her in jail in early September, towards the end of the tour. I went to the prison in Lash, and doubled it up with a check on a detainee, caught by the British, who had been sentenced and put into the prison. I asked the prison governor if I could visit the girls in the prison. It is the same prison as the men but the women were held separately. I was led through a myriad gates and compounds and eventually reached the women. There were five girls with some little children because they take the children into prison with them. There was a female prison warder, and they were all dressed in civilian clothes. I was asking, through an interpreter, why they were there. A seventeen-year-old girl had been given a seven-year sentence for adultery and a fourteen-year-old had been accused of adultery. She was awaiting sentence, but she was so shy and frightened, she kept hiding her face. You could see she was a young teenage girl. I remember thinking there was no way that girl had committed adultery or, if she had, it had not been of her own volition. It was awful to see her. In the UK, if everyone got locked up for committing adultery, half the population would be in prison!

There was a female medic who had gone with me to the prison as well – we took some toys and sweets for the kids because we knew there would be children in there. To start with, the sixteen-year-old we had gone to see wasn't there, but while we were chatting, she came back. She had just been in court and I managed to speak to her. She was very feisty: I was quite impressed with her. She talked through an interpreter but you could tell from her tone of voice that she was quite defiant. I asked why she had run away from home. She said she had gone to Kandahar because she wanted to be a policewoman. In Kandahar, there were a number of policewomen but there were none in Helmand province. All police were male in Helmand. She said she wanted to become a policewoman and she wanted to get married but she was adamant that she did not want to be released to her brother. I asked her if she would be in danger and she was quite non-committal. I went back to the chief of police and I passed on my concerns to him, but he was in a difficult position because it was going to be dealt with by the courts and Afghan law. I often think about Leila because I have no idea what happened to her. I passed the information on to a lady working for the Foreign Office, so she was aware of the case before I left.

September 2006

McNab: *Christopher 'Has' Hasler was told that he had become the first flying officer [he is now a flight lieutenant] since the Second World War to be awarded the Distinguished Flying Cross (DFC). This is his previously unpublished CO's report in which Hasler is recommended for a gallantry award:*

In May 2006, Flying Officer Hasler was detached with his Flight as part of the Joint Helicopter Force (Afghanistan), JHF (A) in support of Operation HERRICK. Hasler flew initially as a co-pilot, owing to his relative inexperience, but soon proved capable of fulfilling the role of aircraft captain. Hasler was actively involved in many high-risk sorties and displayed consistently the highest standards of gallantry and professionalism. Towards the end of his tour he was appointed captain for a number of key missions.

At dawn on 7 July 2006, Hasler led a formation of

two Chinooks into the area of Sangin. The mission was to provide an essential resupply and extraction for a 3 PARA BG [Brigade] Company. The dangers involved were extremely high. The day before, Hasler had attempted the same mission, but he had to abort because a Paratrooper had been killed by enemy fire while securing the helicopter landing site. To mitigate the risk to the aircraft, Hasler elected to land in an 'unlikely' site in order to achieve surprise. The site was surrounded by buildings on three sides and would make the landing particularly difficult. Undaunted, Hasler displayed great bravery, maturity and handling skills well beyond his experience, in leading his formation into Sangin and landing his aircraft successfully, just after dawn. He then safely off-loaded the vital stores before manoeuvring his aircraft quickly, but with supreme accuracy, to allow a number of troops to embark. Again, Hasler needed the highest degree of skill and composure to do this. As he repositioned, he intentionally placed the aircraft's rotor disc just above a single-storey rooftop. Any error would almost certainly have resulted in catastrophic damage to the aircraft. The mission proved to be a complete success.

On 14 July, Hasler commanded the third aircraft of a five-ship Chinook assault into Sangin, a Taliban stronghold and area of recent high enemy activity, as part of Operation AUGUSTUS. Hasler's aircraft was the last of three to land in the first wave; the second wave of two Chinooks eventually aborted their landing due to the heavy weight of enemy fire on the landing site; fire from enemy who were awake, fully alert and expecting the landing. Although a heavy fire-fight against 30–40 Taliban was already under way, and there was a strong possibility of the assault force being split and over-whelmed, Hasler displayed tremendous bravery and commitment and skilfully landed his aircraft, even though small arms and Rocket-propelled Grenades were being fired at his and other landing Chinooks. Whilst under effective enemy fire, Hasler held his nerve and his aircraft on the ground to allow his troops to disembark into the hottest of the helicopter landing sites, before taking off. Hasler's brave decision to do this enabled over-powering numbers of friendly forces to quickly suppress the enemy positions and for the mission to succeed with minimum UK casualties.

Throughout his 10-week detachment, Hasler dis-played great courage and composure, despite his relative inexperience. He maintained the highest standards of professionalism and airmanship in what was an extremely arduous, high-tempo flying tour in the most demanding, high-risk environment in which the Chinook Force has operated in its recent history.

September 2006

Colour Sergeant Richie Whitehead, Royal Marines

I was taking out one of the multiples. The intended multiple commander [MC] was still on course back in the UK so, because I was a spare floating MC, I was helping out everyone, showing people the lie of the land. We – a section of twelve blokes – were out on the southern side of Lashkar Gah, the southern side of the airport. We had recently had IEDs handed in so we were looking around the airport making sure there was no suspicious business. Even though we had got GPS [global positioning system] and maps, it was pitch black and nine times out of ten you made a wrong turn – and I did on this occasion.

In and around a built-up area, I came to a dead end. It was around midnight. I said: 'It's my fault. U-turn.' Everyone was giving me numerous shit over the radio so we turned around and started to come back. But as we'd turned our headlights had gone over the horizon at some stage, and this had been picked up by somebody. So we were just about to drive out of the built-up area, a dead-end alley that I had gone down, when all of a sudden there was Dushka fire at our vehicles from the left. A Dushka is a 12.7 Russian machine-gun. A big, heavy, slow thing. So, obviously, we stopped, switched our lights off. I was in an open-top WMIK and we reversed back in. All the lads had broken cover, contact reports had been sent, etc., etc. As soon as it happened, I thought: No, they [the Taliban] do not drive up to you this close in a town centre and have a pop shot. We were on the south side of them – they were closer into town. If it had been the other way [around], they could have escaped into the desert, but they were not going to escape into town. They wouldn't have done that because they knew we could call other people in.

There were three of us in the WMIK: me, a driver and a gunner on the back. Within a minute, I knew it was a police check-point that had fired on us. From the position and knowing where I was, I realized they were ANP. I had visited the check-point days before. All the lads were getting ready to fire back but I held them off. I told them to chill out. We put lots of para illum [parachute illumination flares] up in the air so they could see us. We were four vehicles – two WMIKs, two Snatch [lightly armoured Land Rovers]. We did this but they kept firing at us. We were not firing. The outcome of me firing or killing ANP at that stage would have wrecked all the hard work that 16 Air Assault and 3 Commando Brigade had done. There were about eight of them. It took forty minutes. Every time we went to move, I was stuck. They were firing at us, mistaking us for Taliban even though we had lit up the area. They could see our vehicle. Whenever we moved forward or back, or put up para illum, or flashed our lights – the Snatch vehicles had spotlights on the top – they fired at us. None of the vehicles got hit but we were pinned down. They were 350 or 300 metres away. Not far. But I couldn't go forward or back. I let zero – the Ops Room – know. They wanted to send out more people but I said, 'No,' because it was gonna cause more chaos. Then they [the ANP] were going to think they were getting attacked. So our interpreter – he was at the back of one of the vehicles and his English was reasonably good – he turned the air blue. He was swearing about these 'poxy, useless police'. So we called them on his loudhailer. And I said to tell them: 'We are British servicemen.' I told him that they must stop firing because, if they didn't, we were going to have to fire on them and we didn't want to do that.

So he spoke to them. All of a sudden the firing stopped. You could see the interpreter was irate and I was trying to calm him down. So I got everyone back on the vehicles, put our hazard warning lights on and we lit the sky up with the last of our para illum. Then we drove down. The ANP were all laughing because they thought it was hilarious. I was obviously not laughing. I grabbed their commander, took his name to pass on to the chief of police. And our interpreter was still swearing. We cleared it up and all came back. Thank Christ for that. For forty-five minutes they were regularly firing with their AK-47s, their Dushka. It was a genuine mistake, but that one was a bit too close for comfort.

9 September 2006 [email home]

Captain Charlotte Cross, Territorial Army

Sorry I haven't been in touch for a bit but I'm sure you've heard there have been quite a lot of deaths/serious injuries out here, and so Op Minimize has been on ... constantly. Plus there's been a bit of a siege mentality in camp ... We had reports of hordes of Taliban on the horizon getting ready to surge into Lashkar Gah, so everything stopped while we waited to be attacked ... I admit I didn't sleep very well for a few days. My body armour is SO heavy. I don't think I'd be able to run very fast or very far in it.

So life's been eventful since I got here 2 weeks ago. We had our first 'incident' on camp on my first night here ... having had no sleep the night before I was pretty knackered, but was woken up at midnight by my new boss dressed in full webbing and helmet, etc, complete fighting order, telling me the camp was under deliberate attack and could I please get dressed!!! Plus we had a casualty. The medical room is down the hall from my room, and I recognized that strong smell of disinfectant. So I got up, got dressed, and then basically we all spent a few hours hanging around in the corridors wondering what was going on ... Mainly I was worrying about my lack of ammunition, because having just arrived I'd only been issued one magazine [more magazines were due the next day]. Eventually we were all sent back to bed. I slept in my clothes, just in case.

The next morning, we were told the ANA in town had decided to shoot a group of stray dogs. The ANP or some other ANA thought they were being attacked and returned fire in the general direction of our camp – and some bullets came over the wall, went through one of the tents and hit a captain in the leg. Apparently he'd jumped up when he heard firing, but if he'd stayed in his bed he would've been okay!

Workwise, there is so much to do and everything takes so long. Plus we're a bit short-staffed, most of my PsyOps section were sent down to Garmsir with about 17 other Brits and a few Estonians helping about 100 local Afghan forces beat off a Taliban advance. Constant fighting for 6 days. And I mean constant fighting. One of the Royal Marine corporals from my team got sent down there (I rather hopefully gave him a video camera, but he didn't get it out of his bag). He manned a 50-cal gun and fired 1,600 rounds. And a sgt major from my battalion got shot in the arm. Garmsir is incredibly strategically important because it's the furthest south ISAF [International Security Assistance Force] have been and it's the main crossing point down there over the Helmand river.

We had a visit on camp from a woman from a Canadian NGO, who told us about the state of the IDP [internally displaced people] camps on the out-skirts of town ... children starving, people being recruited to the Taliban for the price of a day's food, the usual desperate plight of those displaced by war. The politics, though, is phenomenally complicated in that we as ISAF troops cannot be seen to help these people unless they become a military threat. We can't just go and give them food, because they can't become dependent on us. It's up to the Helmand governor to do that, to help his own people. But nobody seems to be doing much about it. Aid, when it's given, often ends up being sold in the bazaars – still in its UN wrappers. We see it as we drive by. What can you do in a country which blocks your efforts to help at every turn? It's very frustrating.

September 2006

Corporal Fraser 'Frankie' Gasgarth, The Royal Engineers

Corporal Fraser 'Frankie' Gasgarth, The Royal Engineers, is thirty-two, He was born in Carlisle, Cumbria. The son of a sales rep for an agricultural feed company, he has an older brother. Both his grandfathers served in the Army during the Second World War. Gasgarth left school at sixteen to start an apprenticeship in mechanical engineering but, after completing the five-year course, gave it up to travel around the world for four months. On his return, he made award-winning cheese while his application to

join the Army was considered. He eventually went into the Royal Engineers in 1999, aged twenty-two. During his time in the Army, he went on tours to Northern Ireland and Iraq, before being sent to Afghanistan in September 2006. Gasgarth, who is engaged, is based at RMB Chivenor in Devon. He got his nickname from comrades and was named after Mad 'Frankie' Fraser, the gangster – because he was always volunteering to do crazy tasks.

My arrival in Afghanistan was relatively straightforward – and was, without doubt, considerably less dramatic than an incident shortly after I had first arrived in Iraq, just after the start of the Second Gulf War in 2003. Now that was an adventure: the day two of us accidentally took a wrong turn and ended up being repeatedly shot at as we mistakenly headed towards Basra, Iraq's second city.

In contrast to Iraq, my first few days in Afghanistan were a piece of cake. We went out as a full squadron – as 59 Commando Squadron – and took over from the Paras out there. Our role was to support 3 Commando Brigade. My job was as a fitter section commander, responsible for maintaining and fixing plant kit. I took over twenty-eight bits of kit and, out of that, one bit was 'roadworthy' meaning – back in the UK – you could take it on the road, one piece was 'taskworthy' – you couldn't drive it onto the road but could take it onto site. The rest was 'U/S': unserviceable. Yet we had to get it all up and running. The kit consisted of everything from JCB diggers, medium-wheel tractors (which have a massive bucket on the front), excavators and graders. A lot of the kit gets sent to out-stations and is used for fortification. All the kit would be used for things like putting up Hesco [bastion] walls, building protections for the [Afghan National] police and building new forward operating bases.

I was primarily based in [Camp] Bastion but we went anywhere – on a road-move – where plant went with us. Perhaps you would build a temporary FOB. From there, the Royal Marines would disappear and do strike attacks but they would have a base to come back to in the desert. As soon as they had finished, we would collapse it all and take it with us. In Bastion, we would have fitters in every out-station and they would look after kit in each plant station. Kajaki was where I spent most of my time – two months in all – and that was where the 'hypothermia incident' happened. But that's another story . . .

September 2006

Major Maria Holliday, QGM, Royal Military Police (RMP)

I'm a bit of an animal lover. There was a cat in Lashkar Gah that we adopted. She became pregnant and had four kittens. The rumour was that she'd had some during the last tour and they'd all died. Anyway, she gave birth in a cardboard box in the Brigade Headquarters but we had to move them out of there. We moved them into an area where there was an Afghan gardener and he kept an eye on them. She got really bad flu symptoms and she was so weak she couldn't feed them. I was trying to give the kittens some dried milk powder made up. Of course, it wasn't the right thing but that was all we had. I also used a bit of cod liver oil but kittens are notoriously hard to hand rear. I was on the phone to the UK vets to get some guidance on what to do with these kittens but, unfortunately, despite all my best efforts, because I couldn't get any proper stuff for them, they all died one by one. The longest one lasted ten days. The gardener buried them all in the little garden in Lashkar Gah. I felt very sad. They had a harsh existence but that's just life in Afghanistan.

The mother eventually pulled through. I managed to get her some human antibiotics from a local who claimed to be a vet, but I was having to guess on the dosages. She later became pregnant again. She was a skinny little ginger cat. She was quite feisty. She used to chase the search dogs. There was a Labrador who was quite frightened of her and used to run away from her. I called her Nagina: she was a wild cat but she was getting fed. Lots of people's mums and sisters were sending her cat food [in the post]. I managed to move her at the end. I was in contact with a rescue society in Kabul that was run by a female American journalist. They said that if I could get her to Kabul, they would take care of her and try and rehome her. Then the cat became pregnant again and it was coming to the end of the tour so I thought: Nothing ventured, nothing gained.

I managed to get her to Kabul at the same time as I was also escorting some Afghan police. So I had a pregnant cat in a cat box in a bag. I took her up to Kabul in September, close to the end of the tour. She went on a helicopter from Lashkar Gah to Camp Bastion; it was a really hot day and she was terrified by the noise of the helicopter. Then she went on a Hercules from Camp Bastion to Kandahar and another Hercules from Kandahar to Kabul. I had some help from the RAF and she went finally in a Saxon [armoured vehicle] from Kabul airport to the British camp. Then I contacted the cat rescue place. She almost escaped at the camp right at the end: she made a bid for freedom up the wall and I just managed to catch her. I contacted the rescue society and they came to the camp and collected her. It was sad to say cheerio to her. Much later, I contacted the American journalist lady: Nagina had had another litter of kittens but, once again, they all died. So they spayed her. I have always been an animal lover. The two dogs I have, Alice and Bumper, are from Croatia and Bosnia.

25 September 2006 [email home]

Captain Charlotte Cross, Territorial Army

Hello ... Still in Kandahar, but getting ready to leave, which is a relief. I've run out of dollars and clean socks, and I can't put my laundry in because it takes 24 hours to come back, and I don't want to lose any of my clothes when I leave because I don't have very many! Oh, the traumas of living in a war zone. It's been okay here in the HQ, though seeing the politics first hand, sitting in on planning meetings, witnessing the absolute lack of joined-up working this Bde [Brigade] has ... it's been pretty enlightening. My days have been pretty dull too. Originally I was staying in a tent in Camp Faraway, so called because it literally is very far away from the rest of the camp. It has rows of tents called things like 'Albert Square'. The ablutions are in metal containers, with three metal toilet cubicles with metal toilets, and three little tiny showers with metal walls and floors, and three metal sinks All very functional. At least the water's been hot, when it's working. Sometimes I've had to trudge to the massive fridge and get bottles of water to wash in, which is freezing. So I wake up at 0645, trudge to the metal washing container, trudge back, pick up my rifle and go and wait at the bus stop to get a lift to the HQ ... Honestly, I thought I'd said goodbye to commuting for 6 months.

Once at work, I check my emails, then go to the

morning commanders' update briefing, or CUB. Everything military has to be reduced to three-letter acronyms, or TLAs. This is fairly interesting: every branch head stands up in turn and briefs the commander on their bit of the war – operations, intelligence, plans, info ops, joint effects, engineers, you get the picture. It goes on a bit. Once that's over, we all go to breakfast . . . I've been stuffing myself here. I usually eat a sausage, some tomato, a Danish pastry AND a yoghurt AND toast. I think it's a case of if it's put in front of you, you eat it.

Then it's time for coffee, and the joint effects meeting – they're trying (at the end of their tour and far too late) to join up the kinetic ops with the non-kinetic, which includes things like media, PsyOps and info ops. Then I spend the rest of the day in meetings, and touching base with the guys back in Lash to feed them information, and get info back from them. We have secure phone lines to do that on, but there's a massive delay so you end up talking over each other. I've also been issued a work mobile, which is good to just phone them up on for morale chats. My boss has had really bad D&V [diarrhoea and vomiting], and was put in isolation for a few days. They want me back there, for their morale, they say, which is nice. At least I feel missed!

Then it's lunchtime (like zoo animals in a cage our days are measured by mealtimes), and at 1730 we have another update brief . . . this time we link up by audio with Lash so the two HQs know what the other has been doing. But the HQ in Kandahar and the HQ in Lash don't really get on, so there's often a few sarcastic comments going between the two.

Then, of course, it's dinner-time, and later everyone kind of hangs around drinking coffee and pretending to work until quite late. There's a ridiculous work culture here of see-how-late-you-can-stay, even though you're not really achieving anything and will be tired tomorrow.

The camp is odd too because there are two 24-hour Green Bean cafés, and a Canadian, Tim Horton's, and people get seriously obsessed about going for coffee . . . I mean they actually talk about coffee like it's an interesting topic. I cannot wait to get back to Lash.

2

Introduction: Operation Herrick 5

In October 2006, the Royal Marines of 3 Commando Brigade relieved the Paras as part of Operation Herrick 5. The entire force totalled about 4,500 servicemen and women. 3 Commando Brigade had the advantage of coming forewarned and prepared for a fight. They also had a better force package than the Paras, with more troops on the ground and a whole regiment of Royal Engineers to focus on reconstruction and development. The Marines hoped to consolidate their positions in the various towns across the province, reducing their presence where possible in exchange for adopting a more mobile approach. There was also considerable inter-national pressure to make progress on the reconstruction effort. Despite the brutal winter conditions, the Taliban maintained their presence and, like the Paras before them, the men of 3 Commando Brigade soon became engaged in some of the heaviest fighting of modern times.

The main combat power was provided by 42 Commando with 45 Commando taking on the Afghan Army mentoring role. 29 Commando Regiment Royal Artillery, 59 Independent Commando Squadron, 28 Engineer Regiment, C Squadron Light Dragoons and the Commando Logistics Regiment all fulfilled vital supporting roles. Close air support was provided by RAF Harriers, air-transport support in RAF Chinooks and Hercules and 2 Squadron of the RAF Regiment undertook the RAF Force Protection.

10 October 2006 [email home]

Captain Charlotte Cross, Territorial Army

I'm now surrounded by Royal Marines. You've probably heard that 3 Commando Brigade have taken over command out here, so pretty much EVERYONE is a Royal Marine. That took some getting used to. I even had to sew the 3 Commando 'flash' – like a Girl Guide badge, or maybe Scouts is more fitting – onto the sleeves of all my shirts to denote the fact that I am part of 3 Cdo [Commando] Brigade. It's an olive green square with a dagger on it. It makes me feel quite hard. Although of course I'm still not, and maintain pink nail varnish on my toenails at all times. But that's slightly ruined by the RSM [regimental sergeant major] who's just arrived with the corps. He's ruled that we're not allowed to wear civvy clothes at all any more – we used to get away with it in the evenings, just sports kit and flip-flops, to give my feet a break from heavy socks and boots (bearing in mind it's still reaching 50°C most days). But now I have to wear my uniform all the time, and my feet are actually starting to rot! The skin on my heels is turning yellow. It's very attractive.

One of the Marines stabbed himself with his morphine the other day, which was quite funny. At least, it will be until I do the same thing ... I just carry it around in my trouser pocket (we all do, seeing as you could be shot at any time), checking every so often in a slightly paranoid way that the safety cap hasn't come off ... They're designed to auto-inject a 4-inch needle straight into your thigh.

11 October 2006

McNab: *The first British troops returned home after a summer of fighting in Afghanistan. The Army admitted that the period had seen some of the toughest battles it had faced in fifty years: for more than four months, the task force had been fighting in an intensity not seen since the Korean War. The force in Helmand lost sixteen men, killed, and forty-three were wounded. The amount of ammunition expended told the story of the fighting's ferocity: 450,000 rounds of small-arms fire, 4,300 artillery rounds and 1,000 hand grenades. One senior commander said: 'We went there to carry out recon-struction and we ended up fighting a war.'*

October 2006

Lieutenant Rachel Morgan, Royal Naval Medical Branch

Lieutenant Rachel Morgan, Royal Naval Medical Branch attached to the Joint CIMIC (Civil Military Co-operation) group, was born and brought up in the north of England. An only child, she left school at seventeen and joined the Royal Navy in 1992 where she trained as a nurse. She was working in a military medical centre before she was deployed to Afghanistan. She completed a ten-month tour of the country from September 2006, working in the forward operating bases of Helmand and the Civil Military Operations Cell, supporting the stabilization effort. She is now based at the Naval Command Headquarters, Portsmouth.

Random acts of heroism probably take place far more often than are widely reported – and often can be treated as normal. Sometimes offensive operations happen at night. On one occasion a night-time operation was planned near one of the main towns, Gereshk.

The op was to investigate how far the Taliban were coming into town at night in the area. The plan was to go out and watch what was going on. I was travelling in a Snatch [lightly armoured Land Rover]. We had about ten vehicles and between sixty and seventy soldiers. Unfortunately the Taliban were waiting – or, if they weren't waiting, they got their act together very quickly. It was midnight. We had been out for about two hours and we started receiving small-arms fire.

I was quite well to the rear [of the vehicle convoy] going in. We were deployed outside the vehicle and I was in a position on the far left of our location. There was an incident and we were contacted from enemy forces to one side. Appropriate call signs returned fire and after a while the Marines started to push forward but quickly there was a change of plan. In the confusion, one of the vehicles, a Pinzgauer, an open-top vehicle, overturned. It was a hilly area and it got stuck in a stream, or wadi. In the ensuing rescue one of the officers became lodged under it. There was no panic and the Marines were in constant radio contact with what was going on around them.

The Afghan night was as black as you can imagine. Most of the soldiers were operating with night-vision goggles which I didn't have that night but I could hear what was going on around me. In a very short space of time we could hear on our radio that somebody was injured and being recovered.

It was a young Royal Marine officer, not long out of training, who had been trapped, completely pinned down, under the vehicle. It turned out that the driver – who was a Royal Marines' sergeant – in the space of fifteen or thirty seconds got a wheel jack underneath the vehicle to lift it off his chest. The injured officer was so badly crushed he couldn't breathe. They lifted the vehicle up enough for him to breathe and squeezed him out from under it. They rescued their man even though there were bullets flying all around them. They managed to focus enough on getting the jack, making it work, getting to this officer, dragging him out from under the vehicle and bringing him back to the helicopter landing site. Within forty minutes or so he was picked up by a MERT [medical emergency response team]. He was taken back to Camp Bastion, where he was treated in the hospital and lived to tell the tale, and later made a full recovery. The quick thinking of that sergeant, and those Marines around him, undoubtedly saved that officer's life.

30 October 2006 [email home]

Captain Charlotte Cross, Territorial Army

We're in the middle of supporting a big operation, so I spent a few hours this morning chatting to a local mayor – otherwise known as 'Key Leader Engagement'. He came in to see us in his full Afghan dress and silken grey turban, with the long end draped stylishly over his shoulder ... He's a Spingiri, which means 'white beard', a reference to his actual white beard, which denotes him as a respected elder. We discussed politics and security for a while, then put him in our radio studio to record a message for local radio, and gave him a can of Coke and some chocolate Hobnobs we bought in the Naafi ... at which point he became very animated, eating handfuls of them and saying he would take some home to show his wife. He also said we should air-drop Hobnobs if we want to win over the local people. We gave him some ISAF freebies, and another packet of biscuits to take home. He told us that his voice on the radio would put his life in danger, and his two sons have to stay up all night with AK-47s protecting him while he slept. But he was happy to do it. He phoned us up later that day to invite us to his cousin's wedding ... Unfortunately, due to the security situation, we had to politely decline.

Other than that, we're really concerned about the schools at the moment, especially the girls' school. Because we keep going on about it, and sending up our reports highlighting our concerns and the impact it would have if the TB [Taliban] managed to blow up a school in supposedly safe Lashkar Gah, finally they're starting to do something about it. They've been doing threat assessments and plans for improving security and teaching the staff what to do if there's an IED at the school. Yesterday we conducted search training at the women's centre, because even if they have ANP guards, men cannot search women. Jen [a friend] put on a burka as part of the demonstration, which made the women giggle. The headmistress of the girls' school gave me a night letter she'd been sent, threatening to kill her for (a) teaching girls, (b) teaching girls infidel subjects, (c) allowing infidels into her school. It's a nasty situation. These women just astound me: they're so brave.

31 October

It's actually been pretty quiet, due to Ramadan, certain 'agreements' being dealt and done by elders, shuras [meetings] and the governor. I'm sure you heard about the suicide bombing and the death of one of the Marines on the camp. That was a surreal experience. When the news came in from the Ops Room, Sky had it flashed up on their screen within 10 minutes, before the family had been informed – the fools. They were told to take it down pretty sharpish. I can't imagine what my poor mother thinks when she hears things like that. My role that day was to phone around locals to find out what their perception of the bombing was, interview people who were nearby at the time, write statements for the press, get on the phone to the radio stations and push out the ISAF angle (the TB reported they'd killed 8 soldiers) . . . through our interpreter; hardly anyone speaks English. And through the 'minister for youth culture and information affairs', a chap called Jan Gull, the Alastair Campbell of Helmand province!

I got told later on by an unfeasibly tall and muscular RMP bloke that he apologized if we got any complaints from the Afghan reporters at the scene, whom he had personally grabbed by the scruff of the neck and carried away because they were trying to film it. I saw the footage on Sky, while I was eating my dinner that night, of the burning Snatch. It actually made me feel quite ill. Apparently the bomber was chatting to a stallholder, lots of children were playing in the street, he saw the convoy and just ran at it. One of our interpreter's cousins was killed, a little 10-year-old girl, so he took an hour off in the afternoon to go to her burial in the cemetery just outside camp. He cried when he told me.

We held a memorial service for Mne [Marine] Wright on the HLS [helicopter landing site]. The padre led the service and the commanding officers gave readings and the colonel made the most emotional speech ... The whole experience was very powerful, and unreal, and sad.

10 November 2006 [email home]

Captain Dave Rigg, MC, The Royal Engineers

Captain Dave Rigg, MC, of The Royal Engineers, is thirty-three. He was born in north Wales and grew up in Hong Kong. The son of an RAF officer turned commercial airline pilot, he is one of four children – three of whom joined the armed forces. After attending Sherborne School in Dorset, Rigg obtained a master's degree in engineering from Oxford University. He initially worked for a venture capital bank but quickly

realized it was not for him. Seeking adventure and wanting to travel, he entered the Army in 2001. After officer training at Sandhurst, he joined the Royal Engineers. Rigg did one short tour of Iraq before being deployed to Afghanistan in 2006. He left the Army in late 2008 for a career as a civil engineer. He lives in Winchester, Hampshire.

The rolling surf, lazy chai rooms and wild exotic parties were beginning to become a distraction and so the Big Boss has moved us to Lashkar Gah, the capital of Helmand province. We are now far better placed to direct activity, with a clearer understanding of all the various dynamics. However, nothing comes without a cost. The camp that we have moved to is in the middle of a D&V outbreak, partly because it is already crammed to capacity. Which means that the uplift of 160 people is having to be accommodated in a line of hastily erected tents sited between the inner and outer wall – known colloquially as 'Killing Area Lines' or 'Death Row'. We have been assured that the site is perfectly safe because at either end of Death Row there is a sangar with clear fields of view over the potential danger area. What wasn't immediately clear was that the sangars are manned by Afghans. Apparently these guys have been vetted and are deemed to be on the ball, many of them having been fighters for one side or the other for most of their lives.

There has only been one incident that has caused us concern and that was some time ago now. Early one morning after a particularly peaceful night, one of the sentries must have grown a little restless and decided to shoot a few dogs. On hearing the gunfire, his fellow sentries assumed there was some kind of attack going on, and so, regardless of the obvious lack of targets, they followed suit. At the time the gunfire started, Major Green had just got up and was bent over pulling his trousers on when he was struck in the backside with a stray bullet. From our perspective, the funniest part of this story was that the injury was not deemed serious enough to warrant him being sent home. Now that we live within the firing arcs of our friendly Afghan sentries, we awake each day with a strong sense of relief, then stay as low as possible until within the safety of the galley.

It's not all bad news, though. We do have an al fresco dining area, which gives it a dangerously mis-leading holiday feel. Of particular note, we also have a permanent goat detachment. Sadly we are currently without any goats, but that is soon to be rectified. The elders from Sangin ate the last residents, and the officer in charge of goats (OiCoG) is in the process of resourcing some more. (Major Cliff Dare had left a successful property-development business and committed to a three-month stint in Afghanistan to pursue his love of goats. He underwent arduous exotic livestock training at a secret farmyard in the Brecons in order to receive the coveted post of OiCoG.)

The goat-acquisition operation, Op BILLY, is now a routine drill. The OiCoG moves downtown in an armoured Land Cruiser with three accompanying armoured Land Rovers and associated personnel. Once at the bazaar, the vehicles take up defensive positions surrounding the livestock section and the OiCoG moves swiftly to the Goat Man to begin negotiations. The local elders are very important in our dealings with the more troublesome provinces and it is important to provide a goat that meets with their approval. Fortunately the OiCoG is UN Goat Authentication, Selection and Screening (UNGASAS) trained, and within minutes of having made contact he has got the goat on its back and made a full assessment of the beast. The negotiations then ensue, and, if successful, the goat is swiftly recovered to its new living quarters.

We are keen to procure two goats so that we can initiate some goat racing now that we have had to forgo attending the weekly camel racing. This is a particular blow to me because the Mustphuk/ Mustafette duo proved to be a winning com- bination. They came in first two weeks on the trot and now the beers are on me. Unfortunately, Club Lash is without booze (a concern with a load of pissed-up squaddies being in close proximity to the town and only a wall to restrain them). Instead we have placed wagers on the peak number of D&V

cases. Numbers currently at 41 and climbing. I've gone for 75 but some have gone as high as 140. These are the fellas you don't accept a cup of from.

That's it for now. Off to Death Row, where I hope to sleep soundly until about 0500 when the tone-deaf mullah wakes us. God knows what they're chanting about (excuse the pun). On second thoughts, it's probably best we remain ignorant on that one.

20 November 2006

McNab: *Tony Blair admitted that Western leaders had underestimated how long it would take to win the 'war on terror'. His admission came, amid tight security, during his first visit to the Afghan capital of Kabul. He conceded that the West had wrongly presumed in 2001 that, when the Taliban fled, the war was in the bag. At a press conference with President Hamid Karzai, Blair said: 'I think we are wiser now to the fact that this is a generation-long struggle.' He was speaking after the death of eighteen British troops at the hands of the Taliban in six months. Earlier he had visited 2,300 British servicemen and women based at Camp Bastion.*

13 December 2006

McNab: *It is revealed that Corporal Bryan Budd, a Paratrooper who launched a sole charge on Taliban lines after his platoon was ambushed, will be awarded a posthumous Victoria Cross. The VC is Britain's foremost gallantry award. Budd was part of a twenty-four-man patrol from A Company, 3 Para, which was sent to clear cornfields in Sangin. The Paras came under heavy fire with several soldiers suffering gunshot wounds. Budd ran at the enemy position with his SA80 assault rifle on fully automatic. He was shot and killed while launching the attack on 20 August 2006. Just the night before he died, he had been talking quietly to Lance Corporal Matt Carse, a Military Policeman, about his wife and the joy of her becoming pregnant again. Carse said the next time he saw his friend was when he helped recover his body. 'He was one of the best and bravest soldiers I had met – he had taken on the Taliban virtually on his own,' he said.*

December 2006

Colour Sergeant Richie Whitehead, Royal Marines

During October I had been given another 'Dirty Dozen' mission – to train up a group of Royal Engineers from 64 Squadron. What we wanted to do was have the maximum amount of input on the ground with Royal Marine multiples. I got given these volunteers and these lads who had been pinged in from [Camp] Bastion [to Lashkar Gah]. They all rocked up – they didn't have a clue what they were doing, or why they were doing it. Plant drivers, JCB drivers, graders – all young lads, all given to me, and I had two weeks to train them up to a suitable standard for me to take them out safely on the ground. Which we did. They were my Dirty Dozen and they were absolutely brilliant because they didn't know any better. So, whatever I said, they did, which was great because there were no arguments. It was brilliant.

So we went out at night and during the day and we used to visit the ANP and ANA positions. There was a plan of building eight or ten new check-points, which had once been mud huts. We were going to build a nice one for all of them with services and electricity and paint them pink (the schools were painted yellow) to brighten up the place. Just to protect Lashkar Gah. So off we went one night in December and there were major rains: it was really, really rainy. It was a hellish night but we were touring around the check-points. Now you couldn't see for love or money with the rain and we went out to north of Muktah. There were only so many routes you can take, and in the rainy season these would diminish because the rivers would rise and you would just get stuck – and you don't want to get stuck out there. We were all in Snatches because the suicide threat had gone up and we had already lost one of the lads: Gaz Wright, from 45

[Commando] in October down in Lashkar Gah.

I had been there over six months now and we had not only learnt a lot but they [the Taliban] had learnt a lot as well – about us. The threat of IEDs and suicide bombing was getting a lot higher and there were more incidents downtown – not against us but against anyone who was having anything to do with us. The clerical departments, the ANP, the governor's compound and all of this kind of stuff were getting hit quite regularly. So, sooner or later we were going to have to come across it.

Anyway, I was out at silly o'clock in the night in the rain with my patrol. And we drove up a normal route, which was one of four we could take. Out one way and back in by another. The lads were out on top [of the Snatch]. We were doing our thing. There were moans and groans and laughter because everyone was getting pissed with rain. We were only out for an hour and a half or so. We went through this certain area of Muktah. We stopped to watch the crossing point of the river Helmand.

We chatted with our ANP [check-point] that we wanted to see. I had a quick cup of tea with them. Everything was fine: they did their normal complaining – not enough diesel for the electricity, not enough ammunition – and then we came back on a different route: it sort of ran parallel to the one we went out on. And I had literally been out twenty minutes past this certain check-point in Muktah, when suddenly there was the almighty explosion to my right – towards the back of the patrol. Straight away I am asking for a sit [situation] report. Comms were not as good as they could have been, due to the weather. It felt like the explosion was a couple of hundred metres away – but it was probably more like five hundred. I knew we were in contact, but all my vehicles were safe so I was happy. I quickly drove into camp, reported it, went to the sangars. They reported a big explosion, fire and stuff, and they pointed in the area of Muktah and I was like: 'Well, we've just come from there.' And I'm thinking: Was this a delayed attack, or an attack on the ANP? So we got in touch with the chief of police, who you could ring whenever you wanted, and said: 'Look, there has been an attack in Muktah.'

He said: 'Yes, I'm aware of this, but it's not my check-point. It is south of my check-point.' Which meant it was closer to Lashkar Gah than we'd originally thought.

I told the ops officer: 'At first light I'm going to go back and investigate that because I believe it's something to do with me.'

So we went out the next day, on foot with vehicles as support, and we were asking all around as we retraced our steps. Basically, where we had driven, there were two anti-tank mines either side of the track, and they'd had the old metal plates underneath dug in – so when they got pressured, they'd come together and form a contact, which would set the two anti-tank mines off. This was all there still.

There was a little trench going off to the power pack. It was a well-rehearsed, planned and set IED situation. And we had driven over it. Amazingly – all we could do was put it down to the weather – we had enjoyed a lucky escape. The sand and stones were moving under the rain. It was flooded. And this had actually got in between the two pressure pads. So when we drove across it, it didn't make contact at that point. Yet twenty minutes later – when we were driving back – this had washed away and the contact had then come together with the weight of the mud and the general weather and the IED had gone off. It made a hell of a mess of the area. There were two big craters. The power pack had been taken out but if you pulled a wire out of the soil you could see a line so it was probably on a remote control. We spoke to the locals and they said they had seen people digging it in. And we had to say: 'If you see this, you have to tell us, especially if we're driving around. We're here for you. They wouldn't have cared if it was one of you that had driven over it instead.'

I had been in the first vehicle. I prefer to be the first. I could get hit, but I want to lead the patrol from the front. And I knew the ground so much better than the rest of the lads. It would not have been fair to put them first. We were lucky. It was a close shave but my attitude was 'Fag, quick. I need a smoke and I need one now.' But my mentality is you're there to do a job. If you start losing mates or anything like that, there's no point in getting upset about it. When you come back, that's time for it [contemplation] but if you do it out there, it's going to have an effect on you and possibly cause more casualties. With a near miss like that, I think: Let's turn it around to something positive. We're still here. Let's take photos of it [the device]. You can go home and tell your mates what you want. I tried to make light of it: 'Laugh and joke about it, learn from it if you can and just let it go – worry about it tomorrow. There is absolutely no point in getting yourself tied up about it.' If I'd got myself tied up every time something happened, I wouldn't have lasted six weeks [in Afghanistan] – let alone eleven months.

22 December 2006 [email home]

Robert Mead, Ministry of Defence press officer

Robert Mead, Ministry of Defence press officer, is thirty-six. He was born in Colchester, Essex, and was raised in a country pub run by his parents near the town. He has an older brother and a younger sister. He attended St Helena comprehensive school and Colchester Sixth Form College before graduating in philosophy and politics at Liverpool University. After a series of temporary jobs, he worked as a telephone insurance adviser. He became an English teacher in Greece, then

a reporter for a local newspaper group. In 2005, he left to take up a job as Ministry of Defence press officer for the Colchester garrison. Mead, who is single, volunteered for a three-month tour to Afghanistan starting in December 2006.

So, then, down to business. You join me on my third night in Stan [Afghanistan]. It is 9 p.m. and I am sat at my desk in the Press Information Centre at Lashkar Gah, home of the Headquarters of UK Task Force in Helmand province, Southern Afghanistan. I have just opted out of the Friday night quiz. Rock and roll.

For all those that don't know, I have taken over the post of chief media adviser to the Task Force, which sounds quite grand. It is a three-month posting and Rolf Harris only knows what will happen.

Stan is so far proving to be a fairly placid host. No gunshots, no mortars and no RPGs (rocket-propelled grenades – the favoured weapon of the Taliban). I have experienced one flight in a Hercules, one flight in a Chinook, had a couple of decent meals courtesy of the RAF, discovered my brand new 3–4 season sleeping-bag, apparently capable of easily withstanding on any normal day temperatures of down to –6°C – can do nothing of the sort – and watched Gordon Ramsay get mauled by a sniffer dog at Camp Bastion. Welcome to my new job.

He's hallucinating already, you're thinking.

Possibly on other matters, but not this. Gordon Ramsay was on my flight out here – travelling with two other chefs and the *Daily Mirror* to cook Xmas dinner for the troops at Camp Bastion. In return the Marines laid on a three-hour display of military bollocks, including allowing Ramsay to fire a few guns, blow up a few things, drive in a tank and, best of all, he got dressed up in an anti-being-bitten-by-a-dog-suit and was told to run in that direction before they set an Alsatian after him. Read all about it in Saturday's *Daily Mirror* or the *Mirror* website. And if you look very carefully you might see me in the background of the video footage. I do have a photo of me and Gordo (he's got a very big head) but it was taken after we landed at Kandahar at 4 a.m. and I had been up all night so I was not looking my best.

Double jet lag has set in good and proper as I only got back from Oz five days before setting out here on Wednesday morning. Seems I was lucky as the winter cold has set in back home and all flights from UK were stopped shortly after we took off. Thank chuff for that. I know this cos we have Sky News. We also have Sky Sports – ylpppeee!

My new accommodation is a tent along with 6 other media ops chaps, conveniently located in a lane known as Grenade Alley as it is less than 15 feet from the perimeter wall with the town of Lashkar Gah the other side. I am assured, because the wall is 12 feet tall [and] I can't see over it, that we shall be woken at 5ish by the sound of the Imam calling the local faithful to prayer from the nearby mosque.

I shall attempt to send back regular messages while here, and in return I ask only this of you:

Ladies, if you wish to help a man suffering in his long hours of solitude with only a member of Her Majesty's Royal Marines for comfort, please feel free, and I say this out of necessity, to send me regular updates on your daily movements, avoiding the urge to include those from your bowels. Those of a particularly charitable disposition could keep an ageing man more than entertained by attaching to those messages any pictures of you naked, or intimately clothed, in either compromising or uncompromising poses. I'm not fussy. They'll be our little secret. You all know you can trust me. (Think of it as practice should any of you fall on hard times and be forced to make a few extra pennies via the admirable medium of Internet porn. Should any of you subsequently go on to succeed in your new-found side-line profession, don't forget Uncle Robbie, who gave you your start.) (Please disregard this section of the message if you are a member of my family.)

Men, send me any comic ditties, works of Shakespearean prose and knowledge of any Internet porn sites undetectable by the might of the British military IT machine. And bearing in mind the speed of this Internet link it isn't very mighty at the moment.

Hopefully the quality of these messages will improve with time once I have perked up a bit.

It leaves me only to say Merry Christmas and a Happy New Year to you all.

24 December 2006

Captain Nick Barton, DFC, Army Air Corps

It was Christmas Eve. A pair of us [Apache helicopters] were on a routine task at FOB Robinson. We knew there was a patrol out in Now Zad, but we were not dedicated to support them. We had an hour and a half of fuel. We got a call from the Ops Room – 'Troops in contact in Now Zad'. We were probably fifteen minutes' flight time tops [from the contact]. So we would have been able to provide half an hour to forty minutes on station with what we had. I was commander of one of the aircraft. As fast as we could, we diverted straight to Now Zad. We were given the check-in frequency, the call sign and their rough grid. We got the spot map out for Now Zad to write down the grid and work out where they were. They had been contacted near ANP Hill. They had a call sign out on the ground and, as they were trying to work their way back, they were contacted.

At the time, there was a high threat in Now Zad. One of our other aircraft had been hit a week or two weeks before. I was the wing aircraft – the lower one

– and we were at 2,750 feet. I was doing 102 knots: we knew we were in a high threat [zone] so we had stepped up our speed rather than orbiting at min power speed, which would give us the best endurance as well as hard targeting.

As we arrived, it all went quiet for five or ten minutes. It was the Green Zone but quite mixed [terrain]. They [the troops on the ground] had about half a K to get back in. The next thing we knew was we had a sledgehammer hit on the side of the aircraft. We called 'contact' on each of the [four] radios. We definitely knew it [the hit] was low left. We had a whole lot of aircraft faults. As I looked out of the window low left, I could see muzzle flash still firing at us and called it on the spot map: 'Contact muzzle flash between blue sixteen and seventeen.' They [the Taliban] were lucky that on their first burst they hit us. After being hit, we were in shock. Initially, no matter how many times you have been hit in the simulator, this was slightly different. But then you quickly focus on flying and checking the aircraft. We had lost our electric load centre one, high-power switching module one, we had lost our fire-control radar, we had an anti-ice fail, an outboard rocket launcher fail, as well as numerous other faults.

So we broke clear of the Green Zone by two to three kilometres and thoroughly checked our systems. Both engines were working normally, no over-temps or over-torques and no signs of fires. We worked through it as a crew. Fortunately, I had called where it [the enemy position] was. The other aircraft had got eyes on to the firing point. He [the other Apache's pilot] kicked himself slightly because he waited for clearance to engage from the ground call sign, who was quite a way now from the contact area. He was slightly annoyed with himself for waiting because he saw the firing point and he could have engaged straight away in our self-defence under the Rules of Engagement. So he took a minute and a half, then engaged with rocket and gun – 30mm and PD7 rockets. On the ground there were two guys with some sort of Dushka [Soviet-made anti-aircraft machine-gun]. The other Apache then fired and put 200 rounds and at least eight rockets into it. Neither of us could see on the subsequent video footage whether we had confirmed hits or not. And they [the Taliban] are pretty good at shooting and scooting.

So we took two or three minutes checking the aircraft and it was fine. We had a couple of rocket problems so we elected not to fire them. We picked up the fall of shot from our wing aircraft and ended up firing off 140 rounds. By now, the patrol was safely back in the FOB. We had a slight difference in engine temperatures and pressures and things were starting to settle down on the ground. We had a couple of jets turn up so we handed over to them and came home. We got the wing aircraft to look at our aircraft [in the air] and our whole side panel had been blown open, unknown to us, because you cannot see underneath. So we returned to base and did a very careful landing. Subsequently, we saw a round had hit one of the electronic units, there had been a small fire and it had blown open the door.

Unknown to me, it [the incident] was written up [by a commanding officer for a bravery award]: I guess it was because we stayed, we saw the enemy [despite being hit], and we dealt with them. I still feel humbled by it all and must mention my co-pilot who was very much an equal crew member and a far more experienced pilot than myself. I, however, received the award [DFC] because I was the aircraft commander on that day. Needless to say, I get him a beer every time I see him.

December 2006

Corporal Tara Rankin, 16 Medical Regiment

I had been back from our tour of Afghanistan for about two months. I was working in Colchester [on the Army base] and I bumped into Sergeant [Paddy] Caldwell [whom she had seen badly injured three months earlier] in the corridor. I was shocked but pleased to see him. He was looking really well compared with the last time I had seen him. I told him I had been with him on the day he was shot, but he didn't remember – he wouldn't have been able to remember anyone from the point of his injury to [being treated at] Selly Oak [Hospital]. He's a really popular guy. I read [in a newspaper] how his commanding officer, Lieutenant Colonel Stuart Tootal, had been to see him in Selly Oak in October [2006]. His CO wrote: 'Sergeant Paddy Caldwell's words came in short, gasping breaths, as he struggled with the ventilator tube in his throat that was keeping him alive. "I regret nothing, sir. I would do it all again if given the chance."' That's typical of Sergeant Caldwell – he's a real fighter.

30 December 2006 [email home]

Captain Dave Rigg, MC, The Royal Engineers

Merry Christmas and Happy New Year from Lashkar Gah.

Who wants to spend New Year in Lashkar Gah? Despite all of my invites, not one individual has made the effort to come and see me and now I'm starting to wonder whether my real friends are here amongst the goat traders and camel racers of southern Afghanistan. During the build-up to Christmas, there was much debate about whether Father Christmas and his band of intrepid reindeer would brave war-torn Afghanistan. The other concern was whether or not he would purposely exclude us for having partaken in the extravagant parties that momentarily swayed us from the virtuous path that we had now found. On balance, we felt that Father Christmas was partial to a bit of drunken lewd behaviour – indeed, how else does one pass the long winters in Lapland? The next issue was a practical one: we lived in tents which did not afford him the conventional point of access. Most agreed that he was a resourceful chap and would naturally adapt and overcome. However, the less optimistic built chimneys just in case. Anyway, to cut a long story short, he did make it and I woke up to find a very nice pair of red boxer shorts and matching hat. The local infantry company now use me to draw fire when they need a diversion – thanks, Mum, I mean Father Christmas.

Christmas Day was spent in southern Helmand province visiting the local police and generally spreading a little Christmas cheer. The troops were obviously disappointed at having missed Katherine Jenkins and Gordon Ramsay so the Top Brass deployed me in my red undies instead. Sadly, they couldn't fit a turkey into the ration packs so we made do with pork casserole and biscuits brown, which is actually quite tasty, but more importantly (when sharing the same field toilet with 40 others) acts as a natural blocker. Some bright spark managed to knock up an improvised oven, and so we did manage a hot mince pie with our hot chocolate. As we travelled around the police posts, we doubted that the police were aware that we were celebrating a very important Christian holiday. Although they did hungrily scoff the mince pies we offered them as we tried to coerce them into manning their check-points. Then we recognized the overwhelming smell of ganja and realized they just had the munchies.

Anyway, that's enough of that. Time for my cold shower before venturing into town. The locals are throwing a Wet Burka night.

Happy New Year, everyone, good luck with battling with those crowds, paying inflated prices and then nursing those heads – not for me, thank you very much.

3 January 2007 [email home]

Robert Mead, Ministry of Defence press officer

Afternoon all, Happy Festival of Eid and welcome back to work.

Some of us – i.e. me – have been at work, defending the good name of the nations' armed forces, at 8 a.m. every morning for the past two weeks, come rain or shine, be it Christmas or New Year, the Muslim new year festival of Eid, or whatever the Islamic world does around Christmas time in order to mourn the birth of a small, devilish, messianic charlatan in a food trough somewhere in glorious and unjustly occupied Palestine approximately 600 years before the birth of the Prophet Muhammad, peace be upon him.

Let me talk you through a typical day during that

period. The day begins with the annoying beep-beep of one of my MoD-issue mobile phones at 7.20 a.m. I now have two almost identical Nokia models of this little baby. I say almost identical as my Afghan-issue one has the interestingly quaint feature of all the letters being in Arabic as well as English.

I say this is when my day starts, though that would be a white lie as technically my day has already had a couple of early preludes, highlighted by the need to get out of my actually-not-too-cold-sleeping-bag-now-but-cold-enough-to-induce-the-need-for-the-lavatory-at-least-twice-each-night. This is bad. This is bad because it necessitates having to get up and get half dressed to brave the approx. 100-yard walk to the nearest bloody lavs. And it ain't warm at night in winter Afghanistan, I can assure you.

So, the alarm awakens your hero, who stirs heroically in his lair, ready to pounce should the nation call upon him to leap to its defence at the drop of a small incendiary bomb. Leaping with energetic vigour and zest he then towels up ready to make the morning stumble back along the track to the lavs, or ablutions, as they are so formally known in the military.

Any semblance of sleep is evaporated by this cold morning march. Yet it is nothing to the return leg, as one jumps out of the shower (because, yes, there are showers, hot ones at that) and – in order to avoid the need for a manly moment of standing naked in front of your peers to towel yourself down and dress, in what is already a cramped area, coupled with the fact that being Marines these chaps make my already puny frame look like Mr Bean – has to walk with only his travel towel (ex large, my arse) to protect his dignity back to his tent. Yowser. Corduroy sack, anyone?

One thing I don't do in the morning is shave as my one true aim for this tour is to grow a beard. So far so good. Disappointingly there is the odd grey hair poking out but I like to think this merely adds to my distinguished air.

Breakfast then follows. A relatively simple affair of two Weetabix and a croissant. Very continental.

Then the first engagement of the day is the morning update at 8 a.m., all huddled in a tent as the mike is passed around to each dept in turn to report to the chief of staff the night's doings. This can be anything from how much contact there has been with 'Terry Taliban' to a meteorological report. All very rock and roll. Or at least it would be, were it not to be delivered in impenetrable military speak of acronyms, acronyms and more acronyms – or should I say TLAs (i.e., the acronym for three-letter acronym). A few examples are:

TiC – Troops in Contact
IRT – Incident Response Team
IX – Information Exploitation

(and my personal favourite)
FOB Rob (pronounced Fob not F-O-B) – Forward
Operating Base Robinson

Woe betide anyone who isn't down with this lingo,
and death was only a whisker away for my colleague,
who is RAF, when he made the mistake of calling 29
Commando 'twenty-nine' instead of 'two-nine'. And
we just about managed to save him from the gallows
when he almost called I Company Ivory Company
instead of India Company. Oh, how we laughed.

Bearing in mind that we are 4 and half hours
ahead of you there isn't much to do in the media
department from then until the UK wakes up
around lunchtime other than look at my emails and
suchlike and read through all the early editions
from the UK papers for the afternoon repeat of the
morning's brief.

Still your hero soldiers on until lunch, a relatively
impressive affair with a range of choices from curry
to burger and chips to salad and pasta and all that
gumph.

Then it's back to it in the afternoon. I hope you're
all deeply impressed with the bravery being demon-
strated on a daily basis.

The afternoon is normally punctuated by a short
snooze back in the tent. Ah, yes, the tent, my home
for the next two and a bit months. The interior is a
relatively Spartan affair but most occupants have
brought a little bit of individuality to their corner

SPOKEN FROM THE FRONT

with duvets, bits of carpet and hanging cupboards. My own slice of individuality is mess, and lots of it. This mess comprises of a stash of empty water bottles (real Nestlé Pakistani tap water), the odd wrapper from an issue bar of 'Italian' milk chocolate (cocoa not included) and the contents of the Xmas box we got from the Govt and you the people of Britain for the bravery we are demonstrating in being out here. Thanks for the flashing red nose and Santa hat. They'll come in useful.

What has perked up things no end is the recent addition of our own mini cinema. We've only just got it but it consists of a super-duper new projector with which we watch DVDs on the wall. Great. You can pick up cheap bootleg copies of DVDs dead easy out here. The Saturday market at Kandahar airfield is a good place to buy them.

This is in itself an experience. Kandahar is a massive base, mainly resembling a building site, which has around 10,000 troops from a mix of nationalities, and wherever the Yanks go so goes commerce. So, there is a big football-pitch-sized dusty playing field surrounded by a wooden boardwalk, cleverly entitled 'the boardwalk', and around this boardwalk is a host of shops selling anything from North Face camping-style clothes and Afghans selling hats, blankets and rugs, but there is also a Burger King, Pizza Hut, Subway and Canadian donut chain Tim Horton's. Not to be outdone the Canadians have rigged up a mock ice-rink so they can play dry ice hockey.

To add to this demonstration of rampant commercialism, on Saturdays there is an Afghan market selling everything from knocked-off DVDs, including copies of *Rocky Balboa*, which isn't even out at the cinema yet, to dirt cheap carpets and pashminas, fake watches of all shapes and sizes, jewellery stalls selling huge lumps of lapis lazuli, mummified tarantulas the size of your hand in delightful display boxes, a man selling old weapons from swords to old muskets and bloody great machete-type knives. There were also enough ancient coins on display to keep an archaeologist happy for a year. Place your orders now.

I could have quite easily spent the whole trip shopping.

I visited Kandahar on my way to a whistle-stop visit to Kabul. After a deeply unappealing delay at the large, tented refrigerator, which doubles up as the waiting lounge at Kandahar, followed by an hour in the back of a Hercules, which is actually much better than it sounds, we arrived at 5.30 a.m. to a bloody freezing Kabul airport, with snow piled up by the side of the runways, to spend two hours in a freezing cold tent before travelling to ISAF [International Security Assistance Force] HQ. This was redeemed by the fact we then drove for ten minutes through Kabul to ISAF HQ so I had my first sighting of actual Afghanistan people in their natural habitat rather than washing my smalls. This largely meant people wandering across a dual carriageway, and shepherds with herds of straggly goats by the side of the road. Lots of goats.

I hope I am painting an accurate picture of a life on operations with the military. And I haven't even started on the dependency I have developed for my daily fix of issue custard and the fact that my hands have begun to crumble because you have to wash them thoroughly before every meal and after each lav break with alcohol-based products for fear of spreading dysentery and vomiting.

Must go now. Meeting the Afghan Minister of Information.

May Allah be praised. Or at the very least not insulted by the infidel while I am within range.

11 January 2007

McNab: *Nato forces in Afghanistan claimed to have thwarted a major border incursion from Pakistan by killing 150 Taliban in a night-time operation. It was said that, the previous day, two columns, totalling 200 insurgents, crossed into the Afghan border province of Paktika. This was believed to be ahead of a spring offensive against Western forces. After crossing the border, the two groups were attacked by American planes, which dropped 1,000- and 500-pound bombs on the Taliban. The move all but annihilated the insurgents, according to the Afghan National Army, which found the*

dead bodies. Pakistan claimed it had also bombed and
destroyed Taliban trucks on its side of the border.

15 January 2007

Captain Dave Rigg, MC, The Royal Engineers

The rescue plan to save the wounded Marine had
been worked out. It didn't involve me. I had done
my bit so I decided to get out of the way and have a
'Hamlet' moment. It had been a long night and an
even longer dawn. By now, it was a beautiful day:
the sun was out, the sky was blue, it was about 15°C.
All was calm and tranquil where we were: it was
strange to think that just five kilometres away there
was a huge amount of chaos and destruction, bombs
were being dropped and people were being killed.
But this was Helmand province, Afghanistan: we
were used to trying to get our heads round things
that didn't make sense.

Having enjoyed some fresh air, I went back into
the tented command post. But the mood of relative
quiet that I had left had changed: things were once
again becoming excited and intense but I didn't
know why. The CO [Lieutenant Colonel Rob
Macgowan] was on his JTAC's [joint terminal air
controller's] radio, which meant he must be talking
to one of the pilots. Then, the battle group ops
officer said to him: 'Sir, if you need a volunteer, I'll
do it.' I thought: Do what? Something strange and

160

slightly disconcerting was going on, but I couldn't work out what it was.

Gradually things started to add up. When I had taken my break, there had been an agreed plan on how to rescue the injured Marine – Lance Corporal Mathew Ford – but this was now changing in front of my eyes. Lance Corporal Ford had been wounded during a dawn fire-fight when Zulu Company attacked a Taliban-held fort close to the river Helmand, ten kilometres south of the town of Garmsir. The assault of Jugroom Fort had been delayed, which meant it had lost its element of surprise and had not taken place in the darkness as originally intended. Eight Vikings [tracked armoured fighting vehicles] had stormed across the river, but as soon as they got to the fort side they came under a hail of gunfire, small arms and RPGs.

The stream of casualty reports coming through on the radio told us that things had gone horribly wrong. Eventually the decision was made to withdraw but, in the chaos, Lance Corporal Ford was left lying wounded against the outside wall of the fort. It was only after the withdrawal was complete that he was spotted from the sky – first by an unmanned aerial vehicle and then by one of the pilots of the Apache helicopters. He was lying wounded but, apparently, he was still alive. Lance Corporal Ford had to be rescued or he would fall into the hands of the Taliban. Before I had taken my ten-minute break, the plan had been for four of the Vikings –

supported by two Apaches, A10 aircraft and artillery fire – to go back over the river and retrieve him.

Then someone told me that the Apache pilots had recommended they go in as a pair, with two blokes hanging on the sides of each helicopter. They would fly into position, the four blokes would jump off, grab Lance Corporal Ford, and then everyone would fly off again. It seemed an extraordinary, almost unbelievable, plan. For one thing, I had no idea you could put passengers on an Apache. Where were they going to be? Hanging underneath it? Sitting on the side of it? No one knew at this stage how this would pan out. But the Apache pilots had formulated the plan and they seemed quite confident. Without much delay, the CO decided that this was the way to go. He asked for four volunteers. It was then that it dawned on me, and probably everyone else, that not only were they going to go ahead with the plan but that they wanted us, the manpower in the command post, to carry it out.

Without really thinking about it, a handful of people, including myself, volunteered. It was pretty instinctive, really. Then the CO went through the volunteers. He said to one: 'No, you've got to control the reconnaissance force, you've got to do this, you've got that job. Yes, Dave, you will go.' Oh, shit, I thought. It was one thing volunteering, but quite another being selected.

Another Marine, Marine Gary Robertson – Robbo to his friends – who had just turned up, raised his hand and he was chosen too. Then the RSM of the battle group came in, WO1 [Warrant Officer Class 1] Colin Hearn. He'd been dealing with the casualties. He walked in as four volunteers were asked for. 'Yes, RSM, yes, good, you'll go too,' said the CO. The RSM nodded dutifully, oblivious to what he had just become part of.

That gave us three 'volunteers'. Then the 2IC of Zulu Company, which had attacked the fort, was keen for one of his men to join. He found one of his signallers, who'd just woken up and was making himself a cup of tea. When asked, Marine Chris Fraser-Perry immediately volunteered – but he didn't know what for. So this confused bunch of volunteers gathered around me outside the tent and it was left to me to explain what they were being asked to do. I had been part of the planning for the attack on Jugroom Fort from the start and so was familiar with the lie of the land, which gave me an advantage. But I had also watched [on computer screens in the command post] enemy reinforcements streaming in from the south and suspected that the Taliban were regrouping in anticipation of our return. Going back in was a bold shout: I reckoned our chances of success were about fifty:fifty. It didn't matter; we had to do something to get Lance Corporal Ford back.

I looked at the three men in front of me. Despite being a bit bewildered, they were all raring to go.

ANDY McNAB

Everyone wanted to help, but it was the four of us
who had been selected to do the job. We didn't want
to let anyone down. I said: 'Okay, do you know
what we're going to do?'

'No, sir,' came the reply from all three men.

'Right. Well, we're going to get on to two Apaches
and we're going to fly to where Lance Corporal Ford
is, we're going to collect him and then we're going
to fly out.' I tried to disguise my concern, attempting to sound confident and in control.

Judging from the expressions facing me, my
fellow volunteers were equally worried. Everyone
looked pretty stunned. The silence was awkward so
I carried on: 'Right, I'll pair up with Chris. RSM, you
take Robbo. Grab your weapon and body armour:
the faster we are, the greater the chances of our
success here. We've got to get in and out really
quick. We'll have loads of supporting fire-power,
but we must avoid getting caught in a fire-fight. We
just need to go in, get him, and get out.'

Without any hesitation or further questions, the
boys ran off to get their stuff. Pretty soon, the two
Apaches came swooping over the top and landed
behind us. The ops officer stepped out of the tent.
'Right, here they are, everyone. Go, go, go: we
haven't got much time! The helos are low on fuel.'
So without really thinking about it or compiling any
kind of plan, we were sent into action. I had my
SA80 with six magazines of ammunition, a smoke
grenade, a frag grenade, my Osprey body armour

and a helmet. And everyone else had similar kit.

We'd all volunteered, but my main worry was that the lads hadn't been briefed well enough. They didn't know where exactly Lance Corporal Ford was, what precisely we were going to do and, at this stage, I didn't know how we were going to sit on the helicopters. So I was pretty nervous about the whole thing. I asked the CO what the plan was and he told me that the pilots would brief me.

I jogged off towards the two Apaches and the pilots both slipped open their canopies. One of them was leaning out and greeted me as I ran up to him. He gave me the thumbs-up, as though to say: 'Shall we go?'

I thought: Is he mad? Did he expect me to swing my leg over the rocket pod, and off we'd go, do the job and come back and it's as simple as that? As it turned out, he did. But the pilot registered my concern. He shouted a load of instructions at me, gesticulated, pointed at the fuselage, handed me this green strop [to tie Lance Corporal Ford to the side of the helicopter once he had been rescued] but I couldn't hear a word because the helicopter engine and the rotors were still turning. However, I soon got the gist of what he wanted us to do and realized that, with time running out, it was up to us to make it work.

With the other boys, I moved away from the helos. We drew a little sketch in the sand and briefed the others on what to expect: 'Right, here's the large outer wall. Ford's there. You boys form the reserve and cover us. We'll go and get him.' Then one of the pilots joined us and said a few reassuring words. Needless to say, they fell on deaf ears.

Feigning confident optimism, we ran in two pairs to our respective helos and jumped on board. I was on the right, Chris Fraser-Perry on the left, and before we knew it the helos were taking off. We just sat there. The fuselage of the Apache has got a horizontal platform that juts out just below the cockpit – later I was told that it was the fuel tank – and I could get a bum cheek on that. We sat one each side of each Apache. I had my right foot on the Hellfire missile rails and there was a grab-hold on the side of the cockpit that the pilots use to climb in.

It was ridiculous. I almost laughed. The helicopter took off, hovered momentarily, then accelerated over the HQ. I looked down at my colleagues who were waving and photographing us from the ground. I even waved back. I didn't expect to see them again. Here we were, sat on the side of a helicopter gunship, about to fly into a heavily armed Taliban fortress defended by an estimated 200 men. The sheer audacity of it was hard to believe. I forced myself to stop thinking about the possible morbid consequences and instead focused on what had to be done . . .

We flew off and the plan changed immediately because our helo, instead of being the first as intended, became the second in the pair. Both helos flew low over the desert, hit the river just south of Jugroom Fort, then followed it. We were only doing about fifty knots, quite low – about 100 feet. You could see everything below as clear as day, camels and shepherds going about their business, and here we were sat on these helicopters about to fly into a heavily armed Taliban fortress. It felt just unreal.

I also realized, just after taking off, that I hadn't fired my weapon since arriving in Afghanistan on 24 August. I thought: Oh, shit. I'd been cleaning it and doing the usual routine, but I thought: What if it's jammed or not working? So I had a couple of test fires from the wing of the Apache. I don't think many people could say they've fired their personal weapon from the wing of the Apache.

But it alarmed the pilots. They must have heard the gun going off from right outside their cockpit. They looked around shocked, wondering what the hell was going on. They saw me and I must have looked a bit like a naughty schoolboy sat there having just fired my weapon. They probably thought I'd had a negligent discharge – when you fire your weapon by accident. I hadn't. I was just test firing it and fortunately it worked.

As we approached the fort, I could see all the dust and smoke, trees burning, buildings bombed to bits, craters. It was just an awesome image of destruction and chaos. The bombing from our air support had stopped just before we got there, but the air was still thick with clouds of dust and smoke. The first helo went straight in and disappeared into the smoke. We hung back and paused. I remember feeling very vulnerable. I sat on the side looking down and seeing this copse of burnt trees but there were still muzzle flashes coming out of them, so there was still live enemy down there.

I was doing my best to blend into this helo so they wouldn't know there was someone sat on the side of it. But basically I'm sat there looking at the gunfire below and thinking: Fuck, I'm completely vulnerable here. I wish he'd just move forward to get this over and done with. And he did. As the smoke cleared, it became obvious that the first helo had overflown the perimeter wall – and had actually landed inside the compound, which was not the plan.

But the two lads on either side of the wing hadn't seen the wall, so they didn't know they were inside – not outside – the compound. They'd been told to run forward to the wall, but what they were actually doing was running forward to the inner wall, and into the lions' den. They were being fired at from point-blank range from little firing holes cut into this inner wall. And, not surprisingly, they were utterly confused. They kept going but in doing so they ventured further into the fort. By now, there were two other Apaches supporting us. One was overhead of the first helo, providing covering fire for the two guys on the ground. The Apache was so close that the empty cases from the 30mm cannon were falling around our lads as they were running around the compound. By now, the other Apache had joined in the fight and their thumping cannons were deafening.

One of the pilots in the Apache that had landed realized the mistake. He jumped out to go and get the two Marines who were now in danger of coming face to face with hordes of Taliban. They were utterly confused after being shot at – and, with the Apache providing intimate fire support right above their heads, the situation was pretty intense.

Fortunately we landed outside the wall, about seventy metres short of Lance Corporal Ford. I leapt from that Apache and sprinted as fast as I could across this horrible, rough land up the hill. My body armour weighed about fifteen kilos, and I also had my weapon and ammunition, so I was pretty weighed down. By the time I got to Lance Corporal Ford I was already out of breath.

He was slumped over. His body position was limp and it was pretty obvious he was dead. But I rolled him over – and the first thing that struck me was how heavy he was. Just rolling him over was a real effort and he was a pasty grey colour. He had been shot pretty much in the middle of the head; it was just a small entry wound.

Lifting a dead body from the ground is not easy, especially as he was wearing all his kit: he must have been a fourteen-stone bloke. He had a radio as well and he was just incredibly heavy. I could not get him off the ground, not properly, not enough to get him onto my shoulder. Panic set in. I thought: Fuck! There's a lot of gunfire going on and I can't move this bloke. I started to do what I should have done immediately and dragged him by his webbing.

But it was a very slow process. I was running backwards dragging him. My weapon was getting in the way. Initially I had him under the armpits, but there was a lot of blood and gore so he kept slipping. And I was alone. I didn't know what had happened to Chris, but I thought that maybe he was disoriented and had run in the wrong direction. I had dragged Lance Corporal Ford's body about twenty yards, when suddenly Chris caught up with me. By now I was absolutely exhausted – and making very slow progress. Together we made better progress, but only marginally.

I think it was because we'd come from a safe environment and we were thrust into a very intense combat zone, then presented with a dead body, and I wasn't psychologically prepared for it. It was bothering me that my weapon kept hitting Lance Corporal Ford's head. We were a bit too gentle and considerate, which was putting everyone at risk. I could hear my heart beating against my breast-plate and feel the adrenalin pumping through my veins, but despite the obvious urgency we were making painfully slow progress.

As we were struggling to get Lance Corporal Ford back, one of the pilots from the Apache saw what was happening. He jumped out and came running forward. He was more tuned in and he said: 'Right, fellows, don't fucking worry. Forget about the gunfire, it's all ours. Let's just get him back.' And it was then that we suddenly switched on, grabbed hold of him and just dragged him back. We all got him to the helo.

By which point the other two from the helo had done their full lap of the Taliban garden. In fact, it was three of them because one of their pilots was with them, and they took up positions around us. But we were pretty much done now: we just tied the strops around Lance Corporal Ford's torso and attached him to the undercarriage of our helo.

I thought I was tired, but the three from the other helo looked absolutely exhausted. They were buggered. But, having survived their unplanned tour, they now had to run to the helo on the other side of the perimeter wall. Which they somehow managed to do unscathed.

Our pilot jumped in, we jumped on the rails again, took off and disappeared. The relief was immense. But it was very sad because, as we flew over the river, all of Zulu Company were lined up on the west bank, waiting and hoping. But they could see our helo flying over with Lance Corporal Ford's body hanging limp from beneath it, obviously dead. It was a pretty solemn moment for everyone. Seconds later, we landed and put Lance Corporal Ford on the ground. Later, the Chinooks arrived and flew his body back to [Camp] Bastion.

15 January 2007

Captain Nick Barton, DFC, Army Air Corps

At this time, I was on a rota: I would spend three days on deliberate tasks, three days on high readiness, three days air testing, three days doing spare work. On this day, I was on deliberate tasks. We were well read into Op Glacier. We had all the sat imagery and spot maps for the Jugroom Fort area. I remember thinking: What are they [the Vikings and men] going to achieve by crossing [the river] and then withdrawing? But my job was just to provide the best support we could. It was a 1.30 a.m. lift and on station for 2 a.m. It was a twenty-five-minute flight down there from Camp Bastion to just south of Garmsir.

It's much harder flying at night, no question. It's much harder to pick up people moving around. It takes you longer to get oriented. You see through thermal imaging but the night-vision system in the Apache is not particularly easy. We make sure we separate each aircraft by 500 feet so we can concentrate.

We were up in the air and initially we were just providing the ISTAR [intelligence, surveillance, targeting, acquisition and reconnaissance]. We had offensive Rules of Engagement and it had all been cleared. But then we could see [Taliban] sentries – guys with weapons – out around the fort and we divided them up between the two of us. I was mission commander for the pair [of Apaches]. We were cleared to destroy the sentries under direction and we were talked on to targets. We opened fire with 30mm on to the sentries. I only got one out of the two of mine: my gun was slightly off. Our wing aircraft was bang on every time, whereas mine seemed to be falling off fifteen metres to the left. Once you get that, you just have to adjust. They [the sentries] could have heard us but they wouldn't have known where we were. But when we opened up, they started running so we needed to get first-round hits or second-burst hits. Once a target starts running, it becomes quite hard. But there was quite a lot of fire coming up at us from across the bank. There was quite a lot of activity [Taliban] going on.

Then, shortly after 3 a.m., it started to go quiet. The Ops Room were talking to us throughout and then we went back to refuel. They said they were looking to cross the river at such and such a time – 5.30 a.m. I think. So we were back up [in the air] by then. I remember thinking: This could be quite interesting. I wasn't sure they had tried fully laden Vikings on a major river crossing before.

As mission commander, I concentrated on providing cover for the 'friendlies' as they crossed the river in their Vikings. I watched the Vikings cross from about 2,000 or 2,500 feet. The wing aircraft concentrated on enemy movement in and around the fort. Bear in mind, it was well synchronized before they crossed. There was a B1 dropping approximately

five 2,000-pounders [bombs] on all the key buildings there. As soon as they crossed the river, the first
of eight Vikings was opened up upon from the three
sides at three different points. And I was watching
that – there was tracer coming from everywhere. It
took a few moments for the lead JTAC to assign us
tasks amid the confusion, bearing in mind there
were six or seven controllers on the radios, all from
various parts. Each aircraft worked to a different
JTAC and also monitored the lead JTAC or battle-
space manager, as well as talking inter-aircraft and
giving updates to our Ops Room.

Eventually, they cleared us to engage. We were
probably firing some eight minutes after the Vikings
were shot at. We fired 30mm only: it wasn't 'danger
close' but it wasn't far off. The 'friendlies' were only
150 metres away from where we were firing, so you
have to be pretty accurate. The guys [on the ground]
were happy with us: they were getting fired at so
they just needed [Apache support] fire. We fired
lots. I didn't fire any rockets on that wave, but I
fired all my 30mm bar forty [rounds]. I fired two out
of four of my [Hellfire] missiles. The other aircraft
did the same. At some point in the initial fire, they
received four or five casualties, including, unfortunately, Lance Corporal [Mathew] Ford. They
[British forces] recovered the casualties, got in their
vehicles and went back [across the river]. To start
with, they confirmed all 'friendlies' were on the
west side of the river. This came over from the JTAC.

Then they proceeded to give us targets of all the locations they had received fire from, to put missiles in and fire, which we did. Ten minutes later, with shock we received 'Ugly, Ugly: cancel. Cancel. One man still missing. One man still on the east side of the river.'

You can imagine, my heart was thumping because we had been putting down all this fire. By this time, we were low on fuel and we stepped up the other pair [of Apaches], the high-readiness pair. And [Warrant Officer Class 1, now Captain] Tom O'Malley was mission commander for that pair. I gave him a handover, saying we believed Lance Corporal Ford was somewhere in the area. We gave them all the grids. Then they spent their full three hours of fuel providing ISTAR, looking for Lance Corporal Ford. Then they found him. While the Marines were working out their plan, Tom [and other Apache pilots] came up with their [alternative] plan [to rescue Ford using two helicopters]. We got back to Bastion, landed, refuelled, rearmed and shut down. We got out and we were just walking back when we got a call from the Ops Room: 'Get back in, power up.' I had spoken to the OC. He said: 'You may be needed to provide fire support and go back in for one more wave.'

We had already flown six hours and you're only allowed to fly for eight without having an extension. But we couldn't have been better read into the scenario. By this time it was about 11 a.m. We heard the plan [that two other Apaches would fly in with four men clinging to the sides], divided up, worked out a time line: absolute maximum ten minutes on the ground [for the two Apaches], but try and be off in five minutes.

We knew one aircraft would fire to the north of the fort and around, while the other would put suppressive fire down on the south. We were just up high [in the skies] co-ordinating it. It took a 2,000-pounder from a B1 to initiate the surprise. There was a massive smoke cloud, dust – the place was absolutely obliterated, really. The other two aircraft were coming in low at fifty feet and we were on either side. We were close enough to feel the blast from the 2,000-pounder as it went in. I don't think it's anything I'll ever see again.

The wing aircraft put a load of suppressive fire down on the northern compound and around, whilst we fired 30mm, initially to the south of the fort. We didn't fire any of our missiles that time, but the other aircraft did. We then did counter-rotating orbits at various heights. We stepped lower than we should – about 1,400 feet – and the other aircraft was even lower at 800 feet. We tried to vary it a bit.

But it worked. If you'd planned the whole thing for days, you probably couldn't have co-ordinated it any better: to get all the surprise and fire-power there. However, because of all the dust, it meant that Tom had to land slightly further forward. After he landed, Tom was like: 'Ugly Five Two. I am being shot at. My three o'clock, fifty metres.' We were: 'Stand by. Confirm three o'clock. Fifty metres from your aircraft.' By this time, because we were so close, it was hard to target with the sight. It was much easier to look out of the window with your eyes and link the gun to your helmet. So the rear seat took over firing with a manual range on the gun. We called: 'UG Five Zero, This is UG Five Two. Stand by, firing now.' UG50 came back with: 'Good rounds. Just in the corner, thirty metres, just where the wall is, one man.' We repositioned slightly and fired again, this time only thirty metres from our wing aircraft on the ground. Fortunately, they were good rounds. That was probably the most sporty firing we've ever done. The margin for error was not very much.

They were about seven minutes on the ground. Then they got back up and lifted off. The other aircraft went Winchester: got rid of everything. I didn't fire any missiles, but we fired our rockets. We came back with [just] two missiles on board.

We remained on station for a bit before returning to Bastion. It was a good two or three hours before we heard that Lance Corporal Ford had died.

You can always pick things out you could have done better. But I was pretty pleased with how the flight had done. Morale had been high up until the point we had heard that news [the death of a soldier]. When they [the two Apaches] went in, I thought: This is ballsy, this is very ballsy. We had a lot of assets [fire-power] in there, but this was not stuff we had ever done before. This was high risk: there were a lot of enemy in the area with RPG and an aircraft on the ground makes an easy target. It is satisfying to take part in an op like that. I have done two tours since, but I have never seen anything like it. Unfortunately, we did not save Lance Corporal Ford but we had tried everything and beyond to get him back.

16 January 2007

Captain Dave Rigg, MC, The Royal Engineers

At 7 a.m. – some twenty-four hours after Lance Corporal Ford had died – we all had a service in the desert to commemorate him. It was very moving.

By now I had taken in the enormity of what we had done. Some people might wonder why we went to such lengths to recover the body even when I suspected he was dead. But once we had set off on our mission, we never once considered pulling out. Leaving our own in enemy hands was inconceivable; we were utterly determined to bring him back. And quite rightly so. It would have sent a very bad message to our soldiers, had we left one of our own behind to the mercy of the Taliban. They are known to be brutal and despicable in their treatment of enemy bodies. It was also important to deny the Taliban the opportunity to capitalize upon the fact they had a dead soldier for propaganda purposes. And it was important for Lance Corporal Ford's family that we got his body back. It was only right that they were given an opportunity to mourn, to grieve over a body.

By now, I had also had a chance to think about my own role. To be presented with a situation like that, and come through it, is a very satisfying experience. You learn a lot about yourself – it answers a lot of questions you would never otherwise have asked.

There's no doubt that an experience like that engenders a lot of satisfaction: knowing that, when push comes to shove, you can keep your head and produce the goods. But that's different from saying, if faced with the same scenario, I'd be able to do it again. I'm just glad that things didn't turn out worse. But, having said that, I also know that I could have done a lot better. There were times when it didn't go that well because I hesitated. There was a lack of coherent thought and decisiveness, perhaps, which caused more delay than was necessary. But, then, how do you plan for something like that?

I also had time to ponder what would become the biggest regret of my military career. During the process of recovering Lance Corporal Ford's body, my weapon – an SA80 – kept slipping off my shoulder and whacking him in the head. It was bothering me for some bizarre reason and it was slowing us down. So I took it off and put it to one side, intending to go and get it. Well, obviously I never did go and get it – I left it lying in the sand. For a soldier, that's a mortal sin.

So, from that moment onwards, I got a lot of stick. Whenever I met someone it was never 'Oh, you're Dave Rigg, the guy who helped to recover Lance Corporal Ford.' Instead, it was 'Oh, you're Dave Rigg, the guy who donated his weapon to the Taliban armoury.' Weeks later, when one of the Taliban commanders was spotted roaming about with my SA80 slung on his back, I became known as 'Mullah Rigg'. I even had to complete a police report: the RMP wanted to know why I hadn't recovered it. In response, I asked them why they hadn't visited the scene of the 'crime'.

January 2007 [diary]

Corporal Fraser 'Frankie' Gasgarth, The Royal Engineers

Who dares wins – or gets hypothermia trying.

At 3,100 feet high and some 60 miles north-east of Camp Bastion, Kajaki promised to be quite different from the barren, windswept, arid dustbowl that had offered Plant Section a place to call home for so long. So I eagerly joined the long queue to board the Chinook, which was to deliver myself and the rest of my section to the promised land of such mystical things as birds, trees and grass. Indeed, if it was good enough for the now long-extinct Afghan royal family, then who was I to decline?

The RAF's obligatory one-and-a-half-hour delay seemed to still catch us off guard, as we stood aimlessly, resembling a school of six-feet tortoises carrying everything but the kitchen sink into the Tardis, which is my bergen. Now let me tell you a little about the tortoise: the tortoise has scant regard for evolution, has no interest in the latest high-tech air-flow bergen strap-device thingies, but still manages to carry its entire sleeping system on its back and shows no sign of stress or strain for one good reason: it stays put, has no airs of grandeur to travel any further than it takes to hunt down and kill anything more energetic than a lettuce. I think we could learn a lot from the tortoise!

When you think of the official residence of a royal family, the plush and privileged abode of Buckingham Palace or the impeccably managed estates of Balmoral might spring to mind. They did with me too. It quickly became evident that the Afghan royal family had been somewhat further down the status ladder than our own beloved Queen. But as Mr Einstein so correctly put it: it's all a matter of relativity. By comparison to the locals, with our erratically powered 60-watt bulb, running water and outdoor swimming-pool, we were living the high life.

To a squaddie, an outdoor pool is a source of great attraction, even at an altitude of 3,100 feet, even in the depths of an Afghan winter, even when during the hottest of Afghan days the water doesn't even reach the official temperature of 'Oh, my God!' But the challenge had been met by members of the Field sections, who had managed a very respectable 16 lengths before being hauled out with their extremities a pale tint of blue. With the original tasking at Kajaki completed, Support Troop had time on their hands, which is a very dangerous prospect indeed. In fact, let me tell you a little about squaddies. Soldiers are not in the Army to serve and protect, like the well-publicized propaganda would have you believe. It is, in fact, a very handy way for the government to keep like-minded people together and safely away from the rest of normal society. It is the same government's job to keep this 'special' group of people busy – hence Iraq and Afghanistan. The last recorded incident of squaddies being left to their own devices was in Germany back in 1939, when several thousand decided to 'pop over the border' to see what was happening in Poland. And we all know what happened then!

On entering the swimming-pool, I can honestly say it was on the chilly side and, with hindsight, I should have come straight out, there and then. But pride (which has always been overrated) and determination to show that not only is Support Troop better than the Fieldies but also way, way more stupid stopped me.

The following twenty minutes played out as follows:

1. At the 10-lengths point, I had to stop doing the front crawl, as my head was beginning to freeze and I could no longer actually see where I was going.
2. After 16 lengths, even though looking composed on the surface, underneath I secretly wished I hadn't seen the bloody pool.
3. After 25 lengths, my fingers had morphed into the most inefficient shape for swimming and I was only faintly aware that I had a body to feel the cold with.
4. After 35 lengths, pride was no longer fuelling me. The only thing keeping me going was the fact that I no longer knew what I was doing and swimming was warmer than not [swimming].
5. At the 42-lengths point, I had drunk as much pool water as I could take and, with no significant drop in water level, it was time to get out or drown.

The following 45 minutes consisted of extreme pain, uncontrolled convulsions and lots of gibbering, as three of my section slowly coaxed me out from hypothermia and back to the land of the coherent. The fine line between determination and stupidity had been crossed and redefined in the same instance.

I have subsequently been informed that I might not be allowed to do any of the winter-warfare courses in Norway next year, as I am now more susceptible to cold-weather injuries. So, the moral of this story is: it doesn't matter how stupid your actions might be, there is always a silver lining somewhere. Only summer tours for me – yippee!

January 2007

Lieutenant Rachel Morgan, Royal Naval Medical Branch

I worked with the Civil Military Ops Cell in Lashkar Gar. One of its roles is to help to build relationships with Afghan civilians, and another is to co-ordinate reconstruction and development. The cell supports the people who are not involved with war and tries to help them get back to normality. I was mostly based between Gereshk and Lashkar Gah, but I travelled all over Helmand province. It's quite normal to get embedded with a group of Royal Marines or Army soldiers for the time you are there in this role; it demands a fair amount of adaptability. I am not a war fighter, but it is necessary to go out on the ground with the patrols as much as possible in order to meet locals and build up relationships with the Afghan community. I took my helmet off, wherever I could, so that people could clearly see I was female. This would particularly help when trying to meet women. It was surprising how open Afghan women could be once they trusted you.

I never had any problems in dealing directly with

men – I did explain to one elder in a shura [meeting] that I was the only person available to lead it and I hoped he would support me openly in front of the other men who might not feel comfortable speaking to me. He told me he would tell them to put up with it – and that his mother had been a doctor in Kabul in the 1960s and that he remembered her wearing a mini skirt. He openly criticized families who would not let their girls go to school – everybody needs education, he said wisely.

We had a situation where a woman turned up at the gate of the operating base in Lashkar Gah. I was often called to search women [the military always uses a female to search women out of respect]. But when this woman turned up I had been on a three-day operation and was catching up on sleep. She had come in the middle of the night so she wouldn't be seen [by Afghan locals]. In the morning I met her with an interpreter. I was overwhelmed that she had taken the initiative to find me.

I said I was sorry she had been kept waiting, that she was welcome to be here and that I was delighted that she had taken the opportunity to come and speak to me. I tried to put her at ease and said, 'We don't have much but what we have is yours, so come and share some tea with us.'

As the Afghan interpreter was interpreting, she was looking a bit blank and perhaps a bit worried. Then a [British] corporal on the gate took me aside and said: 'He didn't interpret what you've just said.

What he actually said to her was: "She [Morgan] says you are a very bad woman and can't work out why you are here. She says surely if you were a good Afghan woman you would stay at home and you would not come out because your husband wouldn't let you be here."' The corporal had only done a six-week introduction course in Pashtu but he had worked out that the interpreter had not interpreted properly. Later that day the interpreter was sacked. There is plenty of dishonesty amongst the interpreters and it's often so hard to pick this up. You can see what kind of things the Afghan women are up against.

We took the woman into a hardened area and she took her burka off. We gave her a cup of tea and a KitKat and she sat talking to me like any of my friends would. She was in her thirties and had already had ten children – six were still living. She was a teacher and had come to discuss the roof not being finished in her school. She was wondering whether anyone could do anything to support her with this. In fact, we were able to help. Because of recent military successes, the Taliban had been pushed back from near her school and this had enabled a surge of reconstruction and development in her area. Over the next eight months we did all we could because we recognized what an amazing person she was to have taken this risk, and how much it could benefit her community. Her husband was a taxi driver and he was aware of what she was doing. In order for her to get to the operating base, her husband had had to take a big detour out of the area and dropped her five K away [so Taliban supporters would not link them to the British forces]. She lived in a town that was within ten miles of us and walked the rest of the way with her brother and their donkey.

Her bravery was inspirational. If the Taliban knew what she had done, they might have kidnapped her or her children, or worse. At the time, male and female teachers were all getting night letters. These were anonymous letters through their letterbox saying, 'Don't work with the British. They are working for the [Afghan] government. You know what will happen to you or your family if you continue to work.' To the Taliban, the government were as much the enemy as we were.

17 January 2007 [email home]

Robert Mead, Ministry of Defence press officer

Forgive me, children, for it has been almost two weeks since my last confession. In that time much and little has happened, though it's still freezing at night and the beard's still coming along nicely, so no need to worry there. But two weeks is clearly too long a wait for you all as at least one person has been pining for my heroic tales and made a personal plea for me to pick up the mighty quill once more.

But let me first say it has not gone unnoticed that there are still several of you lucky people receiving these tales of derring-do who have yet to put finger to keyboard and reply. Now I know this sounds shocking to those who have, not least for those of you who know how self-important I can be. Pull your fingers out. Don't you know how many bullets I had to dodge to make it to the McDonald's Internet café at the end of the road?

So here I am. You join me at the four-week juncture, which means I am just over a quarter of the way through. Yoicks.

The extent of your hero's heroic heroism hasn't gone much beyond a trip to the lavatory cubicle as a beefy Marine just leaves and one is left in the momentary uncertainty of turning round and leaving the man thinking you have only come to perv, or soldiering on and then having to sit on a warm seat engulfed by someone else's noxious vapours. And bearing in mind the dried fruit they give us for roughage, this is not a pleasant experience.

I was due to take a day trip to Camp Bastion last Saturday only for the small matter of a fatality to tie me to the desk instead. As it happens, there isn't much for us to do in the event of a fatality, other than spend the rest of the day in negotiations with the other authorities we have to deal with over who and when should release details.

Lummy, that was a bit serious.

Last Thursday was a long day. A long day. For once it did not begin in the early hours with me being awoken by my bladder wishing to make an entrance stage left. Instead I had to thank a member of the local insurgency as we were woken at 2.15 a.m. when a bomb went off 150 metres from Grenade Alley (you remember Grenade Alley – the delightful wall-lined avenue in which I live). I say I was woken by the bomb. I wasn't. I slept through it, but was woken by the rest of my tent when the alert was sounded. Was this upsetting? Too bloody right it was upsetting, as I then had to sit out in the mother-lovingly freezing cold for the next three hours in my helmet and body armour huddled in the bomb shelter. I say shelter, it provides possibly slightly less shelter than the average non-stick cake tin. And it provides even less warmth at 2 in the bloody morning after one has only been asleep for an hour and a half. I went dressed for a long night just in case as, thankfully, your hero sleeps in his armour-plated thermal vest and long pants, so I was already half dressed when we had to helmet-up. The first hour or so was OK but, by crikey, I was rigid by the time we were eventually given the all-clear. Next time I shall be sure to take my hat, gloves and MP3 player.

The day perked up with the chance to write some proper war-y stuff after an attack on a Taliban HQ early in the morning allowed me to get my teeth into things.

However, the highlight of the day occurred when Mead received his first post of the tour (take note, family, hang your heads in shame). On this occasion the boys had come good and I was treated to a parcel of porn from *EG* [*Colchester Evening Gazette* – his former colleagues], Gawd bless 'em. Well done, the 70s throwback super-group of Clifford, Jones and Palmer.

Then I had gammon steak and egg for tea. Lovely. What more can I tell you?

I am getting fat, or at least fatter. Coupled with my beard there is every chance I may well resemble Ricky Tomlinson/Jim Royle by the time I return. My feeble state of fitness was exemplified last Wednesday when I was on the verge of free-vomiting. I am told this is a popular sport in Army camps, what with the fear of dysentery and vomiting always being only a squirt away. (Not here but when I was in Iraq – oooh, get me – one camp always set aside a Portaloo for those struck down by the liquid laxative so prevalent was it.)

On this occasion, my being doubled up was all of my own doing. I had agreed to take part in a bit of circuit training for charity, organized by our combat camera team. I started with a 1.5 kilometre cycle ride and moved on to a 500-metre row. Both of these were, I see the stupidity of it now, undertaken alongside a very large Marine with a high volume of muscle definition. Mead being the macho-competitive type and always up for a challenge, decided to attempt to match the pace that this trained killer adopted. After the first two disciplines, in which I was a mere couple of seconds behind our well-honed adversary, I moved on to the floor mats to attempt 60 press ups, made it to 11, stopped, lay down, had my photo taken and lost a fair amount of facial colour as my body went into meltdown and I had to take myself off to a well-ventilated area and collapse. I am now a laughing stock.

You will be pleased to know the deficiencies in my expensive sleeping system have been rectified, thanks to a $15 duvet bought from the camp shop, which provides considerably more warmth than my bloody expensive sleeping-bag.

And I know you liked them last time so let's take a few moments for today's lesson on TLAs (and TLA stands for . . . ?)

SAF – Small-Arms Fire
PID – Positively Identified
MSR – Main Supply Route
ISTAR – Information, Surveillance, Targeting,
    Acquisition and Reconnaissance
EF – Enemy Forces
FF – Friendly Forces

Put it all together and you get: 'Using ISTAR, FF PID EF on MSR and engaged with SAF', and so on.

And answers on a postcard as to the definition of

today's phrase, 'dynamic unpredictability', which sounds about as far removed from a definition of my good self as one could imagine.

In such an environment, where every day seems strangely like any other, the little things become important. Each day is currently being given meaning by the 'Chick of the Day' poll, conducted by an engineer clerk who sits a few feet away and who, each day, changes the screen-saver picture of a woman on his computer. The few moments, which are often stretched as long as possible, spent looking at the day's picture are important reminders that women who don't dress solely in combats and who aren't disguised as men and, in most cases, it's a pretty thin disguise, do exist.

Next time we speak I hope to have finally been out of camp as I am due to go into Lashkar Gah in the next few days. I might have even had my hair cut by an Afghan who charges $4. I hear he uses one of the rusty machetes you can buy at Kandahar airfield market. These are warrior people after all. Pictures to follow. Grrr.

January 2007

Lieutenant Rachel Morgan, Royal Naval Medical Branch

The soldiers on guard duty at the FOBs [forward operating bases] try to make themselves quite approachable. However, if people come in looking for food or medical support, they are usually turned away. We had a guy who often came into an FOB in Gereshk to give us intelligence – about what was going on with the Taliban in the area. One day he had given us some information and one of the soldiers thanked him and enquired as to whether there was anything we could do for him. He asked if there was a doctor available, as he was suffering from a headache and perhaps he could take a pill to make it better. The [British soldier] explained that we don't provide health care for everyone we meet, but he'd see what he could do. When he [the Afghan] saw the British doctor he told him that there was a piece of shrapnel in his head which he had had for twenty years, since an injury sustained when fighting with the mujahideen. The British doctor agreed to take this shrapnel out of his head. He [the Afghan] did not receive any anaesthetic for this. The doctor just cut his head open and yanked it [the shrapnel] out. He [the Afghan, in his late thirties] just chanted all the way through, praying, and got himself into an almost hypnotic state that most of us cannot imagine. It was an incredible thing to witness. The British doctor gave the Afghan, a Hazara tribesman, his shrapnel in a plastic bottle to take away.

20 January 2007 [email home]

Captain Charlotte Cross, Territorial Army

I went on a really long patrol to an IDP [internally displaced people] camp north of Lashkar Gah the other day. A female elder there has been threatened because she and her daughter work at the school ('school' being 5 UNICEF tents with nothing inside). The woman's very feisty. She's been beaten up before and shot in the leg. Apparently her phone number's been given out to somebody who's now phoning her up and threatening her, and she said she'll drink the blood of the person who betrayed her by giving her phone number away – these people don't mess around. So a colour sergeant asked me to go with him to the camp, to try to find out what's going on, and to speak to any females we might come across. We already know the Taliban infiltrate the camp; it's right next to the Helmand river and they use that area as a crossing point, and hide out in the camp before moving into Lashkar Gah or further south.

It was a really cold windy day, and even in my thermals and body armour and webbing, I was freezing. We drove through Lashkar Gah town, then up through Mukhtar, and when we stopped the vehicles and got out we were in the middle of a maze of mud-walled compounds, some with UNICEF tent material for a roof, some with little chimneys made of hollow tree branches, and smoke pouring out. We went over to where some middle-aged men were sitting against a wall, and suddenly we had about 20 children crowding round us as well . . . These were definitely the poorest Afghans I've met so far. The kids all had bare filthy black feet and red, streaming eyes . . . and huddled miserably in the howling wind. Some smiled when I spoke to them, but mostly they just looked desperate. So did the men. We asked the kids if they go to school, and they all replied yes, and one older boy held up a little black bag with a school exercise book and a couple of pencils. It was obviously his pride and joy, pathetic though it was. The men denied the Taliban were in the camp and said everything was fine, no security problems here, but we didn't believe them. They said nothing ever happens on this camp it's very quiet . . . so we said what about the mine we found here 2 weeks ago . . . and they said oh apart from that. And we said what about the fire-fight at the police check-point down the road . . . and they said oh yes and apart from that. The CSgt told them he wanted to help them, but while they continue to allow their elders to give what little food aid they get to the Taliban, and shelter the Taliban in the camp, the Taliban will fight us and we won't be able to help them. The men listened intently and looked very sheepish. They didn't argue. We left them and walked through the streets to find some different people to talk to.

The interpreter showed me some long, green

leaves he'd taken from one of the little children. Apparently the child had been thinning out the poppy plants somewhere, and had come back with spare poppy leaves to make into soup. That's what poor people do, even though it puts opium in their bloodstream. It's like nettle soup I suppose.

Anyway, we came across another group of men, sitting next to a small, mud-walled building, which they said was their flour mill for making their bread. And again they told us there were no security problems in the camp, no Taliban here. This time the elder sent a tiny child off to bring us some chai and a little dish of colourful sweets, and we stood in that desolate place with the wind howling around us, and we drank chai with them, and I thought even though they have nothing, they give us what little they have ... I felt quite guilty taking it, but it would've been incredibly rude not to, that's their culture. Then one of the men asked us to help his son, who was knocked over by a car and is paralysed in a wheelchair. The crowd wheeled him out to us, and they all stood round expectantly, like we'd have some magic medicine to cure him with. We called over our medic to take a look, and apparently the young man had a huge bedsore on his hip, so he gave him some aspirin and put a dressing on it. The interpreter told the crowd the dressing cost $16, so they were all very pleased and were beaming at us and thanked us. It was as if we'd made him walk again. Eventually, we thanked them for the chai and we moved on.

The next group of men we came across were sitting on a wall by a little shop, which was selling a few apples, and some bread, and that was about it. One of the men was quite old, he was a Spingiri, and he told us he was from the Kuchi tribe. He said before the Taliban he lived in the deserts in the north, near Kabul, but when the Taliban took power, his people were attacked by the Uzbeks and Tajiks, who hated them because they were Pashtuns, like the Taliban. So they moved south, and their live-stock was looted by the Taliban. They headed for Helmand, which is traditionally the Pashtun heart-land, and they came to Mukhtar and built themselves mud houses and compounds and settled there. But now the government is telling them they'll have to move on, and this old man was saying: 'Where can we move to? We have no land, we have nowhere to go and we're happy here.' Apparently the government stopped the UN pro-viding aid to this camp a year ago, because it wants the people to move on. It hopes they'll leave if they become desperate enough. It's heartbreaking, and you can understand why they end up harbouring and supporting the Taliban. What choice do they have?

And then I come back to the office, and Sky News is on, and I see the world is in anguish about what Jade Goody's said on *Big Brother* . . .

24 January 2007 [email home]

Robert Mead, Ministry of Defence press officer

Salaam aleikum, my children.

Peace be upon you all from Muhammad's mountain retreat and all his Pashtun brothers and sisters.

Morning, all.

You join me as the tour-clock ticks into the second third. Irritatingly my colleague to my right has just pointed out that he has 8.72 days to go according to his personal 'chuff chart', whatever the hell one of those is.

This may sound like I am counting down the days but it's all been so far so good: I have not been shot, I have not developed dysentery, I have been out to meet the good people of Lashkar Gah for the first time, I have clean sheets on my bed. All is perfectly average with the world. Apart from having to look at Jade Goody seemingly every minute of every day for the past week.

Yes, my children, the past 7 to 10 days have been exceedingly interesting. No doubt you will have read and seen much about the heroic deeds taking place in this fair and slightly-chilly-at-night country, but more of my antics with the locals later.

In the meantime, I hope you all read the Sunday papers for my exclusive interviews with those daring chaps what risked life and limb to agree to be grilled by me on what was a bit of a hairy situation when they rescued their fallen comrade on the wings of an Apache. I was privileged, and I don't use that word lightly, to speak to five of the eight who took part in the rescue.

As my 'bootneck' colleagues would say, it was 'hoofing'. Yes, as if one incomprehensible and slightly irritating language were not enough, the Marines have two. So in addition to TLAs (all together now . . .) I am subjected to such sentences as: 'I'm off to the heads before scran then it's back to the grot to get my head down in the scratcher – hoofing.' Remarkably, this isn't a quote from my 'Five Fucking (sorry, Auntie) German Students' porn video sent by the boys which, incidentally, does exactly what it says on the tin. It roughly translates as: 'One is going to visit the lavatory before the evening meal, then it's back to the abode to sleep peacefully in my bed – marvellous.'

I also have to listen to people talk about 'granularity', telling me to 'crack on', 'talk off line', get things 'squared away', and generally be 'threaders' if things don't go to plan.

In something of a backlash against this brain-washing and in a bid to integrate and enjoy the moment more in this ancient land I have decided to attempt to be at one with the locals. To that end, rather than now, like my heathen infidel room-mates, who bemoan the 'wailing' of the local Imam as he calls the faithful to prayer at 5 a.m. each morn-ing, I now awaken at 4.30, wash with sand, as the Prophet Muhammad would have done, and dress in a simple garment of muslin, a free T-shirt from the *Sun* saying 'Page 3 stunner', and leftover Christmas wrapping paper. I then scale the wall before venturing out into the streets to take my morning prayer.

I have discovered the one thing that is less enticing in the morning than my regular 100-metre dash with only a small towel to protect one's dignity is doing it in the rain.

One thing the good men of Afghanistan have in common with those in Blighty is how to loaf. Particularly good practitioners are the construction industry, clearly the same the world over. Currently we have many Afghans apparently digging random holes and ditches all round camp. One assumes this isn't a less than cunning plot to join up with Taliban trenches and allow the insurgents to infiltrate the camp under cover of darkness. For every two men digging the hole, there is always at least four times that many stood or sat around enjoying the sun, having a fag or gently discussing last night's nan bread. It's just like being back home.

So what of my tales in Lashkar Gah? Up until last week, apart from a quick 5 mins through the streets of Kabul or looking out the window of a Chinook helicopter, which incidentally is an awesome ride, especially when it whizzes along at low height, I had yet to see what Afghanistan actually looked like up close. I have now not only seen it up close, I have also smelt it, and at times it hums. I went out on what turned out to be a 6-and-a-half-hour patrol with a team of Royal Engineers who were accompanied by someone from PsyOps, i.e., Psychological Operations, i.e., touchy-feely propaganda, and CIMIC, Civil Military Co-operation, who try to identify local projects to spend money on.

Then there was me and our cameraman. The deal is you go out with a convoy of three Snatch vehicles (stop sniggering, children, this is serious). A Snatch is basically a Land Rover with a bit of armour plating. Only a bit, mind, as most of the troops killed in roadside bombings in Iraq were travelling in Snatches – so they provide some protection but not total.

Not to worry, in you pop in the back, which is a bit of a squeeze with four of you, plus a driver and commander in the front. You don't get much of a view, unless you're one of the top cover troops. But for that privilege you pay the price of having to wear a bloody great bit of body armour, which not only covers the torso but also your neck and your arms down to the elbow. Still, nice view, I hear. Especially when the kids start throwing stones at you.

All I can see is what can be made out through a dirty window about 10 inches square with bars across it. But what this Pope-mobile lacks in view it makes up for in scratch-and-sniffability. Then we trot off through the streets of Lashkar Gah, though streets is an ambitious term, being as they are more

ANDY McNAB

like dry tracks across a potato field in the height of summer with the only signs of moisture being the human excrement dribbling down the middle. No lumps, mind.

You drive along these 'roads', rocking and rolling all over the shop, and every now and again you can't avoid piling through this mucky stuff, which throws up a truly incredible smell, a viciously potent sulphur-type pong that tastes as good as it whiffs and sticks to your teeth.

Yet local children can be seen running alongside the paths, in a desperate bid to keep up with us and wave, more often than not in bare feet. One particularly unfortunate tyke was caught right next to one of these pungent puddles as we drove by and, like the comedy movie when a car piles through a puddle as you are walking to work in your best togger, this lad got covered up to his bare ankles in black shoot. Nice.

Our intention was to go to a play area so the troops could have a hearts-and-minds-winning game of football with the local kids. The play area was something of a dusty wasteland, the kids weren't expecting us and, upon being handed some balls, clearly had not been taught the rudiments of Association Football by a qualified FA coach. The three balls were hoofed up in the air with packs of kids racing after them. I tried in vain to get some pics but the ball never stayed in one place long enough. Within 5 minutes the first of three balls had gone walkabout and within another 20 the remaining two had been had.

There must have been 50–100 kids running around, many of them bare-footed, most of them looking like they hadn't washed for several weeks. But among the children, not a girl, or for that matter a female of any kind, could be seen.

The CIMIC bloke had got chatting with some elders and we wandered off down an alleyway to what turned out to be a religious boarding school, a Madrassa. Eton it wasn't. I've seen slightly smarter pigsties. The CIMIC man got chatting with the head, and we listened as he told us about his 120 pupils who were basically taught the Koran. But the conditions were wretched. It didn't look much from the outside but there was apparently a basement-type design as grubby boys stuck their heads out from somewhere down below as we spoke to the head. Some of these boys didn't look much older than about 3. Others were in their late teens. We then went inside and down into three classroom/bedrooms. I would have found it hard to believe that 120 boys could stand in the rooms available but apparently they all slept on the floor. Very cosy.

It was not until afterwards that the cameraman, Aidy, a Marine by trade, said we should never have gone into there without first having checked it out and that several rule books were discarded for us just to wander in. Luckily I was oblivious to how death-defying and heroic I was being – 'twas ever thus.

We cleared off and stopped at another spot to generally amble about and engage with the locals. In true Afghan fashion, there was another old chap digging a random hole with a crowd of people stood around. Once again there were masses of kids about, this time with one or two girls. But only girls of at most 5 or 6 because by all accounts any older than that is trussed up and not let out except on official occasions.

Our final stop was a bit of an interesting one: we stopped at Lashkar Gah prison, which is supposedly the current home of the odd Taliban inmate. Though you wouldn't have known as the term 'open prison' could well have been made for this establishment. There was a railed gate. Some turrets and a big wall. Other than that there was a lot of vicious, fairly unhappy-looking chaps being passed several table-sized bits of nan bread through the railings and some equally ramshackle chaps wandering about on this side of the gate who were allegedly the guards.

Bearing in mind that arguably the Taliban are my current worst enemy, I would have had second thoughts before I wished it upon them.

Then it was back home in time for tea. Steak en croûte with onion chutney and veg followed by chocolate pud and custard. De-lish.

And I'd like to leave you with a message from one of the random bits of junk mail that regularly appear in my Yahoo junk box. The subject of the message from Antonio Kelly is: 'with silver, and at the east to their flesh'.

Well, quite.

Now get writing.

February 2007

Corporal Fraser 'Frankie' Gasgarth, The Royal Engineers

In Kajaki, every night you got mortared. You could set your watch by it: it was quite comical. When you were out building the new FOB, you were constantly being shot at too. It was harassment fire: you have Land Rovers with GPMGs [general-purpose machine-guns] or 50-cal machine-guns to look after you. Because you have got them covering you, there is no use shooting back with your pea-shooter [SA80 assault rifle]. So you wait until they've cleared the area [of Taliban], then you get back out again. It was like: they're shooting at us; we'd better stop. The shooting has stopped; right, get back out there. In Kajaki, we built an area there for the police to do road checks and we constantly got harassment fire. It took us two days to build it because they [the Taliban] were just constantly firing at us – on and off – all the time. They would fire and then try and move off. Or some would have the guts to fire and stay there. The lads on the hill-top in the OPs [observation posts] would spot where they were and hammer them. If things got really bad, Apaches would be called in or fast air [support] too.

But, for me, it couldn't have been a better tour. One, you were getting all the incidents – you were getting shot at and all that kind of thing. But, second, everything [the kit] was completely knackered [when we arrived] so I was actually plying my trade. If I had gone there and everything was working perfectly, it wouldn't have been as good. Of the twenty-eight pieces of kit that we inherited when we arrived, twenty-six pieces got fixed. I loved it. Yet as soon as you come home, it's back to normal. It is as if you have never been out there. All you have is the memories.

March 2007

Flight Sergeant Paul 'Gunny' Phillips, RAF

We were doing IRTs [incident response team work with a MERT] up at [Camp] Bastion and at the same time there was a big op going on in the upper Sangin valley. They put a load of troops on the ground to try and clear out a few known Taliban-friendly areas. With the IRTs, you are on thirty minutes' notice to move to pick up injured guys. Anyway, the boss [Squadron Leader Ian Diggle] referred to it later as 'the night of nights' because it was probably one of the busiest IRTs that we have ever had. We had nine call-outs in one night. It was that bad. We had been hoping to get to bed just after midnight but in the end it was just a case of 'Well, I might as well stay up.' Because the minute you got into bed you got another nine-liner [emergency call] coming through. So we just gave up and sat outside the tent drinking Coke and smoking cigarettes all night.

We had been into various places to pick up guys – small-arms injuries or they had fallen over and broken a leg – and then we had the last shout of the night. It was almost dawn when we got a call to go and pick up four Americans in the upper Sangin valley. They were all walking wounded, so they had minor injuries effectively. It took us for ever to find the HLS, because one compound looks pretty much like any other. There were that many friendly troops on the ground you didn't know which [helicopter landing site] was which. So we were flying around for five or ten minutes and eventually found it. We landed in this field – it was an old poppy field. It hadn't been cut back so it still had the old poppies growing in it. I was in the front door [of the helicopter], sat behind the mini-gun. So the ramp went down and these Americans start walking towards the back of the cab.

There was a whole load of mincing going on at the back of the cab. People were saying: 'Who's injured? Who's not? Who's coming with us? Who's staying here?' It was one of those times where no one felt particularly threatened. I actually said to the boss: 'This is a pretty good spot actually.' Because we had a compound directly to the rear of the aircraft, a compound either side of us and then quite a dense tree-line to the front. So I thought the only thing that was going to get us there was IDF [indirect fire] really. And there was still all this mincing around at the back of the aircraft and we got three of the guys on and the boss was saying: 'What's happening? What's happening?' We'd been there for about three minutes by now but they were still trying to find this fourth casualty. I was looking out of the front door and literally just underneath the rotor disc there were three American troops that had been put out to give us a bit of force protection. It sounds cheesy and overused but literally the ground in front of these guys just erupted. It [the bullets] must have been about five feet in front of them. You could see the rounds just splashing right in front of their faces. And of course they let rip and all their mates started to let rip and we were like: 'Fucking hell. Contact!' We just got the ramp up and departed. We could see all their tracer going towards this [Taliban] compound but I couldn't tell where they were firing at. So I couldn't use the mini-gun, which was incredibly frustrating.

But we got back to Bastion and said: 'We just had a contact.' And they said: 'Yeah, we're just listening to the American comm chat [communications chatter] now.' And what had happened was, from the compound on our right-hand side, thirty metres from our aircraft, some little bad lad had stuck his AK-47 over the top of the compound wall and did the old 'spray and pray' [opening up with fire and hoping for the best]. I couldn't believe that their guy had been thirty metres from me and I couldn't shoot him because the mini-gun doesn't elevate very high. If I had been behind an M60 [machine-gun], I could have got some rounds off if I'd known where he was. But in the end, the guy got a proper shoeing from the Americans [who killed him].

7 March 2007 [email home]

Robert Mead, Ministry of Defence press officer

My children.

(Brace yourselves, you may need to get a cup of tea for this one.)

Lawks a Lordy, having just checked the dates, it's been a month, a whole thirty days, since my last update. No doubt those days have been barren, desolate, empty wastelands of sorrow for you all in the absence of words from Mullah Mead. Possibly some of you have even turned to heavy narcotic abuse. If you have, save some for me: I'll be home soon.

Where to begin. Well, let's start with the news that you are going to have to wait just that little bit longer to welcome home your hero. This is because I am so irreplaceable that those blighters at the MoD have extended one's tour for a few weeks. Return date has slipped not once, not twice, but three times, from 20 March to the dizzyingly late 10 April. That's a whole extra three weeks. Cripes, I'm glad I'm getting overtime for this. But, as you can see, the timings of these things change so bloody often that I've got more chance of pissing my name in the sand on a beach and it remaining unchanged.

Now the good news – the beard has gone. The fair to middling news is it will be back by the time I return. One shave a tour is enough for any respectable man. Frankly I did not have enough favourable comments from the ladies to make it worth my while keeping, so serves you right if you liked it and didn't reply to my email, which in fairness was practically all of you.

And speaking of non-replies, while my perfectly decent and not-in-any-way-questionable-or-lurid request for naked photos from my lady-friends was well and truly ignored or, worse, earnest promises were made which have been proven to be total dogs-droppings, one of my colleagues then received a collection of gratuitous happy snaps from some lady doing personal things in personal places. Bloody cheek. He showed us all, of course, but I won't – honest. They'll be just for me.

Instead, to add a slap in the knackers with a wet towel to injury, I have had to make do with naked bloody Marines. Let there be no doubt, there is nothing more tiresome and disturbing than, after having been woken at an indecent hour and having stumbled to the bathroom, to open the door to see a butch Marine standing stark bollock, proudly towelling himself down with one leg casually hitched up on the sink. Every bleedin' morning. This is no way to start the day. What is it with men who profess to be more butch than a bulldog with three penises that they display more woofter tendencies than a team of Kenny Everett impersonators?

Right then, what can I tell you?

What has happened? Pah, what hasn't happened?

Let's be honest, not a lot. Well, not a lot warlike anyway. At least not here. Plenty going on out and about as you can probably tell. Having said that, one day seems largely like any other so it's not easy to keep tabs on events. What hasn't happened is I still haven't been shot at yet, though I am repeatedly and reliably informed this is a good thing. This is largely because I haven't really been anywhere where I could get shot. Most of my past month's activity has taken place firmly behind the walls of camp Lashkar Gah. But, goodness, hasn't it been exciting?

I've visited one of our sentry turrets, for some reason called sangars, which is quite curious, because they don't in any way resemble a sausage, and when you look out of the gaps in the walls you see the town of Lashkar Gah is about 10 feet away and only succeeds in reminding you how close you are to potential nasty people.

What else? Well, we've had some visitors, and mildly famous visitors at that. A few weeks back we were treated to the delights of Jim Davidson and 'Forces' Favourite' opera singer Katherine Jenkins. A right incongruous duo those two were. But this was put in the shade by a follow-up show two weeks later. Not by the two male laddish comedians, whose names escape me, but the lovely Claudia, Megan and Jane, the CSE [Combined Service Entertainment] dancers. Grrr, woof and bark.

As I was beginning to pine, Media Ops arranged a game of football and duly beat the hapless plum-duffs of 28 Engineer Regiment in a rousing game of five-a-side. This was followed by several sharp pains in the lower-leg region for days after, due to the large gap between this game and my last, the poor footwear available, and the utter unsuitability of the playing surface, i.e., a rock-hard square of concrete more commonly used for the landing of helicopters. And, indeed, a halt was called 45 mins into the match for two of the cheeky overblown Flymos [helicopters] to drop their load. Normal service was soon resumed and we smashed the sappers. Huzzah.

This was followed only days later by an un-expected late entry into a six-a-side tournament on the same surface. This time it was against a number of sides from the Marines and a few local Afghan sides. Flushed from our recent victory, and buoyed with, what turned out to be, hopelessly overblown overconfidence, we imagined lots of Afghans rolling up in even more unsuitable clothing for football than ours; namely those long shirts and pyjama bottoms that everyone seems to wear, blankets wrapped around the shoulders (despite it being blazing hot) and either sandals or perfectly normal shoes, which they all seem to have the strange habit of wearing as slip-ons, i.e., not bothering to unlace but just flattening down the heel. (My mother would be livid. She never would have stood for this. I can hear her now: 'Undo the bloody laces!')

We stood waiting on the pitch, all quiet save for the standard friendly banter of 'Give it here, you fat poof', and the distant twang of hamstrings snapping after months of unuse. Media Ops already looked hugely out of place. Most of the Marines, as I have explained before, are, to a man, massive, or at very least, considerably fitter than most marathon runners. Still no sign of our local opponents, though there was a hefty crowd forming. Then, slowly shimmering over the horizon, came a large number of athletic-looking youths resplendent in dazzling bright yellow Barcelona away kits, juggling balls and looking a lot like they knew exactly what they were doing, which was preparing to give our arses a sound kicking.

The first game began. Thankfully we weren't in it. India Company 42 Commando vs the Afghans A side. Seven-minute matches. Hectic stuff. The whistle blew and they were off. Quickly a pattern emerged – the bandy-legged Afghans running absolute onion rings round our hapless Marines. Within two minutes the Afghans were 2 up. The Afghan half of the crowd was going wild. The UK side was either shatting itself among those braced for future games, or falling about in hysterics for those only spectating. The Afghans won. Much cheering and indefinite Islamic praises to Allah followed.

We were third up, also playing a team of Afghans – though, not wishing to be in any way politically incorrect, it could just as easily have been the same 6 players as the first game as to a man they all looked the same. (Is this conjuring up images of the match in Disney's *Bedknobs and Broomsticks*? As well it might.) In the words of our photographer, every time we got the ball it was like being surrounded by a swarm of locusts, so quickly were we smothered by the opposition. How we only lost 1–0 Basil Brush only knows. I think I touched the ball in those 7 minutes for approximately 4 seconds and that was only to retrieve it when it had gone off the pitch. We left with our tails between our legs.

In amongst these latest acts of dare-wing-do, and following on from the pasting my lungs received in the above games, I have arrested the decline of my body shape and taken to the gym on a daily basis. I shall therefore return a lean, mean media-ops machine. Grrr. Though currently everything aches massively.

(This is a long one isn't it? Don't complain: it has been four weeks, you know, you ungrateful lot.)

That's not to say there hasn't been some warlike activity. Only the other day we were minding our own business at about 2 p.m. when a rather loud explosion went off. The ground wobbled a bit. Cor, that was quite loud, I thought. Probably a controlled explosion. Then a major (it's OK, it wasn't me) who knew a bit about these things came scampering into our HQ tent looking more perturbed than was healthy for us all, saying to no one in particular: 'Is there any planned controlled explosion today? Does anyone know?' He came back seconds later saying, 'Put your helmet and body armour on, ladies and gentleman,' in a very dignified fashion, presumably having found the answer to his question. Now I was quite excited as it gave me my first opportunity to wear my new blue-cover Osprey body armour, the stuff troops wear. Until now I had been wearing the version which anyone who has visited my home in the past year will have seen and probably tried on. Bit snug, isn't it? Not to mention the breast plate being somewhat small. The Osprey is the new super-duper one with larger bullet repelling bits, and now I have one of my very own. So, we toddled back to the tent to pick up my helmet, when another explosion, this time a 'kin' loud one, feeling altogether closer, louder and explosiver, went off. Lummy. Make for the hills. The best we could offer was the safe-haven office of the combat camera team for a can of 7Up, thumb through this week's *Zoo* mag and a game of Shithead – which irritatingly I keep losing and had to get up early the other day to bring everyone breakfast in bed. Knobs.

As we toddled off, someone came from the other direction, looking considerably less armoured, who told us it had been a false alarm and it was a controlled explosion after all. Excitement over.

However, this is not your hero's only scrape with certain maiming in the past week. No, sirree. After being holed up here for the best part of 4 weeks, trying all I knew to find a reason to get out on the ground (I offered to cook dinner for the governor, unblock the questionable Lashkar Gah plumbing, sleep with a variety of members of the local hierarchy, you name it) finally I was unleashed for a trip to see two new bits of road, one that has been built, one that is being built. However, upon visitation, the first road was in no way similar to anything you, I or next door's gerbil would call a road. Having said that, most major paths of transport have a closer resemblance to the bottom of a gerbil's cage, hardened and then smashed into lumpy pieces before being doused in more lumpy stuff, with extra lumps in, and hardened again, so any improvement that possesses the basic property of simply being flat is a considerable bonus. This road had that going for it – it had little else. It was a raised dirt/gravel track not much wider than a car's width, which fell away steeply for about 2 metres on either side; a field on one, a river on the other. So we stopped at this road, which I expected to be a bit of a bustling country route, and instead saw ... one old chap come bobbing along on his rickety old bicycle. And possibly a goat in the distance, though it was some way off so we couldn't be sure.

The man agreed to talk to us. It didn't look as though he had much else to do that day. Abdul was his name, and he told us he was 55 but he could have easily passed for 85. Nice bloke, but turned out not only did he not have much to do, he didn't have much to say either.

We bade him farewell as the traffic began to build up and two men in the distance rolled up on a motorbike. They were a bit more enthusiastic telling us how this road had cut their journey time from 1 hr 15 mins to 30 mins as this chap had to go to the doctor and it had been very useful, etc. (See how my sophisticated tactics of subliminal messaging is seeping the MoD mantra into your feeble minds without you knowing. You are all under my power, yesss, under my power. These aren't the droids you're looking for, ooooh.)

After this peak of excitement our convoy of three Land Rovers rolled off along this road heading back to town. I was in the front vehicle, looking out the back, when slowly but unmistakably, the middle vehicle veered gently off course. Its front left wheel went over the edge of the gravel road, slowly followed by the left back wheel. As if in slow motion, the vehicle leant slightly before it found itself on the bank of the road, and decided the best course of action was to roll over onto its side. I tapped gently on the gunner who was sticking his head out of the roof keeping top cover.

'Um, the vehicle behind has rolled.'

'RTA [road traffic accident]!' he shouted.

Oh, the irony. Here we were coming to see a new road to benefit the Afghans and the first time we use it we roll a military vehicle and block it for all the Afghans. Ace. But the irony didn't stop there. Oh, no. Thankfully no one was injured bar a bump on the head for the driver. Anyway, standard procedure here is for all to leap out and form a protective cordon while the emergency response team is called to get us out of here before the Taliban get wind of it and come and get us – or if you're a civilian, huddle down in the back and keep well out of the way. Yoicks.

However, your hero couldn't stay low for long and he clambered out to get a good view, and essentially to take some pictures. We ended up being there for about half an hour, the busy local traffic of a couple of battered 4x4s, a goat-herder and some raggedy children creating a devil of a bottleneck. Until along came a chap in a tractor and, irony upon irony, he kindly offered to pull the Land Rover out of trouble. Phew, dangerous stuff, hey?

In fairness I came closer to facing death a few weeks ago when the chefs decided Friday night should be fish-and-chip night and served up such an artery-busting deep-fat-fried menu, including deep-fat-fried Mars bar (which, incidentally, tastes better than the real thing) that I'm not sure if their intention was to feed us or kill us.

(Nearly there, not long to go now, into the home straight . . . Yes, all right, I do go on, yes, I know.)

A few weeks ago I sent some of you the fantastic website www.alemarah.org, otherwise known as the Taliban website Voice of Jihad. Most of this esteemed organ and bastion of exemplary journalistic principles is involved with concocting fantastical stories of Taliban victories over the infidel. (Not unlike my job in reverse you might say. Yeah? Well bog off.)

One of our Land Rovers gets a puncture, they say they've blown up seven tanks and killed five foreign invaders. It really is a cracking read. Most of it is in Pashtu, but for those not versed in the local lingo, one section is in English, or rather the most comic attempts at *'Allo 'Allo!*-style 'Good moaning' English you will ever read.

A particularly fine example of this garbling of Eengleesh was 12 February when, following an attack on a Taliban leader, the website denied their man had been 'martyred'. Instead it said: 'In airstrike only civilians including women and Chileans martyred.' Which seems a bit unfair on the Chileans.

And finally, this week's instalment of Marine-speak

is a short yet suggestive affair. It has become common to hear in the evening briefings (you remember those, full of absolute nonsensical military shag-pile) reference to: 'The Marines left Charlotte this morning before moving onto Beatrice and Annabelle tonight. They will take up positions in Frances on Friday.'

Fnar, fnar. This, though, is not a reference to sexual deviancy, but the naming of certain areas of the AO (that's Area of Operations) by giving them girls' names. Thus, one large irregular shape of land approximately 10 sq km is called Beatrice, another is called Annabelle, and so on. One curious observation. Should the Marines continue their journey, they will come to AO Thrush. Sounds painful. Perhaps it is sexual deviancy after all.

Titty bang.

PS I have a month to go. Therefore you stinking weasels who have yet to write to me have a month in which to redeem yourselves. Get to it.

20 March 2007 [email home]

Captain Dave Rigg, MC, The Royal Engineers

Letter from Afghanistan

Shortly before I departed Afghanistan, two Artillery men were killed, Lance Bombardier Ross Clark and Lance Bombardier 'Paddy' McLaughlin. They had both been through training together and were good mates. The day they died was another fine, clear one in northern Helmand. As the sun set over the Helmand river, the observation post that they were manning was targeted with a rocket-propelled grenade. The rocket penetrated the fortifications around their position and ripped them apart with exploding shrapnel. They had no chance of survival. They died together. I had previously worked with Lance Bombardier Clark: he was the sort of bloke that would have done well in any environment, a genuinely decent bloke.

Having spent the previous seven months working on the reconstruction and development effort in Helmand province, I have been disappointed and frustrated by the lack of balanced reporting within the press. Not surprisingly, the majority of the world's press seem only interested in generating sensational stories: the plight of the poor Afghan farmer who, when not caught in the crossfire, has to stand and watch while his poppy crop, his only source of income, is burnt to the ground. The deliberate ISAF [International Assistance Security Force] operations, which are conducted to flush out, and kill insurgent forces. These are stories that have to be told, but on their own they have no context, and do not do our soldiers the credit they deserve.

The events outlined below are not quite as headline-grabbing, but when viewed against the complexities of rebuilding a nation that is teetering on the brink of anarchy, they are far more newsworthy.

We are told that Helmand province is the most dangerous place on earth. There are certainly lots of people in the province intent on killing us; our soldiers get shot at from Garmsir, in the south, to Now Zad in the north of the province and everywhere in between. When we are out of contact with the enemy and moving through the desert or patrolling up the valleys, we are vulnerable to mines and other improvised explosive devices. Generally the large towns are more permissive, enabling us to patrol with relative freedom, but this is when we are most at risk to a suicide-bomb attack.

Barricading ourselves in our bases would be far safer, but would achieve nothing, and ten years down the line we would still be peering out from our sangars, wondering where the next rocket was going to come from. We have to venture out in order to develop a rapport with the local people; to understand what it is that makes the process of establishing a stable system of governance so difficult. Once we understand the issues we can start to address them.

It would be far simpler if we could just go in search of the insurgent and kill him. This is an insurgency: the vast majority of the fighters in Afghanistan are from abroad – Pakistan, Iran, Chechnya, Turkmenistan and any other nation that provides disillusioned young Muslim men who

have little to lose and a violent urge to prove themselves. There are local fighters, but generally their
allegiances are questionable and they fight for the
highest bidder.

The vast majority of the Afghan people simply
want to feed their family, send their children to
school and generate a little income through trade or
farming. Sadly, this majority is dominated by a
minority who are motivated by a variety of conflict-
ing causes. There is a highly complex array of
interwoven dynamics that make the matter of
uniting these people under one government a
hugely challenging problem. Tribal feuds, the
blossoming narcotics trade, a despised local police
force, a system of governance that struggles to produce literate ministers, 30 years of conflict, a civil
infrastructure system that is medieval, and, of
course, the Taliban and the associated insurgency.

So, with all of that in mind, where do you start?
Being military, it is not surprising that we focus
much of our resources upon finding and defeating
the enemy. Where we can isolate and engage the
Taliban without causing substantial collateral
damage, we do. Before doing so we spend a great
deal of time and effort positively identifying targets
and developing our knowledge of who the key
individuals are and what their weaknesses are. Then
we hit them hard.

However, despite the careful targeting process
our activity inevitably results in the destruction of

innocent people's homes and sometimes their death. The enemy often move into local houses or mosques to fire upon us and we retaliate. The Taliban then exploit these incidents; their propaganda campaign is generally more persuasive than ours. It is therefore extremely difficult to avoid the undesirable second order effects of our war fighting operations.

As it stands, the majority of the Afghan people do not support the Taliban; they are generally as foreign to them as we are, and certainly a lot less merciful. They want NATO forces to provide them with security and it is vitally important that we capitalize upon this local support. This is where the classic 'hearts and minds' stuff comes into play. In a place as primitive as Afghanistan, it is not difficult to impress or win the consent of a local. Maintaining that consent is a greater challenge.

In the last 6 months we have invested over $4m on reconstruction and development projects, our engineers have been involved in building police stations, roads and maternity wards to name but a few. We do not actually build them; we identify the need, recce the task, design it and then contract the project out to a local company. Giving these projects an 'Afghan face' brings a number of benefits. It generates the impression that it is Afghan led, which builds consent for the local government, helps to develop the capacity of local industry, provides employment and fuels the local economy.

The building piece is not difficult. There is no shortage of demand, plenty of international funding but, more surprisingly, a surplus of capacity within the local building industry.

The Americans are very good at building stuff: they don't mess about, they just get it done. They have plenty of experience, having been engaged in multi-million-dollar projects all over Afghanistan since the early 1950s. However, what they seem less proficient at is ensuring local buy-in. Unless the new infrastructure can be manned and maintained by the local system, it soon ends up as a decaying memorial to foreign investment. Southern Afghanistan is a graveyard of failed reconstruction projects.

Afghanistan has been in turmoil for so long that the people live for today and perhaps tomorrow. Planning beyond that is seen as futile; investing in next year is simply incomprehensible. Therefore nothing gets maintained. The fortunate few who hold the purse strings perceive their time to be limited and therefore why invest in something that may not bear fruit for some time and bring them little benefit when they could invest in their family now? This short-term mindset breeds corruption, and it permeates every strand of Afghan society. Unfortunately this psyche is probably too well engrained in the average adult Afghan and therefore the next generation are seen as the key to providing a secure and stable Afghanistan.

We recently completed the construction of a school for an orphanage in Lashkar Gah. When we returned to the school to visit what we hoped to be satisfied customers, we were surprised to discover that all of the children were now living in the class-rooms. Metal beds, most without mattresses, had been crammed into the new school buildings, there was urine on the floor, and the Asian-style toilets that had been provided were covered with excrement. The patrol commander quizzed the director of the orphanage about the unexpected findings and it became clear that he had moved the children out of the orphanage in order to provide himself with more spacious living accommodation.

In the same vein, we have stopped building police infrastructure until the police demonstrate an ability to look after what they have got and professionally man the existing check-points. Police stations barely a year old have no power because the generator starter battery has been robbed, none of the plumb-ing works because the copper-pipe work has disappeared, and they seem to take a pride in systematically defecating around the toilet before moving into the next room. The police have other far more distasteful habits that are not uncommon in Afghanistan. But it is their general abuse of the civil population that is at the heart of many of the problems faced by Afghanistan.

In the Garmsir district, southern Helmand, it was the foul behaviour of the Afghan police that prompted the local elders to send a delegation to Baluchistan to request the support of the Taliban in freeing them from the daily humiliation of the national authorities. Subjugation to a strict fundamentalist code enforced by foreigners was preferable to being ruled by their own authorities.

Our exit strategy in Afghanistan hinges upon enabling the Afghan to govern himself and therefore they must be taught to do for themselves all of what we are doing on their behalf. Significant progress has been made with the formation and training of the Afghan National Army and steps are being taken to consolidate and professionalize the police force.

Each construction project we engage in has been vetted by the Afghan provincial council and measures are taken to ensure that the local people have the capacity to sustain the project without foreign intervention. The tribal leaders are now beginning to lobby the provincial government for assistance and the very embryonic provincial departments are starting to address the people's needs by employing local firms to carry out development work. This system is closely mentored by British civil servants and military engineers. It is a slow and frustrating process, but without it everything else we do is futile. Racing ahead with grand reconstruction projects would probably suit the average Afghan and appease the international press but it would do nothing towards creating enduring peace and stability.

It is the slow pace of this critical development work that will cause the international community to be committed in Afghanistan for many years to come. In the meantime there will be an enduring requirement for our military to have a presence in Afghanistan in order to reassure the populace and disrupt the activity of the Taliban. Sadly, more men like Lance Corporal [Mathew] Ford, Lance Bombardier Clark and Lance Bombardier McLaughlin will die fighting in remote corners of this alien country. But without their efforts none of the other capacity building activity would be possible; Afghanistan would continue to be a failed state and a breeding ground for fundamentalist activity, led by individuals that despise all that we stand for in countries such as ours.

Given the enormous area of terrain, much of it far from hospitable, and the difficulty in distinguishing between insurgent and civilian, defeating the Taliban with military might is probably not achievable. We must make the Afghan people believe that their future under the Government of Afghanistan banner is better by far than anything the Taliban can offer and compel them to take charge of their own affairs.

3

Introduction: Operation Herrick 6

In April 2007, the men of 12 Mechanized Brigade replaced the Royal Marines as part of Operation Herrick 6. The entire force totalled about 5,800 servicemen and women. As the Afghan summer returned, the fighting once again intensified. The Anglian and Mercian regiments, with distinctive and bloody histories, soon found themselves embroiled in action akin to that fought by their predecessors.

The main combat power for Operation Herrick 6 was provided by 1 Battalion The Royal Anglian Regiment, 2 Battalion The Mercian Regiment (formerly The Worcesters and Foresters), 2 Battalion The Royal Regiment of Fusiliers and 3 Battalion The Yorkshire Regiment, with the Light Dragoons providing armoured reconnaissance; 26 Engineer Regiment, 19 Regiment Royal Artillery and 4 Logistic Support Regiment gave their specialized support. The Army Air Corps flew

Apaches and the RAF Harriers from 1 Squadron provided close air support. RAF Chinooks and Hercules supplied transport while Force Protection was the responsibility of the RAF Force Protection Wing Headquarters and the RAF Regiment.

April 2007

Captain George Seal-Coon, The Royal Anglian Regiment

Captain George Seal-Coon, 1 Battalion The Royal Anglian Regiment, is twenty-seven. He was born in Norwich and grew up in the nearby town of Aylsham. He is the son of a solicitor, who served in the Territorial Army, and has a younger brother. He went to school in Norfolk and, after favouring a career in the military, was awarded a sixth-form scholarship from the Army. Seal-Coon went to university in Nottingham to study French and Russian, then in 2004 to Sandhurst. Afghanistan was his first overseas tour and he was deployed there from March to October 2007. He is single, and based at Pirbright, Surrey. As well as being a full-time soldier, he is a part-time artist and has sketched many military scenes, from on and off the battlefield.

I was platoon commander of 7 Platoon, B Company, in Afghanistan – in charge of roughly thirty men at any one time – although that number dwindled with casualties and times away on R&R [rest and relaxation]. When we arrived at Camp Bastion, we were apprehensive but at the same time we felt well prepared, having trained intensively for the better part of nine months prior to deploying. We were keen to get on with it. Everyone was aware that at some stage we were going to come under contact, and we were keen to know how we would react when that moment arrived.

Initially, we deployed to FOB Rob [Forward Operating Base Robinson] to provide security for the artillery fire base. It was fairly quiet, although we were rocketed a couple of times. It was opium harvest time and the Taliban weren't really up for a fight. So we didn't have any big contacts initially. It did, however, give us time to get out on patrol, work with the Royal Marines' Armoured Support Troop and generally get a feel for the place.

In mid-April, we were involved in Op Silicon – the Viking [tracked armoured fighting vehicle] battle group's first major op. The aim of that was to clear the Green Zone [of Taliban] – the fertile farming area either side of the river Helmand above Gereshk. The plan was to clear it up to the limit of exploitation [LOE]. Further up the valley, we were then to secure the area for the engineers to establish patrol bases for the ANA [Afghan National Army], from which they could then project force.

We deployed with Vikings out to the high ground overlooking the Gereshk valley. We got settled there for the night. It was quite a strange, stormy night. As soon as we were settled, with sentries out, it started to rain – and it got windy: on one or two occasions, we were lying, trying to sleep, when someone's roll mat came whipping past, disappearing into the desert night.

We launched into the Green Zone just before dawn. It was a battle group operation involving well over a thousand men. My company, B (Suffolk) Company, was point at the time. We had A Company on the northern flank, on the edge of the desert. There was an area up there called the Red Fort, a medieval fort, built from red sandstone, which dominated the surrounding area. A Company had to push up there. Our job was to push towards our LOE about six K away, defeat any Taliban we encountered and provide security. Then the engineers would move up and build the FOBs and we would patrol the area.

Initially it was quite quiet. We moved out in the Vikings to a drop-off point on the edge of the desert. A few shots were fired as the Taliban sentries pulled back into the Green Zone. We moved in, on foot, quickly, with very few problems. We had it reported that the women and children had largely moved out of the area, which was often a precursor to the fact that something [a fire-fight] was about to happen. We pushed up the valley, through poppy fields, compounds and dense undergrowth, with an Apache overhead providing some eyes out into depth. The first big contact was on the company's right flank. We had the Vikings there as flank security, moving along a wide canal path. The ANA were supposed to follow up on that flank but had not yet pushed forward. At the time, my platoon was point. We were about to cross the edge of an open field to break into some compounds when the Vikings were opened up on from the south-east, beyond the canal they were paralleling. We also began to take fire from positions to our front. We moved in amongst the compounds fairly rapidly, making use of what cover was available. This was mid-morning and it was already getting pretty hot – about 45°C. We were carrying quite a bit of kit, ammo, body armour and radios: the GPMG [general-purpose machine-gun] gunners were probably loaded down with about forty kilos and the rest of us not too much less.

At first, we came under small-arms and PKM [machine-gun] fire. Then RPGs [rocket-propelled grenades] were fired. The fire was all being directed at the Vikings so we extracted back to assist them. I liaised with my OC [officer commanding], Major Mick Aston, and pushed forward to support the vehicles. Two of my sections and I crossed the canal over a narrow footbridge, with the vehicles and 2 Section providing fire support – we were quite exposed at this time and you'd be surprised at how quickly you move, even with all that kit!

On the far side, we took cover in an irrigation ditch, waist deep in water and taking quite sustained, accurate enemy fire. My personal weapon was a rifle and each section had a GPMG and two minimis [light machine-guns]; a couple of guys had UGLs – underslung grenade launchers. My platoon sergeant 'Woody' Woodrow had a mortar man with him, with a 51mm mortar – an excellent weapon. This first contact went on for three hours, solidly. I suppose, during the entire day, we were in contact for about seven hours.

We identified two positions in a field, about 150 metres to our front and engaged. At this point, I had two sections spread out along the ditch, suppressing the enemy. Not long into the fire-fight we were engaged from our rear. Fortunately everyone was in cover. Between ourselves, 6 Platoon and a Javelin [anti-tank] missile, we managed to silence that threat. It was really a case of winning the fire-fight and providing ourselves with security, guarding against Taliban trying to outflank us. We suppressed them and tried to call in an Apache [attack heli-copter]. They were unable to identify the enemy positions, deep within the tree-lines. The Taliban had about a platoon [-sized force] and they were fairly spread about, using the cover well.

The Taliban tried to push around our flanks and we then had RPGs fired at us. We had a lot of fire-power going down. It was my first proper contact and that of almost everyone there. Initially, it was a shock to the system. The compounds were con-structed of compacted mud walls. The villages were a web of these compounds, often with a couple of alleyways weaving through. The walls were really hard, offering good protection from fire and blast. Every time we breached a compound, we had to use explosives and crowbars. During the day, I fired on a couple of occasions but for the most part I was trying to co-ordinate my sections. My mortar man, Private [Richie] Barke, used his 51mm [mortar] to pretty good effect, getting his bombs on target every first or second shot. We also used it to mark the enemy for CAS [close air support], firing a few smoke rounds on enemy positions and then air – I think it was a Harrier – came in and dropped 500-pounders [bombs].

We had extracted back over the canal using the Vikings as cover and were sheltering, waist deep, in another irrigation ditch, in anticipation. The first bomb was a blind – the second on target. We stopped taking fire on that flank after that. 6 Platoon had been pushed into the village and ended up in danger of being isolated in a compound to the east, with the Taliban pushing forward and attempting to surround them. Effectively, they were taking some fairly accurate and concentrated fire, defending this compound. Ourselves [7 Platoon] and 5 Platoon then broke back into the compounds and cleared through to them. We were clearing buildings on red [aggressively, as distinct from on green: a softer approach], due to the proximity of the enemy from that point. We would breach a wall or door, possibly with an explosive charge, throw a grenade in, then clear the compound in an aggressive manner. We took one or two RPGs fired in airburst [exploding above the men], as we progressed towards 6 Platoon – fortunately they were ineffective. 2 Section were about to grenade one particular compound after creating an entry point, when the grenadier and Corporal Parker heard a noise. A family – mostly women and children and a couple of older men – had been sheltering within a room. They were shaken up and scared but uninjured. We spoke to them, reassured them, and they told us that the Taliban had extracted ahead of us and pointed us in the right direction. One of the men guided us a short distance along the route.

We linked up with 6 Platoon, the Taliban fleeing ahead of us. 7 Platoon became point platoon again and we pushed up towards our LOE. By this stage, it was about 5 p.m. and we had fought through the hottest part of the day, almost non-stop. Spending so much time in the flooded ditches had been a relief – I think that prevented a few people going down with heat exhaustion. We continued to clear compounds. About 150 metres short of the LOE, my lead section commander, Corporal Mann, came back, reporting his lead scout had spotted something. We pushed through cautiously and discovered a wounded Taliban fighter trying to hide in the bushes. He was badly injured in the leg so we secured the area and gave him what first aid we could. We discovered a further three Taliban, whom we took prisoner, and there were a number of enemy dead in the area who had been engaged either by us or the AH [attack helicopter]. There were about seven dead in all. This was on the edge of the built-up area bordered with cornfields. Meanwhile 5 Platoon and Major Aston's tac [tactical] group discovered a number of enemy forces in depth and they killed a further five in that area.

We had gone through the day with a couple of biscuits, travelling light on kit to provide more room for ammo. The guys were pretty tired and the adrenalin rush and exertions started to take their toll. It was seven o'clock when we reached our LOE. We didn't get dry clothes or food and water re-supply until ten or eleven o'clock. Remarkably, there was only one casualty. One man, Private Sheppard, was slightly wounded in the face by an RPG fragment. Bearing in mind the intensity of the fighting, we were very lucky. I was massively proud of my men that day. It was a huge step forward for all of us.

We had taken the Taliban off guard. It was quite rare for our guys to see the Taliban up close. They [the victims] were dressed in drab colours and Afghan traditional dress, with Soviet-style chest-rigs [load-carrying equipment]. We recovered a number of RPGs, AK-47s and a couple of PKMs from their position. Most of the dead were probably in their twenties or early thirties. 5 Platoon had to remove the corpses the next day and for some of the guys it was an unpleasant task. In the heat of the day, the bodies were in quite a state, in particular those that had been killed by AH fire. The bodies did not seem like they had been human beings. Their skin was quite waxy: they almost didn't seem real.

April 2007

Warrant Officer Class 2 Keith Nieves, The Royal Anglian Regiment

Warrant Officer Class 2 Keith Nieves, 1 Battalion The Royal Anglian Regiment, is thirty-four. He was born in Bury St Edmunds, Suffolk, the son of a builder, with a sister, who has died. At sixteen he left school to go into the Army. He had intended to work as a thatcher but his sister bet him £20 that he couldn't join the Army and he took her up on it. He was a member of the junior Parachute Regiment based in Pirbright, Surrey, then progressed to the adult ranks. In 1993, having sustained stress fractures in his legs, he decided to transfer to his local infantry battalion, The Royal Anglians. He has completed tours of Northern Ireland, Croatia, Bosnia, Iraq and Afghanistan. His second tour of Afghanistan in 2007 was as a colour sergeant. Married with two sons, he lives in Pirbright, Surrey.

I had done a tour of Afghanistan in 2002, in Kabul.

My second tour of the country began on 2 April [2007]. This time we were in Helmand province. In the build-up, we knew it was going to be more kinetic than in Kabul. During the Kabul tour, we had a lot of interaction with the local community – there was a lot of PR stuff. But in Helmand province we soon realized we were going to have much less contact with the public and the locals.

When we arrived, the temperature was already warming up – it was up in the thirties [centigrade]. As soon as we arrived, I went to [Camp] Bastion for a while – I was part of B Company. Soon after that we had new orders and we took over FOB Robinson with 5 Platoon and 7 Platoon. That was in a big and untamed valley. I was platoon sergeant of 5 Platoon at the time. FOB Robinson was the main fire support base for the Sangin valley – the artillery was already in. We were relieving the unit that was already there.

The OC at the time was keen for us to get our first contact and he organized a three-day familiarization patrol where we got out of FOB Robinson. We had someone come into the base to man the sangars and provide protection. And we went out as a two-platoon group for three days. It was a case of having a look around the villages, doing an over-watch, seeing the women and kids move out. But nothing happened for three days. There was a seventy-strong patrol, all Brits with the ANA attached. I thought it was going to be another of those tours –

all the hype but nothing happening. I had not been in any contacts in Kabul or Iraq. At this stage, I had been in the Army for fifteen years, but I had still never been in a contact.

April 2007

Lance Corporal Daniel Power, The Royal Welsh

Lance Corporal Daniel Power, of Fire Support Company, 1 Battalion The Royal Welsh, is twenty-six. He was born and brought up in Merthyr Tydfil, south Wales. The son of a builder and a 'full-time mum', he has four brothers and a sister. His grandfather was in the Royal Navy during the Second World War and he has a younger brother who serves with B Company, 1 Battalion The Royal Welsh. At school, Power wanted to join the police or the Fire Brigade. But then a group from the Royal Welsh came to his school, Peny y Dre High in Merthyr Tydfil, and he decided to go into the Army. Power is a fitness enthusiast, and is based at the Royal Welsh's barracks in Chester, Cheshire.

When the Royal Welsh came to my school [on a careers day] I said: 'I want to be a sniper.' They said: 'That's not a problem but you'll have to join the Army first.' I was always focused on what I wanted to do, so as soon as I could after I left school I joined up. I was always quite robust as a kid – into the gym and fitness

– and I used to play a little rugby and do boxing.

The idea of being a sniper appealed to me. It was the idea of not being seen, being quite sneaky around the battlefield, being quite stealthy and picking off your enemy without them seeing you. There is also a fear factor with snipers on the battlefield. Whenever there's a sniper out there, it's always in the back of someone's mind. When I left school I was too young [to join up], so I was waiting around on a prep course to join the Army when I was aged sixteen years and nine months. That's the earliest they'll take you. I was first deployed to Northern Ireland a couple of days past my eighteenth birthday. At nineteen, I was deployed to Op Telic 1 in 2003 – the invasion of Iraq. I had just passed my snipers' course in Aldershot. I joined the Black Watch as part of 7 Armoured Brigade. From the Royal Welsh, there was a four-man sniper team to bolster their platoon.

The standard weapon then [in 2003] was the L96 – a 7.62mm medium-range rifle. The rifle we have now is the L115 – that's a long-range rifle. The L96 has a range of up to 1,100 metres. The L115 rifle has a range of up to 1,500 metres. When you're trained on the snipers' course, you're taught to shoot in various different positions: lying, standing, using shooting sticks. At first, there's quite a lot of maths involved with sniping. You work in a pair but also as part of a bigger organization. The firer will be looking down the sight adjusting it while the number two is basically doing the maths and the radio: working out distance to the target, your elevation, difference in incline, the heat, the wind speed. There is actually a little formula we use to acquire a range. It's all to get that one shot. If you have been given a window for that target, it's important to get it right first time. Normally, we move into position without being seen so we have enough time. But we're talking minutes to prepare – three or four minutes or less. We work as a pair, side by side. If I am looking down the sight, my number two is my protection.

You're firing, judging distance, stalking. We do a cam [camouflage] and concealment training. You have to understand the ground quite well, get to your target area and move into position to take that shot without being seen. I have always enjoyed my work. I feel a pride and privilege doing the job.

I had carried out my first kill in Iraq. It didn't really affect me in any way at the time. To me, it was just a target going down. Afterwards, when you come back to civilian life, you kind of think about it, you have certain dreams about it. But at the time [of the kill] you are happy, excited, anxious – all in one. Time kind of slowed down and then sped up. We had quite a few contacts in Iraq. I remember this guy's face, an Iraqi soldier. I remember looking down and he had been shot. A burst had gone up his body and he had a couple of rounds in the neck and one in the head, which had taken the top of his head off. There was no brain in there but his eyes were sunken and had rolled back. When I got home, it was that kind of image that I kept replaying. It didn't really affect me that day, but sometimes you remember it in your dreams – and that was the face that kept recurring.

I first deployed to Afghanistan with Bravo Company [in March 2007]. We did build-up training in Cyprus. Then we flew to Kandahar airfield. We expected at that point to be in a secure location but with a lot of fighting all around us. It was quite well set up. Our role was as a regional manoeuvre unit, which meant we were going to be mounted up in vehicles and called all over southern Afghanistan to do specific ops.

In Fire Support Company, you have a lot of assets. You have your mortars, your Javelin – an anti-tank weapon. You have your machine-guns, your recce and snipers. We were working with Bravo Company, a rifle company. FSP Company is normally the largest company in the battalion. At one time, it is between 100 and 120 strong.

I remember our first contact in Afghanistan. We were going to move up to FOB Price to do some tasks up there. We were given a time we were to depart from Kandahar, but it had been brought forward. We were going to move by vehicles – for a journey of about six hours to FOB Price. We were travelling in light-skinned WMIKs [armed Land Rovers] and Snatches [lightly armoured Land

Rovers]. I was commanding a Snatch. It was night time. We were travelling in the early hours because that was when the Taliban seemed to be at their rest. We'd come out of Kandahar and we were literally a K and a half out of camp when we got contacted. We had prepped our weapons, done everything. We were in convoy. At one point, we were having difficulty with the grenade machine-gun mount, so we stopped just outside the camp, sorted that out, got it mounted. Then we proceeded off – it was 2 or 3 a.m. There was a fire-support element so there were roughly ten vehicles and about sixty people in the convoy.

We were driving down these streets, shops on either side. They were dead: it was quite suspicious-looking. In some parts, it was quite well lit and in others it was not. I was sitting there – and that was when it happened. When I least expected it. RPGs initiated the contact, three or four. The first thing I saw was a blue-green trail from this RPG that landed on the other side of the road. It came at an angle past the windscreen. It was in between the two vehicles: the spacing was short through the town centre, about fifteen metres. We were kind of in a vulnerable position and they [the Taliban] were in a high position on the left-hand side. They were no more than twenty metres away, firing down on to our vehicles. Some were in buildings, some were on rooftops. The buildings are quite odd in Afghanistan: they have rooftops that lead on to verandas. And they [the Taliban] were spread out down this street on the one side. You couldn't really see how many [enemy] there were.

Our SOP – standard operating procedure – is to put fire down in the killing area, then push through it. So instantly we opened up. The two top cover [in the Snatch] were firing, they had a light machine-gun and an assault rifle with a UGL. We had WMIKs in there too. They have grenade machine-guns, 50-cal; then they've got GMPGs, which are mounted on the vehicles. Everyone was giving it into likely enemy positions. It was at night and they were firing so they [the Taliban] were quite easily identified from their muzzle flashes. My platoon commander and platoon sergeant were in the lead vehicle and an RPG grounded about a metre away from their vehicle – it just fell short. And all the shrapnel from that tore through the vehicle – a WMIK. Hot metal tore through their kit. My platoon sergeant was driving. Shrapnel flew across the bonnet into his hands, into his face. My platoon commander was shot in the arm. There were volleys of RPGs, there were assault rifles. There was a lot of automatic fire coming down on the positions. A lot of the vehicles had bullet holes in them and stuff like that.

I was in the fourth vehicle. My role was to command my vehicle while top cover got fire off – they put a lot of rounds down. It was hard because our platoon commander and platoon sergeant were out of action. But there was also excitement – like we gave these guys [the Taliban] a fucking hammering.

The fire-fight was quick, less than two or three minutes. After our first vehicle was contacted, we put a heavy rate of fire down. Then we pushed through, out of the killing area, and that is when we came up with our plan: how to out-flank them, how to extract from the area. Because of the injuries that we sustained, we deemed it necessary to get them evacuated so we were given a grid. We withdrew to there, where we stayed for the night, and then we had a helicopter come in and lift out our casualties. But we had fought through and it was later reported that there were six or seven [Taliban] killed because the ANP [Afghan National Police] had to go and identify the bodies. This was our first patrol – and all hell had broken loose. This was – welcome to Afghanistan.

I had seen a lot in Iraq, which had prepared me for Afghanistan. But for a lot of the guys there, this was their first contact and it affected them. One or two were shell-shocked – we all knew 'This is what we're in for,' but they all reacted as they were trained. My platoon sergeant, Mark Moore, and platoon commander, Matt Hughes, were casevaced back to Kandahar, then shipped [flown] on to the UK. They both received shrapnel injuries to various parts of their body. My platoon commander needed an operation on the injuries to his arm.

We left for FOB Price the next morning. I took over the vehicle that my platoon commander and platoon sergeant were in. I commanded that WMIK down there. We drove without incident. I was happy, really, because when I was in the Snatch I was in an enclosed vehicle. You cannot do anything except command and get the guys to do their job. But when you're in a WMIK, you have got your own machine-gun on your commander's seat. So, eventually, I was more than happy to get out of the Snatch and into a WMIK – even though there was less protection in a way.

April 2007

Captain George Seal-Coon, The Royal Anglian Regiment

On day two of Op Silicon, we fortified a compound in the Green Zone, near Gereshk, where we stayed for a few days, patrolling and gathering intelligence. There had been a cow living in the compound with a number of chickens. We ensured they stayed alive, and were fed and watered during the few days. This was despite 2 Section's attempts to convince me to allow them to cook the chickens. I didn't think it would be great if the owner turned up and we had barbecued them – and there wouldn't have been enough to go around anyway.

The nephew of the owner eventually turned up to take his cow away. The nephew and the owner himself arrived a couple of days later to pick up his valuables. We had conducted a fairly extensive search of the area when we moved in, only finding a few Afghan dollars. That was it. We put them to one side, ensuring they were safe as we lived there. We showed them through the rooms, apologized for the sandbags on the ceiling and the doors we'd forced open.

The owner then paced out to a spot in the centre of the compound. There was a field of dead and dried opium poppies. He marked a patch of ground and instructed his nephew to dig. After a couple of minutes, he pulled out this bucket of opium resin, which was a bit of a shock to all of us. I'm not sure what the street value was, but that had been beneath our feet all the time. As it was, due to the 'hearts and minds' policy, we decided not to destroy any drugs. I think if we had done so, we would have ended up fighting considerably more than the Taliban. We weren't the Drugs Squad. We were stuck in the middle of their community and we needed as much goodwill as we could get from the farmers and locals – so we left them to it.

April 2007

Warrant Officer Class 2 Keith Nieves, The Royal Anglian Regiment

Shortly after we had established ourselves in FOB Robinson, we had orders for the first big operation from the battle group. We moved back to Camp Bastion where we started the battle procedure. Our first op was Op Silicon. There were two companies forward and one in reserve. Primarily, the aim was to clear the Green Zone north of Gereshk and then to establish PBs [patrol bases], thereafter to provide more security. We had to push through the Green Zone and had to then go 'firm' at the limit of exploitation [LOE]. Then the engineers were to come in and build the PBs. There were about 240 Brits altogether, with the ANA in the rear.

Anyway, we were pushing through and clearing the Green Zone – in mid- to late April. 6 Platoon had moved into a small compound in a village area – and that was when we pretty much had our first contact. It was fairly hefty. 6 Platoon was cut off and I had my platoon in the ditch taking fire from three directions. We were taking some quite serious fire. It was about eight thirty in the morning when it kicked off. The first thing was hearing the gunfire from a distance. Then it echoed around and, as we pushed up, we started taking fire as well. It was hard to pinpoint where the fire was coming from. We couldn't see the Taliban but we could hear the crack and we could hear the thump. We could hear RPGs coming over and we could see the trails.

I was the platoon sergeant and it was our first major contact. I had a brand new platoon commander so I was trying to control things, making sure the platoon commander was all right. I was also trying to get amongst the blokes to make sure they didn't get excited and waste all their ammunition. I had three heat casualties at one stage and I was trying to get them sorted out. It was a manic situation.

We were pinned down for a good hour and a half in this ditch taking constant fire, sometimes sporadically and sometimes heavy. Then we got the call – we were told we needed to push forward to link up with the platoon that was cut off. We prepped for that, pushed forward and broke into the village. We then started fighting through the village. From that point on, we were fighting to the LOE.

I was controlling the mortar fire and I got some rounds off at the end. The Vikings had been forward of us and then we started taking fire. To my immediate left was the OC's tac [tactical group]. That was when we identified the Taliban. So, with a few of my guys, we swept through this poppy field. I don't think they [the Taliban] expected us to push that far.

At one point, the Apaches were called in to take care of the Taliban we had spotted in a tree-line. Then there were some Taliban in a compound and the fast air [support] dropped a 500-pounder [bomb] but it didn't detonate. There was a big confab on the radio about what to do. They [the pilots] said: 'There are Brits only 350 metres away. Is it safe [to drop a bomb]?' In the end, they dropped the 1,000-pounder and it was so loud you felt the shock waves. I was about 350 metres away. It was the first time I had experienced a bomb that size go off. We were down in a ditch but what struck me about the Taliban was, almost immediately the bomb had been dropped, they fired some rounds off as if to say: 'We're still here.' All through the day we saw muzzle flashes but we didn't really see the Taliban.

We finally reached the LOE at about 1830 and we were still fighting with a fleeing enemy at that stage. It was a whole-day battle, very intense. One of the young guys – a private of twenty-two or -three – took a nick of shrapnel under one of his eyes. It was nothing serious – it didn't even warrant first aid. Other than the heat casualties, that was our only small injury. But there were twenty to twenty-four casualties [on the Taliban side]. We caught the Taliban on the hop that day. I counted twelve bodies at the LOE – how many we got [killed] extracting I don't know.

It is hard to explain how exhausted we felt at the end of the day. The minimum kit we had was 80–85 pounds plus the Osprey body armour, which weighs a good 35 pounds on top. It soon weighs you down – especially with a heat of 30°C. The adrenalin got most of the guys through but the following day everyone was: 'Fuck, what happened there?' I went around with a camera and got some good photos of all the boys, looking physically exhausted, sat up with all the kit on.

Because it was the first time we came across so

many dead Taliban, we had to seek advice from higher up on what to do with the bodies – so that we respected their religion and everything. It was the first time we had pushed that far forward – they [the Taliban] are usually pretty quick about extracting their own bodies and you don't get to see them [dead bodies]. But this was different.

We managed to establish contact with some of the village elders. We got the bodies centralized so the village elders could sort out the burials, which they did. It took me, the company sergeant major and some guys I had hand-picked to move the bodies. It wasn't nice but it had to be done. The smell – you can't train for it. It was not so much the bloodied state of them, it was the smell that will always stay with me. It's hard to describe but I have never smelt anything like it before. After, the men were washing their clothes in a stream because they could still smell it. Later on, we stayed firm for a while to do clearance patrols and I could still smell that smell.

That night we pushed down. There were a couple of small buildings that we had got into. The guys were sleeping beside the vehicles [Vikings]. I certainly didn't get much sleep that night. You were sleeping with one eye open. After fighting all day, it was hard to get to sleep.

7 April 2007 [email home]

Robert Mead, Ministry of Defence press officer

The moment you've all been waiting for is upon us. Today is my last day in fair, sunny, and getting sunnier, Lashkar Gah (I hope – unless, of course, I get bumped off the helicopter flight).

You will all be delighted to know that I don't have time to compose my usual 5,000-worder as my helicopter departs in a few hours and I have vital packing to do, smalls to wash and prayers to Allah, peace be upon him, to complete.

However, there is still some uncertainty concerning my final arrival back on the green and pleasant soil of olde Englande, namely that I was told there was a flight on 10 April, provisionally booked it three weeks ago, only to ring yesterday to confirm and while doing so was rather irritatingly informed that: 'Eh, sir, there isn't a flight on the tenth.'

Great. The flights are now on 9 and 11 April, so I am provisionally booked on the flight home 11 April, arriving Blighty early hours of 12 April or, if I am very lucky, they may be able to squeeze me on to the flight tonight, meaning I will be back at home in the early hours of tomorrow, i.e., Tuesday. Gosh, even to the end it's so exciting.

Either way, for all those who can join me, I shall be having a Great Boo's up in Colchester on Friday where you can all gather round like an episode of *Jackanory* and I shall regale you, my select selection of bestest chums, with my stories of bravery and gallantry/bore the bleedin bejesus out of you, or at the very least all those who can be orsed [sic] to come out on the pretence that I may buy them a drink. Fat chance.

Whizz-bang (which hopefully is the closest I will come to this sound in the next 24 hrs).

30 April 2007 [diary]

Captain Adam Chapman, The Mercian Regiment

Captain Adam Chapman, 2 Battalion The Mercian Regiment, attached to 4/73 (Sphinx) Special Operations Battery, is twenty-nine. He was born in Gillingham, Kent, one of three brothers. His father served in The Royal Engineers, and they settled in Chesterfield, Derbyshire, when Chapman was five. He left school at eighteen and went to the University of Manchester to do a degree in social policy. It was there that he decided to work in the military, something he had long considered because of his father's career. He eventually joined the Army in early 2003, aged twenty-two. He visited Cyprus, Belize and Malawi with the Army before going on tour to Afghanistan in 2007. Chapman, who is engaged, is based at the 2 Mercians' barracks just outside Belfast.

It's the night before I deploy to Afghanistan on Op Herrick 6. I am taking B Troop of 4.73 Bty [Battery] to bolster the 12 Brigade Recce Forces [BRF] on what is recognized as one of Britain's most demanding deployments in recent years. Not only is it a dangerous op, it is also a dangerous job for all of us and we know it. Our job will be to go and find the enemy. The BRF, already in theatre, have suffered their first casualties: one gunshot wound and three shrapnel wounds after an incident on one of their first missions. This is obviously not the type of news you wish to hear before deploying, but it has to be expected, unfortunately. All I can do is get on with the job. We have been training for this for some time and I am confident of what we have got. My soldiers are volunteers from across the Army, and they are motivated and focused and, most importantly, trained for the job.

Anyway, I'm almost packed and there is little to do but wait. I'm full of anticipation, anxiousness and trepidation. I think the waiting is the worst part but at least my journey begins tomorrow.

3 May
Journey complete. After a relatively comfortable flight on a Tristar to Kandahar, which took seven hours, we then stayed overnight in a very basic terminal. We took a Hercules for the final journey into Camp Bastion. The further the journey went, the more apparent the danger was: coming into Kandahar, we all had to don our helmets and body armour with the lights turned off: a very strange

sensation indeed! Then it was helmets and body armour all the way to Bastion.

Camp Bastion is a large, purpose-built camp in the middle of the desert. It's flat, dusty and full of tents and equipment. There's constant activity with construction and movement taking place all over. However, it was relatively quiet as the majority of fighting troops are out on the ground. There's a big op taking place so I wasn't able to see any of my mates from Battalion (who are also on this tour) . . .

Bad news today: a young soldier had his leg blown off by a mine on an op (from the Royal Anglians) and a Grenadier Guard was shot in the head. He was flown back to Camp Bastion where he later died. It's strange having this go on close by, especially after getting used to seeing the news on TV. It's not a nice feeling knowing that it could happen to anyone here. Pessimistic as that sounds, the likelihood is that we will come into contact with the enemy – everyone knows that.

We're in temporary accommodation at the moment, but we may not even have any when we return from our first op. I have been sharing a ten-man tent with no air conditioning. It's basic but it's comfortable and that's the main thing. The heat here is intense: at one point the thermometer on my watch read 35°C in the shade! It must be over 40°C at its worst and it's only going to get hotter.

The heat will be a massive factor on how we operate, especially when carrying kit. Even just sat around at lunch I was sweating profusely. We will get acclimatized to it, however, especially as we begin to increase our fitness. There are also flies and bugs everywhere, which are another issue. I'm taking malaria tablets, but there are plenty of other nasty diseases, which have already sent some people home. Finally, the sand and dust: it's so dry and when the wind blows the dust gets everywhere. It leaves a thin layer and gets up your nose, in your eyes . . . everywhere!

5 May
Starting to acclimatize now. Obviously the longer you spend out here, the better. We do some phys [physical exercise] every day before 0700 or after 1800 – it's far too hot in between. Yesterday there were another five serious casualties flown back into camp, a combination of gunshot and shrapnel wounds. It was part of a big op in the Sangin valley. During the battle, the mortar platoon fired 600 high-explosive rounds – that's an indication of the severity of things. Every day we hear reports and news of contacts and events. And it's only going to get worse as the summer progresses.

Historically the summer months are the worst for fighting as the opium harvest finishes and there are more fighters, also the winter months are harsh weather-wise. Last summer was bad for the British – a lot died unfortunately. I can see this summer being equal to, if not worse than, last year.

The hospital is in Camp Bastion, so all the casualties (friendly and enemy) are flown in by Chinook, which has been very regular since we've been here. Whenever there is a serious casualty or death, the camp shuts off all ties with the outside world – i.e. Internet and phone – so as yet I've not been able to reach anyone. But I think the phones are working so I will try tonight. I know my parents will be keen to speak especially as they have been worrying a lot – Lisa [his girlfriend] as well.

I received my first letter yesterday, off Scotty [a friend], of all people. Full of humour as usual.

We had our RSOI [reception, staging and onward integration] package today, basically some lectures on Afghanistan, and then we went to zero our weapons [adjust the sights so they are accurate by firing rounds]. It was very hot and the mile or so out to the range was surprisingly sweaty, especially carrying all that kit: the new body armour is massive and extremely heavy. Just found out that a soldier has accidentally shot himself in Garmsir: I'd better use the phones [to ring home] soon!

May 2007

Captain George Seal-Coon, The Royal Anglian Regiment

We were involved in Op Kulang – a big battle group op in the upper Sangin valley. Prior to the main phase of the operation, B Company was tasked to conduct shaping operations south of Sangin. I went out with my OC and another platoon commander for a brief recce to an area called Hyderabad, in the Green Zone, south of Sangin and north of Gereshk. We married up with a company from the 82nd Airborne – Americans. They had just conducted a battalion air assault into this area as part of Op Silicon and had taken part in some fairly heavy fighting. It gave us a good chance to see what they had encountered and get the lie of the land.

We came back to Bastion, had our orders and then pushed out with two platoons' worth of Vikings. On the ground were 7 and 5 Platoons, our mortar-line, FSG [Fire Support Group] B and the OC's tac. The idea was to find concentrations of the Taliban, to disrupt them, and to damage their combat effectiveness. It started off fairly quiet as we headed out into the desert.

The plan was to raid into the Green Zone over a period of four to five days, find and disrupt the Taliban, then extract back into the desert. We started off in a town called Zumbelay, which had been known for some heavy contacts in the past. The other platoon commander and I were expecting things to be fairly serious. That first day we contacted a few sentries who fired RPGs at us. They then legged it. We cleared into Zumbelay a few hundred metres and encountered little else. We then extracted back to the vehicles and moved back to a leaguer [harbour or short stop-off point] in the desert.

The next day we went into Pasab and set up our over-watch. On this occasion, 5 Platoon were kept back on the high ground in reserve. As with the day before, the mortar-line and the FSG, under Company Sergeant Major Snow, set up on a dominating feature. There was a canal that ran along the edge of the fertile Green Zone, separating it from the desert. The village was mostly spread out in the sand with a few compounds dotted amongst the trees on the far side of the canal. We had seen the women and children move out and, getting the familiar rush of adrenalin to the stomach, we began to patrol through the compounds. There were a few elderly people about who told us the Taliban weren't there, had never been there and would never be there – which made us instantly suspicious.

It was not too long after meeting these locals – at about 7 a.m. – when we were contacted from beyond the canal. We engaged this firing point: 1 Section moving quickly into fire positions to suppress it with GPMG and rifles. The Taliban were engaging us with automatic fire – probably from a PKM and AKs. We used an 84mm – a light anti-tank weapon. We saw muzzle flashes and movement amongst the compounds on the other side of the canal but it was often difficult to pinpoint precise enemy positions. As we more or less silenced the first position, 3 Section began to take fire from our left flank and a couple of RPGs crashed into the ground nearby. We had to cross a bit of open ground to properly engage these positions, so I got 3 Section to put heavy fire down onto the enemy as we moved to a better position.

The Taliban were often very mobile, not carrying a lot of weight, and they liked to try and get around our flanks. We occupied this compound and continued to suppress these two positions. It became apparent there was movement in the branches of the trees about fifty metres away. Corporal Parker gave his whole section 'rapid fire' into this new target, whereupon two Taliban fighters dropped dead from the trees into the canal.

With these two fighters gone, it quietened down for a couple of minutes. We got orders to put in a bit of deception as if we were going to cross the canal, to try to draw some fire from the enemy, the idea being to pinpoint their position and to engage them with the FSG. We threw a bit of smoke, notionally to give cover, then ramped up our fire and shouted a few commands. This seemed to work and the Taliban began to fire into the smoke, giving their positions away. They were only thirty to fifty metres away, on the other side of a ditch. We and the FSG poured a heavy rate of fire onto them, quickly silencing the positions. We had effectively done an arc around this village and the OC gave the orders to pull out. But I was not keen to run my guys over the open ground, in full view of the enemy's old positions. The Vikings were sent forward and we piled into the back of the vehicles. During this time, we fired mortars onto the positions to cover our extraction. At a guess we were fighting a little over a section's worth of Taliban [eight men].

On day three, we moved into an area called Hyderabad, setting up our fire support on a higher feature, dismounting and patrolling in on foot along the desert and in the compounds. We saw a number of civilians, some fleeing into the desert, but many who stayed amongst the compounds. We spoke with a few elders, trying to put out the message that we were there for security at the request of the Afghan government: we weren't the enemy. We even arranged a shura [meeting] for the afternoon.

It was an hour or so after dawn. We asked the locals in Pasab if they had seen the Taliban. They told us they had never been there. At just that moment, we heard a burst of automatic fire, from 5 Platoon's position ahead of us. We got close enough to support them. This involved a dash between compounds and along narrow alleyways. 5 Platoon had pushed up to a couple of fairly large compounds and it was there they had taken fire from a medium machine-gun. We also received intelligence that the Taliban might be moving around to strike us. 5 Platoon established a fire-base on the roofs of the two compounds and started to suppress this enemy position.

I was concerned about hanging around to the rear of 5 Platoon, with so little cover. Spotting a deep irrigation ditch to our flank, I moved the platoon there. It was a bit too crowded. Within seconds, there was a very large explosion – from a mortar – twenty or thirty metres away, on top of our last position just as one of the section commanders, Corporal Stef Martin, was getting down into cover. He landed pretty much on top of me. He was hit, not too badly but he had taken some frag through his upper arm, passing through his triceps. Another mortar then landed a little further away.

The FSG were up on the high ground and spotted the mortar position – a puff of smoke and the area it came from. We got air to look into it. It was a B1 bomber overhead that properly identified the position and dropped a large 2,000-pound bomb on it. We took no more mortar fire afterwards. Corporal Martin had the medic pick the frag out, bandage him up tightly and he cracked on.

We had orders from the OC to advance into the built-up areas. In some of the bigger compounds we used bar mines to blow our way through the walls as opposed to cutting across open areas in full view. We were moving forward in bounds. We went through house-clearance drills. There was a chance of running into civilians in the area and we didn't want to cause any unnecessary casualties. The OC tasked my platoon to move forwards to the area of a bridge, more or less on the position we'd stayed, during our recce. We closed up towards the canal, pushing through a graveyard. I dropped off one section in over-watch and I held myself and 2 Section back as 3 Section advanced on the left flank through a fertile poppy- or cornfield. It was five feet plus full of crops so it gave a bit of cover from view. They advanced up to a mound forty metres short of the bridge. The ground on the other side of the river was visible. You had about fifty metres of open ground that sloped upwards to compounds on the other side. There were compounds left and right of the slope.

We were being very cautious at this point, having already been in contact and knowing the bridge would be a perfect spot for us to be ambushed. We did have ladders as an alternative means of crossing but they were too short to ford the canal. Just before he moved, Corporal [Stu] Parker said he was going to take a couple of guys to check the bridge out just in case it had been IEDed [booby-trapped with an improvised explosive device]. We had an irrigation ditch on our right-hand side and decided that if we got contacted it would be a good place to take cover. Just as he broke cover from the tree-line on the edge of the ditch, there was a whoosh and an RPG came from the compounds on the far side, shooting over our heads and exploding ten metres behind us. Everyone piled into the ditch pretty rapidly. The Section 2IC, Lance Corporal Stevie Veal, was knocked out briefly by this blast but was uninjured and was dragged into cover. Corporal Parker jumped into the ditch and 3 Section opened up on their side and started to suppress these positions. For a few minutes it felt like everything was coming at us. Parky lost count at seventeen RPGs in the first five minutes of fighting. I jumped into the ditch with 2 Section, up to our waists in water, and pushed forward, trying to get eyes on the enemy position. It was difficult to see forward without leaving cover because of the foliage. Parky had brought a couple of GPMG gunners with him. They managed to scramble out of the ditch into a decent firing position. I pushed forward and got some pretty good eyes on, keeping Lance Corporal Veal's fire team back to provide flank protection. Ironically, the compound we were taking the most fire from was one we had spent three nights in less than a week previously.

I managed to send a full contact report over the radio, having had to scramble half out of the ditch to get comms. We moved back a short distance and Stevie Veal shot two Taliban, trying to outflank us. One of his blokes, Gilly [Private Gillmore], had been injured in the thigh by the first RPG but was still engaging the Taliban with LMG [light machine-gun] fire. After those two [Taliban] had been killed, it quietened down a little on that flank.

At that stage, we were just over a hundred metres from the main enemy position – it was mostly open ground between us. I had not heard anything from

1 Section over the net so I was quite concerned. I couldn't get hold of them [on the radio]. I pushed back along the ditch another thirty metres, leaving Parky to carry on the fire-fight and taking Gilly with me to where I expected to be able to find the OC. I couldn't find Mick [Major Mick Aston] but met with the Viking troop commander who told me that 5 Platoon had also been contacted to the flank. I then heard over the net that we had taken further casualties – two privates injured by fragmentation. I couldn't get hold of the platoon sergeant because he had been trying to casevac them. There was also our medic, Corporal McLaughlan, who was shot in the gut and he was in a pretty serious way. He had been shot just outside the compound and was dragged into cover, under heavy fire, by Private Ronnie Barker, who started to administer first aid. Ronnie was only a team medic, not experienced in putting in an IV drip, and Mac was bleeding pretty heavily. Mac managed to talk him through the process, despite the pain. He was a T1 [critical] casualty so it was absolutely vital that we got him back as quickly as possible. The round had gone under his body armour and exited out of his lower back. The two guys who had been fragged were not as serious but it was still a concern. They were suppressed in the compound, unable to exit through the doors due to enemy fire.

1 Section had an engineer with a hoodlum bar [a large crowbar] and he smashed through the rear

wall of the compound to get the casualties out. Having sustained casualties and completed our task in the area, we were ordered to pull out. I asked the Vikings to push forward so we could prepare our extraction back. It was annoying, not assaulting the enemy, but there was no way we could cross the canal with the kit we had, without taking serious casualties. We put down a heavy rate of rapid fire to give the rear section enough time to get out and enable us to push the Vikings forward, then piled into the back of the vehicles. We were effectively the last troops out of the area. I jumped into the last Viking, nicely burning myself on 2 Section's GPMG as I did so. At least that raised a smile! We stopped for a quick head count and extracted back to an HLS. We got our casualties into the back of the Chinook and away.

Five casualties was quite a big deal – although everyone survived. The contact had gone on for over an hour and, without indirect fire and with 1 Section's casualties, all we could do was sit tight and kill as many of them as possible. We were getting low on ammunition by the end of it. It was one of those few occasions when you think: Hang on a minute. We could be in the shit here. This might be real trouble. In the final contact we saw about eight Taliban killed but it's hard to tell if there were more – I'm not sure about 5 Platoon's BDA [battle-damage assessment]. The Taliban are good at getting their casualties and dead away and we didn't assault into the enemy position. Later that day we received orders to return to FOB Robinson. That afternoon, we had a mine strike and Sergeant [now Warrant Officer 2, Keith] Nieves and a couple of others were badly injured, with Private Nadriva, Keith's mortar man, rescuing him from the front of a burning Viking. Fortunately, no one was killed but it was a fairly hairy day.

11 May 2007 [diary]

Captain Adam Chapman, The Mercian Regiment

I'm finally on the ground, probably as far from home as I could possibly be. I've arrived in the town of Garmsir with an advanced party of TSM [troop sergeant major], patrol commanders and signallers. The rest of the troop arrive in two days. Garmsir is basically the front line against the Taliban. We are the furthest south of any friendly troops and the enemy have to come past us on their journey north from Pakistan. Garmsir is a ghost town: it's seen nothing but fighting for some time now. The Taliban occupy positions to our south; there is a trench system they use to get up close and occupy, before attacking friendly positions.

These positions consist of the main base called Delhi and then two smaller positions, JTAC Hill and the Eastern Check-point, where Guardsman Davison was killed last week. I'll spend most of my time in Delhi, which is an old derelict compound surrounded by a wall and barbed wire. It is only approx. 200 metres in length and width and there are no facilities – it's completely barren. We are very isolated here; as such we must conserve everything. At the moment we will get one litre of [bottled] water a day – the rest comes from a well. There are no fresh rations, electricity, gas, etc. We will get a resupply by helicopter roughly once a week and once a week a large convoy brings supplies down to us.

There are TICs [troops in contact] every day. Just as I arrived, our troops were firing mortars onto suspected enemy positions. But I am calm now and not as worried as I thought I would be. Even on the flight down from Bastion I was fine although I knew I'd be getting off the heli in one of the most dangerous places in the world . . .

I'm really looking forward to this. In a few days, we'll be patrolling and operating, which is an exciting prospect. We're sure to see some action. I don't want to sound flippant or macho but that is what I'm here for, and I know my lads feel the same. It's the pinnacle of soldiering and it beats sitting in an office. I wonder how I'll feel in a few months' time.

May 2007

Warrant Officer Class 2 Pete Lewis, The Mercian Regiment

Warrant Officer Class 2 Regimental Quarter Master Sergeant (RQMS) Pete Lewis, 2 Battalion The Mercian Regiment, is forty. He was born and brought up in Nottingham, the son of a factory engineer. He had two sisters, but one died during his 2007 tour. Lewis left school at sixteen and worked for the next five years as a bricklayer. He joined the Army in October 1990 and has served for nearly two decades in the Mercians. During that time, he has been on four tours of Northern Ireland, two of Bosnia and two of Afghanistan. He is married with three children, and is based at the Mercians' barracks outside Belfast.

Before we arrived [in Afghanistan], it was a constant worry for me how our men would react. How would they react last thing at night before going to bed and first thing in the morning? But from day one, as soon as we were out there, every man in the company was awesome.

You hear of people refusing to go back on the ground once they have been in heavy contact. We had none of that. We were lucky in the respect that we were a floating company. We spent about ten days in [Camp] Bastion acclimatizing, and then we went to Sangin for two months. I was a company sergeant major in Grenadier Company. I would say

I was a dad to the company, some of whom were only eighteen years old. I am the senior soldier. There's not a lot that happens in the company that doesn't come through me in one way or another.

There were anything from 90 to 120 men in our company. My job is about discipline. The sergeant major has got to work closely with the OC. If they don't get on, then the company doesn't function. I was lucky: I had two OCs on the tour and they were both very, very good. They were very soldier-oriented. And because we spent those large periods of time out on the ground, it was a case of hardships shared. The blokes were eating rations; we were eating rations. The blokes were shitting in oil drums; we were shitting in oil drums. The blokes were burning the shit; we were burning the shit. The blokes were in contact; we were in contact. So the cohesion of the company just grew and grew and grew all the way through the tour.

Sangin was relatively quiet. We had perhaps five or six contacts within those first two months. The only casualty we had was an Afghan interpreter, who got shot through the femur. That was after a thirty-eight-hour push-out. We were coming back into the DC [base] at Sangin. It was around 1400 hours so it was pretty warm. We had a heat casualty on the way back in. I was on foot for this op so a quad bike came out and picked him up, which fixed us on the ground for about thirty minutes. In hindsight, this enabled them [the Taliban] to put the ambush in on us. Because we had gone static, they could predict our movements. It was only two and half K back to base and they picked their spot.

They opened up from across a canal with heavy machine-gun. Luckily, we were within the arcs of the DC tower so they had their heavy weapons, which opened straight up. Compared to some of the contacts the boys were in, that was short, only fifteen or twenty minutes. We gave the casualty first aid, then extracted him back on foot with a casevac team. He was picked up in a Chinook. The interpreter was twenty-four or -five and he had worked with us for the first month and a half.

The first confirmed kill we got was at a village near Sangin. We got a Taliban who was quite high up in that district. The boys had gone in to clear a compound and this guy came running out. He had a weapon and he was shot.

Looking back, the only plus about Sangin was that it had a canal running through the base so it was a respite for the boys every day to jump in and cool off.

I think Sangin was a massive reality check for the blokes, me as well. I had never lived on rations for more than three weeks. But we were on rations for two months solid. When we went into Sangin, all our water came out of the rivers from the Royal Engineers' Life Support [and was treated] so it tasted of chlorine. But Sangin was a good staging point for the boys. It got their battle fitness up and it got them used to the heat.

13 May 2007 [diary]

Captain Adam Chapman, The Mercian Regiment

Despite getting up at 02.20, I had a really good day, and saw my first real bit of action, although not personally involved. I went up onto JTAC Hill to watch the other platoon's mission unfold. At first light they hit a compound with several anti-tank rockets and lots of machine-gun fire. The plan was then to extract to ambush positions and wait for the enemy. They engaged an enemy, with covering indirect fire support. I was in a position to watch as the 81mm mortar and 105mm shells whistled over my head and impacted a few hundred metres ahead. Very impressive to watch and the noise was phenomenal! Any enemy on the receiving end would have been pulverized (but I am dubious). The platoon commander is a Grenadier Guard called Andy. He is a really nice bloke and very professional and capable.

I then drove over to FOB Dwyer to pick up the rest of the troop. Dwyer is where the big 105mm guns are located and is basically a shit-hole in the middle of the desert. It's a pain to drive there but there is no heli landing site at Delhi and I doubt the pilots would want to land there anyway. The lads

are in good spirits but some are a little apprehensive. After all, Garmsir is supposedly one of the
worst places to be. To be honest, I think it has been
built up a little and is not as bad as many make out.

I then went out on a foot patrol in the blistering
heat of the afternoon but it was very useful to see
the ground. We patrolled through Garmsir centre,
which was once busy but is now nothing more than
a ghost town, very eerie, almost looked like a Wild
West town. The only people we saw were the
Afghan National Police, who were too zonked out
on drugs to care much!

15 May
We conducted our first patrol last night and it was a
relatively successful operation. Purely in the fact
that everyone came back safe and that will always
be the main thing. I honestly believe that had we
encountered the enemy there would have been
problems. Luckily we didn't. There was a large contact at JTAC Hill before we left. You could actually
see tracer rounds going over our heads in camp and
hear the zip of bullets as they flew overhead. A lot of
rounds were fired over about an hour and fighter
jets flew in to try to find and destroy the enemy.

It was an odd feeling sat here knowing we would
be out there very shortly. I was not as nervous as I
thought I might have been, going into one of the
world's most dangerous places at night. In fact, I
was strangely calm . . .

28 May 2007

McNab: *A sad landmark. A mine strike caused the death of the fiftieth British serviceman killed since Britain moved into Helmand province. Corporal Darren Bonner, thirty-one, served with 1 Battalion The Royal Anglian Regiment. He was a committed Christian and had a fiancée. He had been seen by comrades reading the Bible the night before he died. Major Dom Biddick, the commander of A Company, was in the driver's seat when the mine hit his Viking armoured fighting vehicle, but the blast struck the rear. Biddick said of Bonner: 'He genuinely cared about the people of Afghanistan and it is a source of some consolation to those that knew him that he died on operations contributing to a noble cause.'*

May/June 2007

Warrant Officer Class 2 Keith Nieves, The Royal Anglian Regiment

It was 16 May and we were carrying out 'shaping' operations on the edge of the Green Zone: trying to shape the enemy to let them know we were there. We were trying to push into certain pockets, certain villages where we knew they had enemy strong-holds. It was a show of force. After pushing through in the day, we would then move back into the desert away from it at night. And the next morning we would push into another village. So we were fighting in the Green Zone but we were living in the desert [at night] by the Vikings. We were two platoons strong with company tac [tactical support group] and attachments – the [Royal] Engineers, etc., etc. We are talking about 120-plus men in all – there were 5 and 7 Platoons, and we had an ANA attachment as well.

For the whole trip, we had contacts. We pushed into the first village, Zumbelay, I think. We did a bit of firing and pushed back into the desert, rested up for the night and did exactly the same on the second day, this time in the village of Pasab. On the third day, we went to another town – Hyderabad. We set off at about 8 a.m. – we were running a bit late because we were having difficulty getting in with the vehicles. As we were moving through, I saw some locals and thought: This isn't so bad. At least there are some locals down there. I said to my platoon commander: 'Boss, you need to question that guy to see if there have been any Taliban in the area.' He [the local man] said there had been no Taliban in the area for a long time.

I remember pushing through this small pocket and coming out the other end and there was a massive bit of open ground rising upwards slightly. On the top of a hill there was a compound that stood on its own. And then there was a horrific contact. I'd heard nothing like it in my life. It had come out of nowhere. I got the boys down. But, in fact, the fire was not on us. It was on the vehicles on the high ground, which were over-watching our movement.

By now it was about 11 a.m. We decided to break into the compound on top of the high ground. Once we got into it, we started to take mortar fire onto us. We had broken in because we were keen to have somewhere a bit more secure, to get us out of the open ground and into some more adequate cover. Until then, we had had the platoon spread across the open ground. We pinpointed where the Taliban were and fast air came in dropping 500-pounders. We eventually cleared the compound that the Taliban were fighting from, and it all went quiet.

After that there was a lull. It calmed down so we got the orders from high to move through Hyderabad. The village went into a triangle with a bridge crossing at the point where the village ended. I had my platoon [5 Platoon] in a graveyard and 7 Platoon pushed further forward. Then they got ambushed at the river crossing. They took two casualties at that stage. And the fire-fight we had from there was horrific. We couldn't see the Taliban but they were out-flanking us and it was then we took the call that the Vikings were coming down and we had to get the casualties from the other platoon up. I had one medic with me, but I couldn't send him up because we were under fire from small arms. We didn't see the Taliban at all that day but we knew there were a lot of men.

My instinct was to get the guns up [fire] on the trees, which the Taliban were using as a firing point.

We were firing GPMGs. From there, the Vikings came down and extracted the casualties under fire. We got the casualties back, but it was a frantic moment. Certainly, as platoon sergeant out there [in Afghanistan], I had two big fears – a mine strike and that I would [inadvertently] leave one of my guys on the ground. And at one moment [during the fire-fight], I couldn't account for all my blokes and they were getting thrown in the back of the vehicles to get extracted. It was quite an unsettling moment for me. I was responsible for thirty-four guys, but I didn't have a hand on how many had been extracted. I had my little book to tick people off with all the names on like a school register – for peace of mind for me – but I didn't really have a hand on it until I got back on top. But once I realized all the men were there I calmed down. I said to myself: 'I don't need many more days like this.'

We then took a call, which hit the blokes hard, that we [the British forces] had had our first two major casualties. One guy was shot by small arms in his stomach. The other had shrapnel wounds from an RPG. Then a Chinook flew in and the casualties were extracted. The guy who was shot had serious injuries, but they were not life-threatening. We then took a call that we were going to extract back to FOB Robinson to recoup the boys – give them a rest. It was now 2 or 3 p.m. So we all loaded up into the Vikings. At that stage, I took my belt off – the webbing with all the pouches. On the route back we had the WMIK in front. I was the lead platoon so I had the Vikings in convoy and we were moving across a desert. It was a big convoy: we had a good fifteen Vikings and six or seven WMIKs along with a refuelling truck. I was the fourth Viking in the packet. We were moving forward, and that's all I remember.

Suddenly I woke up as if I was in a dream: the cab was covered with smoke. I couldn't see anything, and I couldn't hear anything. There was a ringing in my ears. I sort of woke myself up. I looked down at the door – where the mine had hit – although I didn't know I had been hit by a mine at that stage. But the mine strike had blasted the doors ajar slightly, just enough to put an arm or leg out, but not to squeeze my body through. I initially went for the door because I thought: Fuck, I've got to get out of here quick. But I couldn't get out so I sat back down. I saw the whole engine block was on fire on my left-hand side. I just remember feeling the heat and I thought: Fucking hell! I have got to get out of this vehicle! We had four of us in the front cab: me, the driver, the gunner sitting on top and I had my 51 [mortar] man sitting on the seat behind me. In the back cab – because it's a twin cab – I had seven guys: five engineers, a medic and an additional sniper, but they were essentially OK.

It was the right-hand door of the cab that I could not get open. The engine block was all ablaze. I saw my 51 man sitting on the floor in shock so I shouted to him: 'Get me out of this fucking vehicle.' Luke

[Private Luke Nadriva] managed, with the driver, to squeeze the [crumpled] armour and I slipped out of the vehicle. As I slipped out, the door shut and all the skin peeled off my arm where it had been burnt. I took a couple of steps and fell over. I had a quick look to make sure my foot was there and it was. So then I started crawling back to try and get away. Being a reserve vehicle, it was full of ammunition. I didn't know where anyone was at the time. It all happened in a split second. And the casualties were starting to get extracted. There were four casualties in total because the front cab got the brunt of the blast. It was me and the driver, who were worst off. The 51 man behind me had minor burns to his arms and the gunner had burns to his arms and his face.

The Viking was smoking: there was thick black smoke. I got dragged to the rear of the sergeant major's vehicle. I was then treated on the ground by a medic and I got put onto the Chinook. I remember flying back. I had this pain in my right foot, but I was more worried about my bloody eyes. The blast had blown all my eyelashes off and I was getting dust in my eyes. I remember screaming out for a damp cloth so I could get all the dust out of them. After that I couldn't take my boot off. I wanted to check my foot was still intact. I didn't have morphine on the ground because I didn't want it. But once I got onto the Chinook and I knew everyone was safe, I had some. I could feel my right foot swelling up. I knew it wasn't right. It was bloody sore. The driver was more seriously hurt than me. He was having trouble breathing because he had a lot of inhalation burns so he was in a bad way.

The MERT [medical emergency response team] was on board the Chinook so it was a case of a paramedic giving me morphine. I don't remember much after that. I remember getting put onto the ambulance at Bastion on the HLS. I remember getting into the hospital. I then went in to have surgery to remove the shrapnel from my wrist and to treat all the burns on my arms. From there, I was fastballed and got put on a plane [still on the same day] and taken back to Kandahar. I got stabilized and then put on a plane to the UK and I was in Birmingham within twenty-four hours, at Selly Oak Hospital. I didn't know the damage to my foot until I got to Selly Oak. By this stage, all my head had swollen up as well because of the flash burns. My eyes had swollen shut. I was put on the burns unit for a week and I had to wait for the swelling to go down in my foot before they could operate on it.

But I had a consultant look at it and I had the X-rays and everything. I knew it was repairable but I also knew it was in a pretty bad way and it would never be the same again. My heel had shattered and was subsequently reconstructed with a [metal] plate and many pins. I have had four operations: two on my right foot, another to repair a tendon in my left wrist and one to take out the shrapnel. Altogether I was in hospital just under a month. I don't feel it's the end of my Army career. I'm on the mend. I have another eight years' service left – so I might as well do them.

18 May 2007 [diary]

Captain Adam Chapman, The Mercian Regiment

Last night and today were significant in that incidents occurred which brought home the realities of war for the first time. I had a section on JTAC Hill that called on indirect fire from the 105mm guns to assist in destroying an enemy position. However, somewhere along the chain, a grave error was made. This resulted in a local village being shelled. Very soon after, a number of civilian casualties were brought to [Camp] Delhi for help, some serious. Unfortunately, some died. The rest were airlifted to Kandahar for treatment. [Chapman has asked for it to be pointed out that the error was not made by troops on the ground.]

The next morning a group of men arrived at our front gate in Delhi, obviously upset, angry and seeking answers. A few of us went out to speak to them and there were some heated debates. I stood back and John (a captain whose job it is to liaise with the locals) and an interpreter dealt with things as best they could. Shortly after this, a vehicle with more men and the body of a young child arrived. Not a very nice scene; emotions were running high and understandably so.

That afternoon my troop was tasked to go down to the village with John on a 'hearts and minds' patrol to see what we could do to help and appease the locals. After all, it's essential to maintain their support. We were worried how they would react so it was potentially a dangerous situation for us.

The patrol was successful: although extremely angry, they [the locals] eventually came to understand it was an accident, albeit a devastating and fatal one. They showed us damage to buildings and a cow that was killed by shrapnel. By the end, I was sat down on a rug with John and some senior local men drinking chai [like tea]. It's a very nice drink. I hope the opium fields and cannabis bushes around the compound had nothing to do with it!

The Afghans are hospitable and friendly, and I felt sorry for them. They live simple lives, in poverty by our standards, and wish only to live in peace. They don't want the Taliban and they don't want us. It's a difficult situation made even more so by dropping [a bomb] on them by accident. But unfortunately that is the reality of modern warfare. It is usually the civilians who suffer the most. But in Afghanistan the support, or at least the acquiescence, of the locals is essential. Without it, we won't succeed. I just hope that we avoid any other incidents. Tonight there'll be some individuals with a lot on their conscience.

I spoke briefly to Mum and Lisa [his girlfriend]

last night as there are satellite phones I can use here. Both were surprised to hear from me, so it's good for them to know I am OK. Reassurance is all they can get really . . .

22 May

Another busy and significant period. Yesterday there were a number of contacts on the check-points and a member of the ANA died on the Eastern Check-point, but not through enemy action. It's believed it was either a heart-attack or a drugs' overdose. His body is in the camp awaiting pick-up.

The troop also took part in its second major op as part of the company mission to stir up some trouble in Objective Snowdon, before air and artillery hit the Taliban. The plan was for my platoon to get into a fire-support position to provide cover for 3 Platoon's strike on the objective: air and artillery would then destroy any enemy in the area. All was going well until we got close to the fire-support location. We then spotted approx. seven to nine enemy in a wood-line to our south. I made the decision that it would be unsafe to move any further south. I got permission to engage the enemy and did so. My platoon fired a few hundred rounds – rifle and machine-gun (I fired about half a magazine). But the real damage was done firing a Javelin anti-tank missile (costs nearly £70,000 and is heat-seeking) and four ILAWs (interim light anti-armour weapons –

about £10,000 each). Total enemy killed was about five with many more injured in the follow-up mortar and artillery strike that covered our withdrawal. We got back to [Camp] Delhi and I was very happy. In my eyes a successful op: we killed and injured several Taliban whilst taking no casualties ourselves.

24 May 2007

Flight Lieutenant Christopher 'Has' Hasler, DFC, RAF

This was a special day. I went to Buckingham Palace to collect my DFC from the Queen. My folks came over from Canada. My parents, Michael and Mary Margaret, flew over from Ottawa. My younger sister, Olivia – we call her Livvy – who works in human resources back home, flew over from Halifax, Nova Scotia. I was so nervous that, even two minutes after getting my award, I couldn't remember a word the Queen said to me. But we all [including other decorated RAF men] went to have lunch at Claridge's. All the boys from work got on their number ones [their formal blue RAF uniforms] and we all got pretty drunk in town. It was a day to remember.

26 May 2007 [diary]

Captain Adam Chapman, The Mercian Regiment

Today is a very sad day here in [Camp] Delhi: the mood is sombre and quiet. Another young soldier [Guardsman Probyn] has died and two others have had to have legs amputated after there was an explosion on their patrol. Exactly what happened is unknown as yet, but 3 Platoon were on a routine patrol when it happened at around 0100. Over the next couple of hours everybody battled hard to get the injured to safety and to the helicopter, and then to Bastion. Everyone did what they could but it was chaotic and frustrating not being able to help more. I've got two soldiers who are a little upset and slightly shocked. They were personally involved in moving the dead and injured. Their angst is understandable: a young man shouldn't ever have to see the bloody and mutilated remains of another young man who was alive and well alongside us only a few hours before.

The scary thing is that it could have been my troop who got hit: we do the same job in the same places, and we've been to the same area. Fate, I suppose.

3 June 2007

Lance Corporal Daniel Power, The Royal Welsh

There is one particular contact that I will always remember. We had been tasked to go up to Tarin

Kowt, in the Oruzgan province, to help the Dutch. They were carrying out a reconstruction role and they were getting a lot of stick [from the Taliban] up there. So we had been tasked to do certain ops up there. It was a full Bravo Company which was sixty blokes, in WMIKs and Snatches. We got there no problem at all. We did ops in the TK [Tarin Kowt] Bowl. There were a lot of Green Zones there: we were trying to draw them [the Taliban] out of the Green Zones and hit them. We didn't really want to go into the Green Zones due to our [small] numbers because it was such a vast area.

We had seen sporadic contacts up there, nothing to talk about. Then, after two weeks, we were due to leave Tarin Kowt for a vehicle move down to Kandahar – an eight-hour drive. This was daytime. We set off first thing – six or seven in the morning. It was still dark when we got in the vehicles.

Prior to this we had had a hint [intelligence] that there were 200 Taliban on the route we were going to take back. They had been seen there earlier. Some hints you pay attention to – and this was one of them because it seemed like good information. It was known that the Taliban were going to do a surge out on the ground – a mass surge. We were quite apprehensive. You think: Two hundred guys. That's a lot. We had between sixty and seventy guys.

But after we had been on the road for about half an hour, it started to come light. We were driving down. We split the convoy into two packets – two groups so we were not one big target. It was planned that if one of the packets was contacted, we could manoeuvre the other to help out if needed. There were about sixteen vehicles: two groups of eight. There was only 150 metres between the two: close enough to support each other but a bit of spacing too. I was in the second vehicle of the second packet – in a WMIK. It was quite picturesque. It's quite funny because you are in one of the world's most dangerous places and there are some quite picturesque views on the way down.

We had been on the road travelling for roughly an hour and a half and then we came to a winding road through the terrain. On the right-hand side, there was a high-rise bank, and there were small buildings dotted around the place. And on our left-hand side there was a lot of foliage and trees that were slightly higher than head height. Then, again on the left, the ground dipped down slightly and there was a lot of dead ground down there. Just beyond that, in the far distance, there were mountains all around us. The first packet had gone out of sight completely, when we heard a lot of machine-gun fire coming down. It then came over the net [radio network] that there was a contact. And that was when we started to receive incoming: mortar rounds landing in and around our position on the road. Then they fired their first RPGs. They [the Taliban's weapons] were set at different ranges.

They like to have their guys set at different ranges.

Normally an ambush is a linear one, but this seemed like a 360°: they were firing from both sides. They were firing from right and left, up the road. So it was like a 360° ambush. The ambush was quite long – I think it lasted for twenty minutes. I was on a WMIK so I was firing and commanding. I was firing my GPMG. The enemy are quite brazen as well – some of them are on drugs. There were rounds landing in the engine block, through the bonnet. Basically, the platoon commander at that point decided to hold back the second packet while he formulated a plan. But due to the terrain, there was really only one way you could go. And that was forward. There was a vehicle in front of us that had gone firm – making itself a hard target for the enemy – and the road was only really wide enough to take one vehicle. My vehicle started taking rounds, so I got my driver to edge forwards slightly, then reverse back slightly, then drive forward. Then we identified a building on the left, where armed gunmen had been seen running into cover. So the vehicle in front got an NLAW – a light anti-tank weapon – and fired that into the position. I got my top cover to fire into the position too, with the machine-gun. The compound was 300 metres away. We were smashing the fuck out of this compound. My bonnet was strewn with empty cases because my top cover had used quite a substantial amount of ammo. Then, as I was firing, these two gunmen ran thirty or forty metres away into dead ground – ground you cannot see between you and the enemy. They must have been withdrawing from [a fire-fight with] the first packet when we spotted them. That was when I had one of them in my sights and I gave it a couple of bursts and that was when he dropped. It killed him. Then the top cover fired at the other one. It wasn't seen if he had killed him.

While this was going on, we received the go-ahead that we could push through. Mortars were still coming down in and around the area. As we came around this corner, the first thing I saw was a WMIK from the first packet on its side – on fire. It was one of the most horrible times of my life. My immediate thought was: Someone's dead; one of our guys is dead. Can we identify whose vehicle it is? We had desert bergen [rucksack] covers – DPM [disruptive pattern material]. There were a couple of them on fire on the floor and, at first glance, it looked to me like a couple of the guys. So at one point I thought that the vehicle had been hit and the crew had been killed. But it turned out that the vehicle had been hit and could no longer carry on so our forces had denied [to the enemy] the vehicle and the equipment that was on there. If we have to abandon a vehicle, we try to take what we can, then we blow it up. You throw a grenade or another explosive in there. That was what had happened.

After the contact was over, we assessed the damage. We had no fatalities but we had four serious casualties. Bravo Company's OC had a serious injury to his face and one of our guys [from Fire Support Company] had been shot in the leg, and later lost it. One of the guys from Recce Platoon had been shot through the back of the leg, which had shattered his kneecap. Fusilier Damien Hields [who was later awarded the MC for his bravery that day] was shot: the round came through the side of his body armour but, instead of penetrating his ribs, it ricocheted around and came out again. He carried on firing his grenade machine-gun despite his injuries. But we secured an HLS to get our casualties back to [Camp] Bastion. Eventually, two Apaches and a Black Hawk helicopter arrived but we were out of contact by that point. They were firing in the distance – engaging contacts – [Taliban] targets that were withdrawing.

A lot of the other vehicles as well had been damaged, including two of the Snatches. One Snatch was no longer operable: two wheels had been blown up on one side and an RPG had hit it but it hadn't detonated. But the windscreens were all bowed in where they had stopped the rounds. We called in an Apache gun-ship which destroyed the Snatch. A lot of kit was denied to the enemy because we couldn't take it back. So, in all, we had to leave behind one of the WMIKs and a Snatch – they were written off.

Basically we were still on this road for four to five hours before we got back to Kandahar. We were quite happy to be out there, quite excited, but still, whenever someone gets injured in your team, you feel for them. But then you have to put that to the back of your mind and crack on with the job in hand. Who was to say that we wouldn't get contacted again? So we got our weapons squared and just moved off. But there were no more contacts after that. We had a report that more than forty-five Taliban had been confirmed killed. It was believed the ambush had involved more than a hundred insurgents.

When we finally reached Kandahar, I took a look at my vehicle. There were quite a lot of bullet holes. I looked in the headrest of my seat and there was a hole there. I stuck my finger in and pulled out a round – a 762 short – the Taliban had actually fired at the vehicle. You could still see the swirls on the barrel [of the bullet] where it had been fired through the rifle. And I remember thinking how different that could have been. A couple of inches to the left and it would have been all over for me. At any time, in a contact you can be only two inches away from life or death.

6 June 2007 [diary]

Captain Adam Chapman, The Mercian Regiment

It seems that I am only writing in this [diary] occasionally at the moment. That's probably as I've not actually done much, just been in the same routine. Unfortunately I've just found out that a soldier killed today in the Gereshk area was someone I knew. L Cpl Paul ['Sandy'] Sandford was in my platoon back in Battalion. He was shot dead today as my old company were in a large contact. I don't know much else. It's very upsetting as I knew him personally. I bumped into him just before coming out here. It was great to see each other and share a joke or two: we always did. The last thing he told me was that he got married; now he's dead and she's a widow. I know he will be sorely missed by all who knew him – he was a great lad.

Rest in peace, Sandy.

June 2007

Captain Dave Rigg, MC, The Royal Engineers

There had been speculation for some time that I might get decorated for what I had done at Jugroom Fort [retrieving Lance Corporal Mathew Ford's body under fire]. I was on a course in Wales, and my colonel back in Germany, Colonel Phil Sherwood, told me on the phone that I had been awarded the Military Cross – the MC. It was a wonderful honour to be recognized. There had been a lot of acts of bravery and exceptional soldiering feats – even during my short period out there – but very few of them receive official recognition. I was very proud but I also felt a sense of guilt that the other three guys who had volunteered weren't honoured too.

19 June 2007 [diary]

Captain Adam Chapman, The Mercian Regiment

This time tomorrow I'll have deployed on Op Bataka, the biggest op down here in a long time and the brigade's main effort. Over 700 [men] will be involved and my troop has an integral part as one of three assaulting platoons. I'm pretty excited as it will be a dangerous op, crossing the canal for the first time and clearing enemy positions. We'll be fixing bayonets, which is not something I ever envisaged doing, especially in 2007 – it's not 1917! But it's something impressive to have done especially as an infanteer [infantryman].

After the op, the [Grenadier] Guards go north and A Company, the Worcestershire and Sherwood Foresters, will take over, which I am looking forward to as they are a different bunch, my bunch.

I received another set of mail yesterday – as always, a great thing. I was hoping to call back home tonight but the phones are out of use. There's been a casualty not far from here and his family needs informing before the phones go back on.

21 June 2007

McNab: *Many servicemen and women prepare for the worst by writing letters to their loved ones to be read in the event of their death. The girlfriend of Guardsman Neil 'Tony' Downes, aged twenty, who died this month in a landmine explosion, received this poignant letter: 'Hey beautiful! I'm sorry I had to put you through all this, darling. I'm truly sorry. All I wanna say is how much I loved you and cared for you. You are the apple of my eye and I will be watching over you always. Jane, I hope you have a wonderful and fulfilling life. Get married, have children etc. I will love you forever and will see you again when you are old and wrinkly! I have told my parents to leave you some money out of my insurance, so have fun . . . gonna go now.' Jane Little said of Downes, who was from Manchester: 'His major told me after he died that he was thinking of asking me to marry him. I would have said yes straight away. He was a perfect boyfriend. I am immensely proud of him.'*

22 June 2007 [diary]

Captain Adam Chapman, The Mercian Regiment

Op Bataka was put on hold for twenty-four hours after there was a problem with the helicopters. It was extremely disappointing at the time because we'd got prepared to go and did not find out that we weren't till the last moment. So we spent the whole of the next day waiting. The worst part was the waiting; knowing that we were taking part in such a huge operation was a buzz.

Fortunately, we finally departed on the op twenty-four hours late. We spent the night in the ground in Eastern Check-point as the battle group reserve. We eventually left at 0300 to attack a small village at first light, quite an exciting prospect.

Everything went according to plan and my troop cleared its objective without incident, meeting no resistance. I got to issue the orders 'fix bayonets', which is a personal highlight as an infantryman. Not many soldiers fix bayonets in this day and age. The lads then cleared two buildings using grenades. There was a massive amount of fire-power support- ing us – and it was proper war fighting with artillery and attack helicopters battering enemy positions. We then extracted. The whole thing was a great experience and the highlight of my military career so far, I think. And overall the whole thing was successful. All our boys came home, but not the same can be said for the Taliban.

I saw my first dead person up close. He was killed by the first platoon into the compounds and we had to pass him. He was a real mess and had been shot up pretty bad. He resembled a mannequin rather than a man. It was quite strange, almost fake. I had a good look at him, probably about my age, long beard, but now no longer. It didn't really affect me. I was just cold to the whole thing. I'm not squeamish and we are just doing our job.

June 2007 [poem]

Fusilier Daniel Wright, The Royal Welsh

FORGOTTEN WARS

Through the valley we tread the desolate sand,
The presence of death haunting this barren wasteland.
All emotions are dead bar discipline and fear,
Unbeknown to us all our enemy draws near.
We mount up and travel through IED alley,
Their ambush is sprung at the shadow of Death Valley.
A sound like thunder, incoming like rain,
Their mortars drop short,
Their efforts in vain.
Countless enemy attacks, but we send them to Allah
For in this company of warriors lies an uncommon
    valour.
Top cover opened fire, like a wall of lead,
In a bloody wave the Taliban crashed down dead.
Another man down in the blood and the dust –
Give covering fire, it's time to de-bus.
Out the back, hit the ground, move fast, stay low,
My rifle lets rip engaging my foe.
Ammo runs low for their pain and my sins,
I throw another wounded soldier on the back of our
    Pinz.
His eyes drift away, their draining of life,
His words of devotion and love for his wife,
He drifts in and out, embracing his death,
'Stay with us, Richie, this won't be your last breath.'

Bullets hail from an enemy unseen
As this hero's red hand gives me a fresh magazine.
Back in open fire as my enemies fell,
Their cut-off position smashed by my UGL.
Bullets ricochet from the Pinz on one side,
RPGs explode, our vehicle denied,
Metallic taste in my mouth,
Face and hands deep red,
My uniform stained with the blood of the dead.
To the lowest depths of hell we've sunk,
Hard to believe how much blood these deserts have
   drunk.
To punch through the killing area the WMIKs break
   track,
The Chinooks circle for the wounded casevac.
Back in the camp all safe, but how long can peace last?
The Union Jack in the breeze, it flies at half mast,
'Royal Welsh, stand together, and you won't fall
   alone.'
Our orders were simple, destroy the Green Zone,
Rifle company push through us, a further two clicks,
Their weapons grasped firm, their bayonets fixed,
Their heads held high, their eyes open wide,
I'd gladly give my life to fight by their side.
A red mist consumes me, my fury is driven,
But behind the front-line fire support must be given.
Our barrels glow from another fire mission,
Our mortars crash down on another enemy position.
The death count rises, our target's neutralized,
'This one's danger close, men, so all be advised.'

The hunters' moon waxes, with ambient light,
In my hand my St Christopher is held so tight.
I think of my friends behind enemy lines,
I fear for the worst, but no prayers spring to mind.
Then hope in the eyes of battle-weary soldiers
As Apaches take flight, like angels on our shoulders.
The battle rages throughout another night,
Illuminated skies as hellfires ignite.
Days turn to weeks before our battle is won
But throughout Helmand province the forgotten war
    carries on.
Will they ever know the sacrifice,
In these bloodthirsty wars,
Safe in their homes behind their locked doors,
Comfy and warm, content in their bed,
Their dreams never haunted by enemy dead?
The reflection of war makes us question our sanity –
Do we fight for humanity, or one nation's vanity?
It's not for honour of queen and country we fight,
But for our brothers in arms to the left and right.
With their selfless courage, commitment and
    unwavering nerve,
In this company of heroes, my honour to serve.

25 June 2007 [diary]

Captain Adam Chapman, The Mercian Regiment

I found out today that my regiment lost another
soldier and that four others were badly injured.

Drummer Wright was killed when his vehicle was blown up. I don't remember him, but I know two of the others who were injured, one of whom is in intensive care. Another sad day for British forces and my regiment in particular.

We've now got Internet access here in Garmsir, which is a massive bonus as it gives us a little more access to the outside world. No bad thing!

RIP Dmr Wright.

30 June

It's been raining. The place has flooded; it's unbelievable how much it has rained. It's nice and refreshing after the heat, but it's turned into a quagmire. The flood water has receded today but there is still a dark cloud over the camp tonight. I've just found out that Captain Sean Dolan was killed today [it was eventually revealed he died from enemy mortar fire]. His vehicle was hit by some sort of explosive device and he was killed instantly. Sean was a friend; he was, more importantly, a husband and a father. He was an ex-regimental sergeant major and a legend in his own right. His death will be felt hard across the battalion.

There has been another dozen or so casualties across theatre in the last twenty-four hours, meaning our ambush has been cancelled tonight, as all our aircraft are deployed to assist with casualty extraction. I suppose this is what you would call a war. Back home there have been a number of terrorist attempts to kill innocent civilians in both London and Scotland. Three British soldiers were killed in Iraq also.

RIP Sean Dolan.

July 2007

Private Tom Dawkes, The Mercian Regiment

Private Tom Dawkes, 2 Battalion The Mercian Regiment, is twenty-three. He was born in Bromsgrove, south Birmingham. His father worked for an air-conditioning company, but was forced to retire after a serious accident. His mother works as a power-press supervisor and he has one brother and two sisters. Dawkes left school at sixteen and worked for a production company, then later as a tool-maker and as a fork-lift-truck driver in a warehouse. He entered the Army in January 2007, shortly before his twenty-first birthday. He had wanted to join at sixteen, but had to wait for an operation that could only take place when he was fully grown. Dawkes, who is engaged to be married in 2010, is based at the Mercians' barracks just outside Belfast, where he has earned a reputation for writing poetry.

I was still training at Catterick when my section commander came in and told us which companies we would all be going to. He said there was a good chance that I would be going to Afghanistan to catch the end of the tour [with the Mercians]. Some were still under eighteen so they couldn't go. It was confirmed I would be going to Afghanistan shortly afterwards. I was scared. It was going to be the first time that I had left the United Kingdom. It was also going to be the first time I had ever flown.

14 July 2007 [diary]

Captain Adam Chapman, The Mercian Regiment

Things were looking up for a short while. A large operation was planned for the end of the month down here. They planned to attack a village known as Madrassa, an objective known to be full of Taliban. Prior to this, they wanted a detailed recce of crossing points over the river Helmand and routes into Madrassa. The best thing is we got tasked to do this, a very important and high-profile job. I spent a few days planning for an MOG [manoeuvre outreach group: it deploys, self-sustained, into the desert for a period]. I planned to go out for four days and see some good stuff: it looked like being a very good op.

It seemed destined for trouble from the start. The medic I was taking out fell ill with diarrhoea and vomiting, so we were delayed until he got better. We eventually deployed a little late. Under my command, I had 10 vehicles, 21 Marines, a field-support team, interpreter, anti-tank team and my own troop: in total 51 men and one woman. Quite a big command for a junior captain. All was going well. We recced the river and were looking at a suspected Taliban village – then we were suddenly told to come back.

The whole operation was being cancelled. All the resources were being sucked up north for an even bigger op as things seem to be going wrong there. I was utterly disappointed, especially after all that's happened previously. It looked like we had finally got a decent job and it was pulled away at the last moment. Nobody's fault, just the way things happen. One never knows what's going to happen next.

Anyway, we're back in [Camp] Delhi now and back in the same old routine. Groundhog day! Worse still, I spoke to the battle group second-in-command and he still doesn't know when we will leave here. The only thing I've got to look forward to now is going home on leave in 3 weeks. It seems such a long time and I know it's going to drag. I've got a lot planned: can't wait to see everyone and do everything I've missed these last few months. It seems to be all I can think of recently – all I can do is wait.

Another soldier was killed a few days ago – a Grenadier Guard attached to my battalion in Gereshk – and things seem to be going from bad to worse in Iraq, where several more have been killed. And I bet they got nothing more than a tiny bit of media coverage. Pathetic.

16 July 2007

McNab: *It was revealed that the rate at which British soldiers were being seriously injured or killed on the front line in Afghanistan had reached that suffered by our troops during the Second World War. The casualty rate in the most dangerous regions of the country was approaching 10 per cent. Senior officers feared it would ultimately pass the 11 per cent experienced by British soldiers at the height of the conflict sixty years ago. The rise was partly driven by a ten-fold increase in the number of wounded in action – those injured, but not killed – over the past six months as fighting in Afghanistan intensified. In November 2006, only three British soldiers were wounded in Afghanistan by the Taliban, compared with thirty-eight in May 2007. The official injury rate given by the Ministry of Defence among the 7,000 British troops in Afghanistan was about 3 per cent. But when the figures were applied only to the three infantry battalions on the front line, it rose to almost 10 per cent.*

18 July 2007 [diary]

Captain Adam Chapman, The Mercian Regiment

The camp was mortared this morning. I didn't imagine they would get this close so soon. Fortunately nobody got hurt. The round landed just outside the perimeter (about 25 metres from my room) and the majority of people were asleep under hard cover anyway. If it had landed another 5 metres in [to the] camp during the day, it would have been a different story.

I was awake on duty at the time and heard the whistle, then the loud explosion. I've heard hundreds of mortar rounds go out, but it was a strange feeling hearing one going the other way – pretty helpless, really. Cpl Green saw the explosion on his way back to the block – his heart rate upped a little!

We had jets in the air pretty soon and it's believed they destroyed the mortar. However, it's thought they [the Taliban] have several others in the area. I just hope they don't get any more accurate. We are pretty defenceless if they do.

19 July 2007

McNab: *It was announced that two Distinguished Flying Crosses (DFC) had been awarded for bravery in Afghanistan. They were to Captain Nick Barton and Captain Tom O'Malley, of the Army Air Corps. Barton was given his award for his bravery when his Apache helicopter was struck by a heavy machine gun round on Christmas Eve while he was supporting troops in a contact at Now Zad and for his part in supporting the Jugroom Fort rescue mission. He calmly kept control of the helicopter – even though it was severely damaged – and even completed his attack on the target. O'Malley received his award for his courage when, under a hail of* *enemy fire, he flew, with another Apache, to retrieve the body of Lance Corporal Mathew Ford at Jugroom Fort in January 2007. Warrant Officer Class 1 Ed Macy (a pseudonym) and Staff Sergeant Keith Armatage were awarded the Military Cross (MC) for their part in the rescue mission. Captain Dave Rigg's MC was also announced for his bravery during the same incident.*

28 July 2007 [diary]

Captain Adam Chapman, The Mercian Regiment

As I count down the days to leaving here, more bad news. I received a message on the Internet from a friend's girlfriend that raised more questions than it answered. But I could guess that he'd been hurt: Martin is a close friend of mine that I've had since uni and we went through our Army training together. He's a Para and now out in Afghanistan.

I had an agonizing couple of hours before finding out what happened. I called her back in the UK. Basically Martin was shot in the shoulder and badly wounded; he's now back home in hospital. He's safe and that's a positive, but the shoulder is in a bad way. I was quite shaken. I've known people who have died out here, but never a close friend. It's quite shocking.

Anyway, I'll be in the UK in about 10 days so, hopefully, I'll be able to visit him. I just hope he makes a full recovery now.

6 August 2007

Colour Sergeant Simon Panter, The Royal Anglian Regiment

Colour Sergeant Simon Panter, 1 Battalion The Royal Anglian Regiment, is thirty-eight. He was born in Great Yarmouth, Norfolk, and was brought up on the Suffolk/Norfolk border, attending Stradbroke High School. His father is a peat salesman and his mother runs her own beauty business. Panter, who has one younger sister, left school at sixteen. After working as a chef for four years, he got fed up with having to work nights at weekends when his friends were having fun so in 1991 he joined the Royal Anglians as a private, aged twenty. He has completed tours of Croatia, Iraq and Northern Ireland, as well as two tours of Afghanistan. He is married, with two boys, and is based at Pirbright barracks in Surrey. His military career is currently threatened by a serious ankle injury he received on his second tour of Afghanistan.

On my second tour of Afghanistan, I was based in Sangin. I was a 3 Corunna platoon sergeant with A Company in 1 Royal Anglian. Our general role was reassurance of the Afghan national population and deterring the Taliban. I was based at Sangin DC. It was relatively quiet because the CO of the battle group had built a ring of steel around Sangin by using the PBs [patrol bases] to take the pressure off Sangin. It had worked: people had come back to

Sangin and it was a thriving market town again, just as it had been before.

On this particular day, our battalion CO [Lt Col Stuart Carver, DSO] was on R&R. Major Charlie Calder, the second in command of the battalion, was at Sangin DC for a couple of weeks while the CO was on leave. Inkerman patrol base, which is three or four miles north of Sangin, was under heavy attack, day in day out. Anyway Major Calder wanted to go to Inkerman to check on the morale and see how the troops were. I was tasked with getting a group of men in four WMIKs to take him up there. We left at 0100 and got there at 0145. We had the route picketed – almost completely lined by the Afghan and British troops – because the 611 was a notoriously dangerous road.

We then got our heads down and were awoken by the sound of gunfire and RPG fire early in the morning when the base was attacked. It was seven or eight in the morning and we had been sleeping beside the vehicles in the open. It all kicked off and we stood to and tried to identify Taliban positions and engage them with mortar. We used all the weapon systems available at the base because it overlooked the Green Zone. They [the Taliban] were probably 200 metres away, 300 max. It was heavy and sustained fire.

It lasted for fifteen or twenty minutes and that was pretty much it. And then we found out that C Company were going out on patrol later that day and so I went and spoke to the OC designate at the time, Captain David Hicks, MC [since killed in battle]. He was in charge while C Company OC was on his R&R. I went and spoke to him and said: 'Do you mind if I get eight men and tag along and help you out on this patrol?' I knew they were under-manned because of the R&R.

He gave orders to go out at 1600. The plan was to reassure one of the local hamlets just out to the front of Inkerman. Within forty-five minutes, we'd got to the outskirts of the hamlet and then the forward platoon saw the Taliban in a position with RPGs and AKs so they opened fire on them. We had in the region of eighty men: twenty to thirty ANA and the rest Brits.

I was with 11 Platoon and I was in their third section. I was at the back and there was a lot of RPG and AK fire coming our way. It was getting quite close and I could hear a lot of firing and RPG fire on our left flank. I was speaking to the platoon sergeant at the time, saying we were not sure whether that was ANA or enemy. So I was trying to get in comms with the platoon commander to let him know that we had got some firing on our left flank. Because I was reserve, I thought I would go over there and check and keep an eye on the left flank. In the end I spoke to the platoon sergeant, who thought it was a good idea, so I took the section of eight men and off we went.

We got in this ditch, no more than fifty to a

hundred metres away from the main body of the company. I could still hear a lot of gunfire and RPG rounds – coming not directly at us but across our flanks. I was trying to still get comms to find out whether it was friend or foe. There was a lot going on. I couldn't get in comms with the OC or the platoon commander so in the end I took it on myself to go up there with the section. The main reason I did this was that I didn't want a blue on blue [friendly fire] situation to happen. I thought we had best make our positions known to each other with a face to face.

We got the section and started going up along the ditch and I was thinking: This is a bit noisy. Just in case it was Taliban, I was worried they could hear us coming. So I decided to get out of the ditch and go along the bank. After no more than twenty or thirty metres, I heard some more RPG fire and a few rounds getting fired. It was not at us, but to our front, and then after another few metres I actually saw four Taliban in this ditch. They were no more than 100 to 150 metres away from me. We positively identified the Taliban, fired straight at them.

We may have got one on the first burst. We were firing SA80 [assault rifles] and LMG [light machine-gun]. They had AKs and RPGs. We had surprised them. A little bit of a fire-fight ensued and then I thought: We have to take the bull by the horns here and dispatch these Taliban. So we concocted a quick plan. With the remainder of the section giving fire support, me and another lad, Private Patrick Casey, pepper-potted along the ditch and encountered a Taliban just fifteen to twenty metres in front of us. We hadn't seen him initially. I killed him: I shot him with my rifle. At this point I thought: Bloody hell, they're getting a bit close. So I put the bayonet and a fresh mag on, and as I was doing that I saw some movement in front. I chucked a grenade towards the initial area where the Taliban were and after that we didn't really get any incoming fire back from them. Then one of the lads spotted a Taliban running to our left. He fired and I fired and the Taliban dropped. But I didn't know whether he had gone to ground or not. Then I spotted him again in the ditch about twenty metres away. I fired some more rounds and he was down. I jumped into the ditch towards him. He still had his weapon – an AK variant – in his hand and he was still breathing. I had my bayonet fixed and I bayoneted him, straight into the chest. Several times. We were taught in training: once you shoot, then bayonet them because they have been known in the past to jump up behind you after feigning death or injury. So it's always good to make sure they're dead. He was probably in his late twenties, no more than thirty. He was in black with a black tie around his middle and he had chest webbing on as well. The first guy was dressed exactly the same.

To our right flank, the company were still having a bit of a bun-fight with the Taliban. I think the

Taliban we encountered had been trying to sneak up on the main company and ambush them from the flank but they got surprised by us because they didn't know we were there. Then we had a quick chat. Me and Casey went up towards the position where we had first seen the Taliban. And there was another Taliban in there. He may have been injured but he still had a weapon with him so he was shot. I shot him. That was that for the time being. We had a mini re-org to call the rest of the section in, covering all our arcs, doing a head count and re-arming.

Whilst this was going on, a fourth member of the Taliban opened up on us, again from the ditch. This was three or four minutes after we thought the fire-fight had ended. He was firing with AK: it was automatic gunfire from under a hundred metres. So we now fired back at that Taliban position. I said to one of the guys who had an ILAW [interim light anti-tank weapon] rocket launcher: 'Fire at that position.' He couldn't get the damn thing to work so I took it off him and fired at the position, and all the other guys fired everything we had for a couple of minutes. We didn't get any return fire so we assumed he was killed in that initial volley, from less than a hundred metres away. I thought: I'm not going to send any guys up to confirm the death for safety reasons.

Then we searched for the [three] dead Taliban. Two of the guys looked like they were foreign fighters. These were the guys dressed in black. They were maybe Iranian or Pakistani. We found grenades on their bodies and mobile phones. They had two grenades and a mobile phone each. And we took notebooks from them with phone numbers in. The third guy looked like he was local Afghan. He was wearing brown traditional Afghan dress. He had a red sash round his waist and a turban that was off at the time. He was the guy with the RPG beside him.

I had killed people in battle before but never as close as this. You very rarely see the Taliban. They are usually at a distance and well hidden. I sat down at the end and said: 'Fucking hell, lads. You only normally read about this shit but we've actually done it.' Then we cleared things up and got the Afghan National Army. They did a search and took the weapons off them [the dead] and then it came over the radio that the fire-fight had died out at the other end.

I had a face to face with the OC. It then came over the radio that a Harrier was coming in to do a bombing run. So we had to extract out of the area pretty quick and we went back to Inkerman. A couple of times I have shot at Taliban and seen them drop and said: 'That's a kill.' But I had never done anything like this where you can say 100 per cent they were killed at close range. We took no casualties. At least three Taliban were confirmed dead, but there were probably four dead – and there might have been others. There must have been at least ten Taliban involved in the initial ambush because of the amount of fire that was coming down.

August 2007

Private Tom Dawkes, The Mercian Regiment

I flew to Kandahar on a Tristar. I just slept on the
plane. I wasn't thinking about what would happen
when I got there. Then after two days we went on to
[Camp] Bastion. My first impression was that it was
hot – very hot! Temperatures were in the forties
[centigrade]. I was an infantry soldier in
C Company, which had already been posted to
Lashkar Gah. We did a few patrols here and there
and then did a twelve-day op in the Green Zone in
Gereshk. Our role was to try to take this area of high
ground that had been controlled by the Taliban.

I had my first contact on the first day of the op. It
was eight or nine o'clock in the morning and we
were going along on foot. I was armed with an
LMG. Then we got ambushed by RPG and small-
arms fire at a place called the Fan. We were in open
ground and two people – I was one of them – had
dropped off their day sacks. Then we took a couple
of steps back just before an RPG came straight out of
the cornfields. To start with I heard the whoosh.
Then it went straight through our group – I was no
more than six feet away from it. Straight away they
[the Taliban] opened up with small-arms fire. So we
just jumped into ditches where there was cover. I
jumped into some water. We were firing back in the
general direction from where they were. But then
they fired another RPG, which hit the wall on the

opposite side to us. I managed to get off almost 200 rounds. But we couldn't actually see what we were firing at because the cornfields were about eight feet tall. So I don't know whether we hit anyone. The contact must have lasted about five minutes and then we bugged out back to the compound. There were no casualties and everyone was laughing saying: 'RPG! RPG!'

We found out that we had just about been surrounded by the Taliban. Others [from C Company] had taken shots from behind us. We stayed in the compound – an open building with no roof – and for a couple of hours we used a small bombardment of artillery and mortar fire. I was thinking: Am I going to get through this? It's more mental than physical once you're out there. I just wanted to do my duty to the best of my ability. It was a real eye-opener . . .

22 August 2007 [diary]

Captain Adam Chapman, The Mercian Regiment

The last three weeks have passed in a blur. I returned to Camp Bastion for a week before returning to the UK for two weeks' (well-deserved) leave. And now I'm back in Camp Bastion waiting to fly down to Garmsir again. I never imagined all those months ago that I'd be back in Garmsir in late August!

Needless to say, leave was awesome. I managed to

see a lot of friends and family and travelled all over the country. I saw Martin [his injured comrade] a couple of times in hospital: he's improving – he was very close to death – but he's strong in both body and mind, and I'm sure he'll bounce back. It wasn't very nice seeing him in treatment. There are lots of injured soldiers there; it's quite depressing. Hospitals aren't the best of places anyway, but there's something upsetting about seeing so many young people in visibly bad conditions. There was one soldier from my regiment who had lost both legs.

The rest of the time was spent travelling, spending too much money, getting drunk, going to weddings and, perhaps most importantly, seeing Lisa and my family. It wasn't that bad being back. I got into the swing of things pretty quickly, but a lot of people were worried about the state I'd be in. I suppose they watch the news back home and hear about things – it's natural.

While I was away some of my troop had a very lucky escape when an RPG exploded when it hit their room: only minor shrapnel wounds, very fortunate not to have lost anyone. And they also had some very big contacts.

The BRF [Brigade Recce Force] have also taken 5 men off me because they are down on men, which is a bit of a sucker punch. The positive thing is I've only got two months to do!

25 August

For some reason, despite having very little to do these last few days, I've been very lazy in writing this journal. I don't know if it's my state of mind after having been on leave or what, but I need to be a bit more proactive.

Three soldiers died on Thursday when an American jet dropped a bomb on them. They call it 'friendly fire'. I call it a tragedy. It's not the first time it's happened, just usually it happens to innocent Afghan women and children who were in the wrong place at the wrong time: extremely saddening. The soldiers were from the Royal Anglian Regiment who have now lost 9 men on this tour. And I think it's over 20 in total. That's just over one soldier dying every week. How long can they keep this up? It's the same thing in Iraq: the Army is undermanned as it is, but men won't be staying in much longer at this rate. I know a lot of men are leaving after going to Afghanistan. I suppose people want a taste of war and then leave it at that. I don't blame them. Especially if they're married with children.

I picked up a new beret and badge today. On 1 September my regiment [the Worcestershire and Sherwood Foresters] is amalgamating with the Staffords and Cheshires to become the Mercian Regiment; a sad day, really. I'm quite proud of where I come from and my regiment – it's part of my identity, and some of that will be lost. But you have to move forward constantly and I think it will be good in the long run. After all, my regiment was formed from the merger of 2 others.

September 2007

Private Tom Dawkes, The Mercian Regiment

We got to meet quite a lot of the local Afghan people. We spoke to them through interpreters. Their culture is very different from ours and in a way I felt ashamed to be there. Although all the Taliban want to do is kill people, the Afghans are essentially a friendly people. They just want to get on with their lives. But we were – through collateral damage – sometimes destroying their lives. It was a great shame. Innocent people were having their lives messed up. But most of the people were on our side – they told us where the Taliban had been and locations of IEDs. Sometimes they had even seen the Taliban plant them so they told us to go this way rather than that way. Most Afghans know that we are trying to push the Taliban out of their villages so they can get on with their everyday lives. So I think they do trust us. I don't respect the Taliban for what they do, but I do respect them as fighters. They are strong fighters. They will fight to the death, and because it is their terrain and their home ground, it is very hard to beat them. They don't carry heavy kit like us so they are able to manoeuvre quickly. Some of them who have been trained have good soldier skills, but others have just been handed a weapon and told to go out. They can't shoot straight – fortunately!

September 2007

Colour Sergeant Simon Panter, The Royal Anglian Regiment

It was the last battle-group op of our tour: to clear the Green Zone. We had cleared the Taliban out and they had crept back in so we were going to clear them out again.

We were going to be out for one week. We marched from Sangin – about eighteen Ks. We left at 1 a.m. to get there for first light. Throughout the day, we had several skirmishes with the Taliban all the way up and then at the end of the day we had got to our limit of exploitation (LOE). We were not paying a great deal of attention because we were fucked, fighting the Taliban all day in the heat. We had been on our feet for eighteen hours – the whole A Company group, about 120 men. We just settled down: the OC got in the three platoon commanders so that we could organize an all-round defence. We got briefed up and I was on my way back to brief up the rest of our platoon when, suddenly, all hell broke loose. It all kicked off.

It was an RPG-initiated contact from the Taliban.

But I had never heard so many RPGs coming our way. It was followed by a hell of a lot of automatic gunfire. We were caught on the hop. Luckily, we had a section pushed out to a compound at the river's edge but it was pinned down. They couldn't move in this compound, getting sprayed with everything the Taliban had, and we were getting exactly the same. But I was in the open: I was caught as I was going back over to my men. My platoon was in a ditch at my left flank – about fifty metres away. I was on my belt buckle – about 150 metres from the enemy – and I saw tracer fire going past in the corner of my eyes. I could hear the whizz of it. The lads were saying: 'Sarge, you want to get over here in cover.' And I was like: 'Fuck, I'm not moving. If I move I'll get shot. There's no fucking way I'm moving.' It was about six o'clock at night. I was caught in the middle of it. There must have been about twenty Taliban. We, the Brits, were very fortunate that day, but the ANA took three casualties from fragmentation – RPGs. One was killed and two seriously injured.

The fire-fight lasted about twenty minutes. But I stayed on my belt buckle the whole time. I daren't move and I didn't even return a single round because I knew that if I moved I was going to get it. Afterwards, I was laughing nervously with the lads but I had several moments when I was thinking: How the fuck did I get away with that?

5 September 2007 [diary]

Captain Adam Chapman, The Mercian Regiment

Since returning from the check-points, we've been back into the same old routine. However, a few significant events have occurred.

We're now definitely leaving Garmsir on 8 September. Finally, after so long (it will be 4 months), we're going, our future as yet uncertain. At the moment, we will be going back to Bastion with A Company, before another large operation up north, then on to FOB Arnhem. Arnhem is even worse than here, by all accounts: lots of mortar attacks as well as IED threat. So, I'm in two minds about leaving. In favour is working with A Coy [Company] again, as well as doing something new. Against is the more apparent danger and learning the ground all over again. But overall I'm glad to be leaving here, and risk is part of my job.

Prior to leaving, there is the little matter of a large op we're doing down here first. We're doing a deliberate company attack to clear a large area of enemy territory. It should be good and a nice, positive way to finish our time here. At the same time, the Gren Guards are taking over again so it will be very busy.

Today started very well but ended badly, in that all-too familiar way. We celebrated/commemorated our amalgamation into the Mercian Regiment. We had a little parade, the padre said a few words, we then had a volleyball competition, followed by some hot dogs – a bonus. It was just a nice day.

However, the OC then informed us that C Company had two men killed and one badly injured; B Company also had two seriously injured in a separate incident. At the moment, we don't know who they are but it's likely I will know them. Another very sad day, and to what end? A lot of people are wondering: is it worth it?

9 September
The op ended in disaster, and became the worst day yet in many ways. All was going to plan until a large contact kicked off. It was almost like an ambush. Fortunately for us, my troop was a few hundred metres to the east of the main body.

Over the next few hours, the company tried to extract out of the contact. There were a lot of casualties and Pte [Johan] Botha was missing in no man's land, and couldn't be extracted because of the enemy. My group engaged one compound with an anti-tank missile, killing enemy in there. But, other than that, we weren't involved in the main fight. It was so frustrating and so terrible listening on the radio to the events unfolding. I could hear the screaming and anguish in people's voices. It was horrible. We eventually caught up and moved forward to provide extra ammo and become the reserve, but we were needed to secure the extraction route. Eventually, jets dropped 4 500lb bombs on to enemy positions only 50 metres away from us. It was surreal; it felt like the world was blowing up. That caused a lot of damage and knocked unconscious Pte Stacey, when part of the wall he was hiding behind landed on him.

I could write about this for pages, but it was hard enough opening the journal. Sgt Brelsford and Pte Botha were dead and seven others injured, some very seriously. I'll write more when I can but, to be honest, I don't think I want to just yet. Seeing all the young soldiers and even sgts and the OC after led me to tears with them. It was such a blow for everyone and it will take some getting over. What a waste of life.

September 2007

McNab: *I know only too well from experience how sad it is to lose a friend and comrade, and the effect it has on the other men so I wasn't surprised that Captain Adam Chapman was reluctant to write in his diary about the events of 7/8 September. Operation Pechtaw had involved A (Grenadier) Company Group, 2 Battalion The Mercian Regiment. On the night of 7 September, Captain Simon Cupples, the officer commanding of 1 Platoon, had been ordered to clear two key objectives. On reaching the second, the lead section was engaged simultaneously from three enemy machine-gun positions, the closest being no more than twenty-five metres away. It was a massive and* *well-planned ambush believed to involve some thirty Taliban. There were immediate casualties. Cupples, his men and everyone on the op had to take life-or-death decisions quickly and show their mettle time and time again. Warrant Officer Class 2 Pete Lewis takes up the story.*

7/8 September 2007

Warrant Officer Class 2 Pete Lewis, The Mercian Regiment

The big one was in Garmsir. This was the day before we handed back to the Grenadier Guards. If you added the contacts up, the boys had probably been in 200-plus contacts by this stage [on the single tour]. And that was deploying every weapon system we had. Casualty-wise, until then we had had a few shrapnel wounds from RPGs, but that was it: nothing worse.

September 7 was the last company op we did down in Garmsir. We were pushing further south than anyone had been on that tour. I left at 1800 hours to put the first check-points in for the blokes to come through me. The boys started coming at last light, which was about 1930 hours. It was a funny day as well because it was quiet around camp. Everybody knew that we were going to get some action that night. Even though we had not pushed that far south, we had recced a lot of places we were going. We were probably going no more than 1,800 metres south and then we were going to swing along and go down to CP [Command Post] Balaclava and clear some of the compounds that we got counter-attacked from on a daily basis.

I counted the company through at JTAC Hill. Less my tac [tactical support group], there were ninety-four on the ground that night. I was in a Viking as my casevac vehicle. At about 2320 the first contact came. That basically was [an attack on] a point section going around. They got hit by small-arms fire. That's where we took casualties. That night we had two dead, six gunshot wounds, and a lot of minor casualties. I was with the doc: he was in one Viking and I was in the other. I can remember going forward in the Vikings. It just seemed to take for ever to get there. I picked up the first casualty who had a gunshot to the leg. He must have got that in the volley of fire that came through on the back of the initial contact so I chucked him in the back where there was a medic team.

One of the platoon sergeants on the ground was Sergeant [Craig] Brelsford. That was the last time I spoke to him because he got shot that night. I said: 'Brels, are you all right?'

And he said: 'Yes. I've got a casualty.'

And I said: 'How the fuck have you got a casualty already? You're not in the fire-fight yet.'

He says: 'He has just picked a stray round up there.'

So I chucked him in the back. Brels pushed on

forward, while I got back into the Viking and trundled forward again.

The area around Garmsir is just a maze of ditches, canals and the like. So it just sort of took for ever getting there in a Viking, weaving around. When I got there, the point section was pretty much out of ammunition. I spoke to the platoon sergeant. At that stage, we had got all the casualties back but we still had a man missing, who was Private [Johan] Botha. I did a quick ammo resupply and started banging the casualties in the back [of the Viking] to the doc. At that stage, I had no dead. I had three T3s [walking-wounded casualties] and two T2s [seriously injured casualties] and a couple of guys in shock. The second part of the casevac were two Vikings down at CP Balaclava, with my colour sergeant Duggie Thomson ['Tomo'] and another team of medics in the back. I had two full Vikings [of injured] so I got on the net and told the boss I was going to take them back. It had sort of calmed down at that stage – it was probably about 2 a.m. I had a couple of unconscious casualties. The one we thought we were going to lose was Private [Sam] Cooper, who got shot in the back of the head even though he had got his helmet on. We also had Private Luke Cole, who got shot in the stomach and the leg. It was my snap decision on the ground to go back with the casualties, six of them, in two full Vikings.

The boys were still taking incoming during this as

well. So another two Vikings came down with a second ammo resupply. What made it worse for me was that it wasn't a massively ambient night. I don't know what smoke the old Taliban were using but it was like a fucking Chinese firecracker. There was just thick black smoke and you could see fuck-all. So it was strange. At that stage [after getting back to the main base – FOB Delhi, Garmsir], I waited for the IRT [incident response team] to come. I remained in comms with the OC on the ground. But by now Brels had gone forward again to try to locate Botha and he had got shot in the neck. I can remember the message coming across from Tomo now. It was: 'The situation in my wagon has changed so I'm staying.' I picked up straight away that somebody had died. At this stage, I didn't know it was Brels. He was one of the platoon sergeants. He was a really good guy. He went out to try and locate Botha, who was still missing. It would be typical of any of the platoon sergeants but Brels got tasked with that and he went forward with it. At that stage, it was three or four in the morning before first light came. The boss [Major Jamie Nowell] made the conscious decision to come back to Garmsir and re-org.

7/8 September 2007

McNab: *With one dead, one missing and four injured, the situation could hardly have been worse for the men of*

1 Platoon. Captain Simon Cupples and his men had already risked their lives time and again to go into the 'killing zone' under fire to extract the casualties. At one stage, Cupples himself had crawled to within fifteen metres of the enemy to place himself in front of one of his wounded men. From there, he co-ordinated first aid, fire support and forced the enemy back using his own SA80 rifle. But at the re-organization, it was clear that Private Johan Botha was still missing. That meant only one thing. The battle-weary men from 2 Battalion The Mercian Regiment would have to go out again to retrieve him. It is rule number one on the ground: nobody leaves a British serviceman – dead or alive – to the mercy of the Taliban.

7/8 September 2007

Warrant Officer Class 2 Pete Lewis, The Mercian Regiment

The boys had just been out fighting for eight hours, but there was no lack of volunteers [to go out and get Private Botha]. We all knew that if he fell into Taliban hands and was still alive – it wasn't worth thinking about. If we had not got Botha back that night, the company would be broken [in spirit] for the rest of the two months there. So, just before first light, we moved out.

The task force that came in [to support the Mercians] went and held some of the buildings we had been holding that night, just outside the contact. And then we went forward in a series of six Vikings. The majority of the Vikings had a commander who had been on the ground that night. In the front of my Viking was Mr [Captain Simon] Cupples, who had already located the body at night but had been unable to get it back. I had a snatch squad of myself, the doc, and men out of Botha's section. There were just six of us in the back [of the Viking].

We went forward. I can remember saying: 'Fellas, if the shit hits the fan out there, we've got enough fire support from the Vikings. So just listen to QBOs [quick battle orders] on the ground, and we'll get Botha and back in.' We located the body straight away as we went forward. Daylight had broken. I got out of the vehicle and had a quick look around. The ground looked so easy and flat in the daylight compared to that night when we'd been there. Botha was there on the ground. We picked him up, took him in the back. We were still hoping he was alive. The doc checked his vitals [signs of life] but he said, 'No.'

I got on the net and said: 'Look. There's a T4 [a dead serviceman].' It sort of hit the boys in the back [of the Viking] hard because they were his best mates. And it was they who had wanted to come in the pick-up squad. A couple of the younger boys started crying, and I said: 'Look, fellas. You've just got to get on with it.' Then I covered Botha in a poncho.

But that was a rough night, all right. Initially, we

thought we were going to lose Coops [Private Sam Cooper] as well, but he's walking again now even though he's still not 100 per cent. [Private Luke] Cole is doing very well too. A lot of boys earned some good medals that night, but it doesn't make it any easier.

12 September 2007 [diary]

Captain Adam Chapman, The Mercian Regiment

The repatriation ceremony [for Sergeant Brelsford, Private Botha and two other soldiers killed in separate incidents] was obviously quite an emotional event. It was difficult seeing the four ambulances arrive with four coffins. It was quite a sight. The padre and the commanding officer said a few words before the plane arrived to take them home. We had the honour to march on to the parade with A Company, which was a nice touch. People are still mourning and it will take a long time to get over it, but I've seen a lot more smiles and heard a lot more laughter from the boys. But it will be hard for them to go out and fight again.

The last few days have been busy, however, as we're preparing to deploy again at short notice. We're taking part in a massive operation to clear an area of the Green Zone called Zumbelay, which is a Taliban stronghold. If this wasn't difficult enough, we still know very little about the how, when, where, etc., which is not exactly ideal! We will be on the ground for some time and it promises to be difficult. We've had to strip down what we can take; there's no room for comfort. I'm not even taking a sleeping-bag or this journal because of the extra weight, so my next entry may be some time away.

My birthday is in four days' time and I'll be away. So I've opened all the cards and parcels I've received. I've received lots of food and goodies, but unfortunately I've got no room to take it away with me: except for a small bottle of port and some sweets (I've got to have a treat on my birthday, really). I'm looking forward to going out on this op but it promises to be very demanding and difficult. So it's tainted with apprehension – only time will tell.

September 2007

Private Tom Dawkes, The Mercian Regiment

I've always liked writing poetry – ever since I was a kid. Whenever I have nothing to do, I've always liked to write poems and short stories. I like reading poetry too – mainly Shakespeare. I particularly like *A Midsummer Night's Dream*, *Macbeth* and *Hamlet*. But I don't really read war poetry. Then when I was in Afghanistan I wrote my girlfriend a poem – and, of course, all the lads got hold of it. Some of them gave me a bit of stick, but I just ignored it. Then a few of them asked me to write a poem for their girl-friends and loved ones – and so I did. I wrote different poems depending on what they wanted in it. Then eventually they got me to write one for the magazine. I write my poems in the evening – usually when I'm lying on my bed. I usually just write them in a pad using a pencil. Everyone's around me – I don't need peace and quiet. I write poetry most nights, but not all the time. If I'm depressed or angry, I'm more likely to write my thoughts down. Even if I spend just ten or fifteen minutes writing poetry, it makes me feel calmer and happier.

A Poem by Private Tom Dawkes

It all began on a hot summer's night
In the country of Afghanistan,
With the Battalion of stars
Called 1 WFR
To go and defeat the Taliban.

The weeks went on and morale was high,
The Taliban didn't know what hit them.
After laying down rounds
And taking compounds,
Nothing in the world could stop us.

Then one fateful day we lost good men –
This was such a loss,

From dusk till dawn,
Everyone mourned
For the brave men that died that day.

The fighting got intense so the enemy fled
As we started to advance.
We pushed on and on
Till the enemy was gone
And there we started to nest.

For every soldier out there fighting
Is doing it to stay alive.
They all want to go home
Where they are not alone,
To be back and to see their families.

We have suffered enough,
Everyone wants revenge,
So when we attack
The enemy crack
Under a force that's not to be messed with.

The battalion is hard, the battalion is tough,
The battalion is also soft,
So when our men die
All the men cry
But at the end of the day we keep soldiering on.

This is for all the brave men
Of 1 WFR,

Who have shared their love
And spilt their blood.
This is the life of all companies.

RIP all men who have died for a cause not of
   their own but to
protect the lives of those around them.

20/21 September 2007

*Warrant Officer Class 2 Pete Lewis, The Mercian
Regiment*

We were on an op in which we had established ourselves in the Fan. It was a massive piece of high
ground in the Green Zone that dominated the area
around it. It had taken us about eight hours to
secure the area. There was sporadic small-arms fire
all the way through but we took no casualties. We
spent the night on the top of the Fan in compounds.
But we had orders to move on at 0600 the next
morning.

I was fucked because we'd been up for about
thirty-six hours. I started to get my head down. I can
remember a Claymore [anti-personnel mine] being
deployed. I got up and said: 'What the fuck is going
on?' There were only two guys on sentry and they
had seen movement so they let the Claymore go –
but there was no fire following it from them [the
Taliban], and there was no fire following it from us.

The next time I got woken up was after the re-supply [vehicle] had left. On the way down the hill, there is a sharp turn before you get to the canal. Unfortunately they took the corner too sharply during the night and rolled the Pinz [Pinzgauer, an armoured vehicle] into the water. I went down on the quad bike with Sergeant Moran while the doc had run off to get the Vikings. When I got there [the scene of the accident], there was Private [Brian] Tunnicliffe [Tunni] on the bank. I checked his pulse. He was dead. Minty [Colour Sergeant Phillip Newman] was trapped in the Pinz, which was submerged upside down. There were only two of us on the ground at this stage. I got on the net [radio] and said: 'I need reinforcements.' A platoon [eventually] came down. But I couldn't get into the Pinz. Tried both doors, but couldn't get in. Whether it was the pressure of the water or something else, I don't know. But the Pinz was upside down in deep water. I went in with full kit to start with. I had Osprey body armour, a rifle and everything. But then I took them off and put them on the bank. I thought: Shall I swim into the back? But then I thought: No. If I get caught up, I'm fucked. The doc came down with Pip, the company medic. There were four of us, but there was no way we could move the Pinz.

When the vehicle overturned, there were three in the back and two in the front. Tunni somehow got out at the front [but was killed]. Whether he jumped before it rolled and landed on its roof, I don't know.

And a couple had come out of the back door and they were fine, but in shock. Eventually, the Vikings came down and pulled it out of the water. We got Minty out. He was dead as well. I thought at this stage: For fuck's sake! I had known Tunni, who had been driving the Pinz, all his army career. Minty was TA and had been attached to us all of the tour. Later, I went round the platoons individually and said: 'Have you heard that Tunni and Minty have gone? But you've got to focus on today, fellas.'

All in all, the tour saw a lot of hardship, a lot of good times. There were a few low points in it but throughout the tour the men were awesome. I took a company of boys and men out there, but I only brought men back. Some of them are little bastards but, out there, they were brilliant. I couldn't have asked for a better company in any respect.

4

Introduction: Operation Herrick 7

In October 2007, 52 Infantry Brigade replaced 12 Mechanized Brigade as part of Operation Herrick 7. The entire force totalled about 7,200 servicemen and women. During this period, the fighting continued to be intensive and the International Assistance Security Force (ISAF) struggled to consolidate President Hamid Karzai's control of Afghanistan.

The main combat power on Operation Herrick 7 was provided by 40 Commando Royal Marines, The Household Cavalry, 1 Battalion The Coldstream Guards, 2 Battalion The Royal Regiment of Scotland, 2 Battalion The Yorkshire Regiment (formerly The Green Howards), 1 Battalion The Royal Gurkha Rifles and 3 Battalion The Rifles. They were supported by 36 Engineer Regiment and 5 Regiment Royal Artillery. The RAF 15 Regiment Field Squadron and 7 Force Protection Wing protected

Camp Bastion and Kandahar, and RAF Chinooks and Hercules provided air transport. Harriers from the Naval Strike Wing and the Apaches of the Army Air Corps gave air support.

20 October 2007 [diary]

Captain Adam Chapman, The Mercian Regiment

It's been over a month since I last wrote as I've only just returned to Camp Bastion after the operation as we ended up spending an extra two weeks on the ground. I didn't bring my journal as we deployed with as little kit as possible because of the weight. Hence we ended up being very uncomfortable for 4 weeks without life's little comforts. But at least we're all back now and I'm flying back [home] in 2 days. I can't wait. It's weird thinking back to the beginning of May and now: a lot has happened.

The last four weeks have been no different in the number of incidents. The op seemed jinxed from the start and this feeling continued throughout with vehicles breaking down and other minor incidents. To be honest, I think everyone was apprehensive as it was the last big op before going home.

I had my 27th birthday out in the desert. I spent most of the day in the lead Viking of a convoy, hoping not to hit a mine or IED. I wasn't actually that concerned, strangely, which is probably a little worrying. Fortunately, all was quiet and I celebrated my ageing with a small bottle of port [illegally] and an equally dwarfish cake. I had to leave all my other birthday goodies back in camp.

The next day was the first proper day of the operation with the battle group, inserting a fire-support group on a small hill to over-watch the Green Zone. My troop were providing some security to the Royal Engineers, who were clearing the area of mines. Unfortunately, one of their soldiers stepped on a mine and it blew his leg off below the knee. He was treated on the spot by a couple of my soldiers and extracted back to [Camp] Bastion without much fuss. When I saw him there was very little blood and it seemed unreal. I felt hardly anything, just: 'Poor bastard. That's his life altered for good.' And we just got on with it.

24 October 2007

McNab: *The wife of Warrant Officer Class 2 Pete Lewis, 2 Battalion The Mercian Regiment, kept a diary during his time away in Afghanistan. An edited version of Fiona Lewis's diary appeared in the* Daily Mirror. *While he was away, he missed his thirty-eighth birthday, his daughter Rachel's fourth birthday and the death of his sister Vivienne, aged fifty, from lung cancer. This was Fiona Lewis's diary entry from 24 October 2007, the day he returned home: 'Pete's coming home today. Rebecca and Rachel have matching new outfits and I've spent ages* *getting ready. I'm as nervous as a teenager on a first date. We all wolf-whistle as our men march back in their combats. It's hard to concentrate on the speeches when all I want to do is run over and grab Pete. He looks thinner, tanned and shattered. But so relieved. Only thirty-six hours ago he was out fighting Taliban. Rebecca and Rachel run to him first, and he scoops them up into his arms. Then we have a hug – I don't want to let go. I'm crying again, this time with joy. I feel like the luckiest woman in the world – but so sad for the wives who can never hug their husbands again. Back home, I make a special dinner while the girls jump all over Pete. When they've gone to bed we sit on the sofa, Pete with a Jack Daniel's and Coke, just chatting, chilling, cuddling. Early night.'*

21 November 2007

McNab: *The Taliban has a permanent presence in most of Afghanistan and the country is in serious danger of falling into the group's hands, according to a report from a Brussels international think tank. The Senlis Council claimed that the insurgents controlled 'vast swathes of unchallenged territory' and were gaining 'more and more political legitimacy in the minds of the Afghan people'. It said that the Nato force in the country needed to be doubled to 80,000 front-line soldiers who should be allowed to pursue militants into Pakistan. The 110-page report said that its research found the Taliban controlled*

54 per cent of Afghanistan. The Ministry of Defence dismissed the report, saying: 'The Taliban does not pose a credible threat to the democratic Afghan government.'

6 December 2007

Captain Dave Rigg, MC, The Royal Engineers

It was a brilliant day. Mum, Dad and Anna – my girlfriend – came to Buckingham Palace with me so I could be presented with the MC [for bravery at Jugroom Fort]. I received it from the Queen. Everyone asks me what we talked about, but I'm ashamed to say that – in the excitement of it all – my recollection of what she said is a little vague. I was surprised at how nerve-racking the presentation was. For a little old lady, she has a huge amount of presence.

The investiture is a day that I will remember for the rest of my life, but I regret that I was unable to share it with my fellow 'volunteers'. I doubt that I will ever again experience the selfless commitment to one's friends and duty that I saw on that day.

January 2008

Flight Sergeant Paul 'Gunny' Phillips, RAF

I can tell you about my worst day. We were out tasking at about midday. We got a message to go and pick up some walking wounded from a mine strike. This was up towards the east of Musa Qa'leh. We had an empty cab and we spoke to the ops back at [Camp] Bastion and said: 'Right, we have not got any medics on board. How badly are they [the wounded]?'

They said: 'It's a couple of T3s.'

So, it was walking wounded, minor injuries. The gen was that it was a patrol that had gone out to the east of Musa Qa'leh and they had had a mine strike. We said: 'Yes, we'll go in and pick the guys up. Just make sure they're all bandaged up and we'll put them in the cab and fly them back to Bastion.' So they gave us the grid and we had an Apache [attack helicopter] with us [as an escort]. So the Apache scooted over, had a quick look around, saw where the guys were. The guys on the ground marked the HLS [helicopter landing site] with green smoke. So we landed on the green smoke: it was on a little ridge. We were facing north and we had Musa Qa'leh on the left-hand side and desert on the right-hand side. I was on the right-hand side, near the door. The patrol had parked their vehicles about 150 metres behind the aircraft. I was standing watching the patrol because there was a lull where nothing was happening. We were saying: 'Where are these guys [the wounded]?'

One of these little Pinzgauers started driving towards us. And I said: 'Guys. This must be them coming now.' There was a little dip just before the

Pinzgauer got to the aircraft, about a hundred metres away. The Pinzgauer started to drive down and suddenly it hit a mine: an anti-tank mine. I watched the front end disintegrate and a corporal was thrown a good fifty or sixty feet in the air. He was that close that I could see his right leg had gone from the hip downwards. He impacted the sand fairly heavily. The front of the Pinzgauer was burning away. I could see the guys who had fallen out of the back. A few of the ground troops started running towards the wagon and then they realized, 'Oh, fuck. It's another mine,' and they stopped.

The Apache then got a message to us saying: 'It is probably best if you get out of there.' So we lifted and went and sat at FOB Edinburgh and we had this big discussion within the crew whether to go back in and try and help them again or wait until the IRT [incident response team] got there. It was a case of some of the guys wanted to go straight back in but I said: 'Look, these guys have just had a major incident. Let them sort themselves out, patch the guys up, re-org. They're going to have to extract out of a potentially mined area anyway. If we go back in, it's just going to cause noise, confusion, a bit more panic. It's going to put pressure on them to try and get the injured guys back to the aircraft. When they're ready, they'll bell us up [on the radio] and ask us to come back in.' While that was happening, they had already got a message back to Bastion and the IRT aircraft actually went up because they had got medics on board with the right kit. When they went to pick these guys back up again, they said that the corporal [from the Pinzgauer] was still alive on their way back. I found that a bit of a surprise but unfortunately he didn't make it back to Bastion.

And for two or three days after that I was probably the lowest I've felt in my life. I'd seen a lot of casualties prior to that event, but to actually see the event itself was incredibly shocking. Not something I'm ever likely to forget. We had one killed, and they picked up two T1s and two T2s. We never went back [to the scene] because the casualties were much more serious and we simply didn't have the medical training or the equipment to deal with them.

If you're feeling low, the option is always there not to fly. Nobody can force you to fly. If you fly when you're not firing on all cylinders, you're more of a liability to the rest of the crew than not being there at all. So, if you're that bad, nobody will think any less of you. It's a very open and honest forum. But then again you don't want to turn around and say, 'I'm unfit to fly,' because it's almost like passing the buck to one of your mates. Because someone else is going to have to fly instead of you. So you don't want to let your mates down. So I carried on then even though I wasn't feeling 100 per cent. All in all, Afghanistan has been a huge culture shock. I tend not to talk about my experiences outside the military environment. My mother certainly doesn't know what I get up to.

28 February 2008

McNab: *Prince Harry flew back to Britain after completing ten weeks of an intended fourteen-week tour of Afghanistan. He had been deployed there secretly to avoid him – and his comrades – becoming Taliban targets. But his cover was blown by the Drudge Report, the US-based website, after the British media had agreed to keep his deployment a secret until after he had returned to the UK. The prince, then twenty-three, described his posting as 'all my dreams come true' and vowed to return to front-line duties. The third in line to the throne said he had revelled in being 'just one of the boys'. Brigadier Andrew Mackay, the commander of the British Forces in Afghanistan, said Prince Harry – known to his comrades as Second Lieutenant Wales – had 'acquitted himself with distinction'. The Queen said her grandson had done 'a good job in a very difficult climate'. I was impressed by his attitude and disappointed for him that he had not been able to complete his tour.*

March 2008

Sergeant Hughie Benson, The Royal Irish Regiment

Sergeant Hughie Benson, 1 Battalion The Royal Irish Regiment, is twenty-nine. He was born and largely brought up in Belfast, Northern Ireland. He has three brothers, two of whom are also serving with the Royal

Irish. Their father, also Hugh, is with The Royal Irish too. Benson left school at sixteen in 1996 and joined the Army the following year. He hadn't intended to follow in his father's footsteps until his final year at school, but he eventually concluded that a military career was the 'best option' for him. All four military members of the family served during the battalion's tour to Afghanistan in 2008. Hughie Benson acted as a team commander for OMLT [Operational Mentor Liaison Team] 1, A Company, training the Afghan National Army (ANA). Before Afghanistan, he toured Macedonia, Kosovo, Sierra Leone, Northern Ireland and Iraq. He is married, with two children, and is based at the Royal Irish's barracks in Tern Hill, Shropshire.

There were four of us from my family on the tour, all serving with 1 Battalion The Royal Irish. My father is a QM [quarter master], and my younger brothers are Sam, twenty-three, and Steven, twenty. You do worry about them but the best thing is not to think about it. It's quite fortunate because my brother Steven is in A Company with me. When I was in Sangin, he was in Sangin. When I was in Musa Qa'leh, he was in Musa Qa'leh. My other brother was attached to C Company. And he was part of Ranger Company. So when we were in Sangin it was all right because we were all in the same place. But when I moved to Musa Qa'leh, whenever I heard that someone had been injured in Sangin, it was a bit of a worry: the fact that it might have been him. We definitely are close as a family.

This was my seventh tour – I've done two in Iraq but this was as platoon sergeant acting as team commander for OMLT 1, A Company. It was my first tour in Afghanistan. I had to work closely to the ANA – I had to co-ordinate patrols and operations with them. When I arrived, I thought Helmand province had a lot less infrastructure than Iraq. There were a lot of mud huts, and a lot of people working the land and fields. I thought it must be a harder life for them than for people living in Iraq.

I was [pleasantly] surprised at what the ANA could do. Prior to leaving, we were led to believe we were going over there and they were people running about with guns. They do have an idea, more than a bit. If you have a strong company commander then that company will know what they're doing. The structure relies heavily on the company commander. If you've got a bit of an idiot as a company commander, then the blokes won't care. There are around a hundred ANA in a company. You will have six in your [British Army] team: so six mentors to a hundred ANA. I was lucky. Throughout the seven months, I had the same company commander so I had the same troops all the way through. You have to trust them. If you don't trust them, you can't go out with them, especially up in Musa Qa'leh. That was the most kinetic fighting that we did. If I asked them to do something they would go and do it. If we were in contact and I asked them to do something, there was trust that they would go and do it. But there are different kinds of trust. Would you go out and leave your iPod sitting on your bed? The answer would be no. But when it comes to trusting them out on the ground, I would.

The co-ordination, the fire-power, and the planning that the Taliban put into their attacks is unbelievable. I don't think they've got the resources to waste them. And they're very good fighters. It's the commanders who know what they're doing; the blokes just do as they're told. And the insurgency, with their IEDs, are getting better every day, which is a scary thing. I would never go out on the ground without an exact plan of what I was going to do because when they do hit you, they hit you hard. And they know exactly what they're doing; there's no rushing them. If it means them waiting for you to move to where they want you – to the ground of their choosing – then they'll wait. That's the way they are – and then they'll hit you as hard and as fast as they can until their ammunition or their IEDs are expended.

7 March 2008

McNab: *It is revealed that Captain Simon Cupples, who returned to the battle zone three times under enemy fire to rescue three wounded comrades, will receive the*

Conspicuous Gallantry Cross – an award just below the Victoria Cross. Cupples, twenty-five, led a handful of men five times to recover casualties after almost a third of his platoon from the Mercian Regiment had been shot when a force of some thirty Taliban ambushed them from a distance of only twenty metres. Sergeant Craig Brelsford, twenty-five, was awarded a posthumous Military Cross for trying to retrieve the body of Private Johan Botha in the same incident. Furthermore, Corporal Michael Lockett and Private Luke Cole, who was seriously injured, were both awarded the Military Cross (MC) for their conspicuous bravery. The Mercian Regiment, who lost nine men in their six-month tour, were awarded thirteen bravery medals.

The courage of several members of 1 Battalion The Royal Anglian was also officially recognized. They included those who had fought on 13 April 2007, when Private Chris Gray, nineteen, lost his life in a fire-fight. Lieutenant Colonel Stuart Carver, the commanding officer, was awarded the Distinguished Service Order (DSO) for the way he led his troops. Major Dom Biddick and Corporal Robert 'Billy' Moore, who was injured during the fire-fight, were both awarded the Military Cross (MC). So, too, was Captain David Hicks, but his award was posthumous. Captain Hicks, twenty-six, was killed on 11 August 2007, during a violent attack on his patrol base north east of Sangin. Lieutenant Colonel Stuart Carver later paid tribute to the nine men from the 1st Battalion who died during that single bloody tour. He said of his own DSM: 'Personally I see the award very much as recognition of the whole battalion's efforts. You cannot give a medal to all 700 members of the battalion, but my medal is to recognize them all. I'm immensely proud of them. That feeling hasn't diminished over time. The real test of our work will come this summer [2008]. I look back and see that we made a huge difference to the overall campaign. I'm not saying we won it, but we changed the mindset from being defensive to taking the fight to the Taliban.' Colour Sergeant Simon Panter, who killed three Taliban in a single fire-fight, was Mentioned in Dispatches. He was honoured in this way for his 'heroic actions, outstanding leadership, initiative and aggression that sent a powerful message to the enemy that British forces would attack to reinstate legitimate government whatever the risk'. The gallantry awards were among 183 medals announced for bravery largely in Afghanistan and Iraq.

7 March 2008

Warrant Officer Class 2 Keith Nieves, The Royal Anglian Regiment

Young Private Luke Nadriva, who got me out of the blown-up Viking after it was hit by a mine strike, has been awarded the Queen's Gallantry Medal [the QGM is the third highest bravery award for courage not in the face of the enemy]. Luke is a Fijian lad in his twenties. He was my 51 [mortar] man [in 5 Platoon]. He undoubtedly saved my life. My vehicle was engulfed in flames, but he managed to get all the armour [plating, crumpled in the blast] free so he could open the door. He had to prise it open. There is no way I could have got out of that vehicle [but for Nadriva's courage]. I will always be grateful to him.

5

Introduction: Operation Herrick 8

In April 2008, 16 Air Assault Brigade returned to Afghanistan and replaced 52 Infantry Brigade as part of Operation Herrick 8. The entire force totalled around 7,800 servicemen and women. A great deal had changed in 16 Air Assault Brigade's eighteen-month absence. UK forces in Afghanistan now used a large number of forward operating bases all over Helmand, which had been built by the Royal Engineers. These were designed to reinforce the platoon houses and provide launching pads from which troops could patrol the surrounding area.

The pattern of life in towns such as Sangin and Musa Qa'leh was far more normal than they had previously seen and large-scale construction projects, such as the Kajaki hydroelectric plant, were taking shape. However, the Taliban had not gone away and in places the fighting was as fierce as the Paras had endured in 2006.

The main combat power of Operation Herrick 8 was provided by 2 Battalion The Parachute Regiment, 3 Battalion The Parachute Regiment, 1 Battalion The Royal Irish, 2 Battalion The Royal Regiment of Scotland, 5 Battalion The Royal Regiment of Scotland and 7 Parachute Regiment The Royal Horse Artillery. They were supported by the Royal Logistic Corps, the Royal Electrical and Mechanical Engineers and elements of the Royal Artillery. Helicopter support was provided by the Sea Kings of 845 and 846 Naval Air Squadrons, as well as the Lynxes of 847 Naval Air Squadron and RAF Chinooks from 18 and 27 Squadrons and Army Air Corps Apaches. Harriers of 4 Squadron Royal Air Force gave air support, and Hercules from 30 and 70 Squadrons, and The RAF Regiment were responsible for Force Protection

April 2008

Ranger David McKee, The Royal Irish Regiment

Ranger David McKee, 1 Battalion The Royal Irish Regiment, is twenty. He was born in Lisburn, Northern Ireland. The son of a steel welder, he has two sisters and a brother. His great-grandfather served with the Royal Irish Engineering Corps and he has an uncle in

the RAF. McKee left school at sixteen. He had grown up during the Troubles and had wanted a military career since he was ten, having seen soldiers patrolling the streets and being supported by the local population. He joined the Royal Irish in March 2006. His visit to Afghanistan in 2008 was his first overseas tour and he worked for OMLT [Operational Mentor Liaison Team] 2, B Company. McKee, who is single, is based at the Royal Irish's barracks at Tern Hill, Shropshire.

Before we left [the UK], I was looking forward to the tour but, then again, I was a wee bit frightened too. We'd obviously heard the news about boys getting into contacts, roadside bombs and all that. But when it comes down to it, you think: It [trouble] can be dodged. It can be avoided if you go back and do what you're taught to do.

When I arrived, I was part of the OMLT. Our role was to train the ANA. We were training them in lots of different subjects: basic field drills, patrolling skills, teaming through their own weapons, and getting them converted from the AK-47 to the M16, the American rifle. We went out on patrols with them. We took them through IED clearance, mine clearance, room clearance, compound clearance. Our aim was that they would eventually be able to do it themselves without the British.

Some of their skills were nearly there [to a professional level] but the thing that confused them was having different [British] regiments coming in with different perspectives. So they ended up with one regiment training them to do something in a particular way and then our regiment, or another regiment, would do it completely differently. And then they would have to try to adapt to it.

Some of the ANA's soldiers were average but many of the new recruits coming in were absolutely terrible. We always spoke to them through an interpreter. Our role was to turn them into an effective fighting force. We knew it was going to be a challenge.

April 2008

Major Jonathan Hipkins, Royal Military Police (RMP)

Major Jonathan Hipkins, of 156 Provost Company Royal Military Police (RMP), is forty. He was born in Nuneaton, Warwickshire. His father worked as a car designer, his mother as a PA to a company managing director. Hipkins, who has a younger brother, left school at eighteen. He hoped to become a fast jet pilot in the RAF but failed a secondary hearing test and was commissioned into the Supply and Movement Branch in 1988. After nearly six years in the RAF, he left to become a civilian police officer in Coventry from 1994 to 1997. During his time in the force, he also became a yeomanry officer – a TA cavalry officer. After a short-service voluntary commission with 9/12 Lancers, he transferred

to the RMP in 1999. In the last decade, he has done tours of Northern Ireland, Bosnia and Afghanistan. Married to a police officer, he has two sons and is based at Colchester, Essex.

The Royal Military Police does a traditional policing role for the military – investigations into crimes, etc. But we also provide Provost support – myriad military police tasks from reconnaissance to route signing and from prisoner and detainee handling to evidence gathering. If a British soldier is killed in Afghanistan, that incident has to be investigated for a UK coroner by the RMP.

The role of the Royal Military Police in Afghanistan is often unsung but it is hugely important. There was an incident when, in a convoy of vehicles, the first vehicle hit a mine. Everyone in the first vehicle was killed. It was a Snatch armoured vehicle and four service personnel died. In the second vehicle, I had two members of the Royal Military Police who then had to get out and conduct the preliminary aspects of a murder investigation in a hugely threatening environment. Then they literally had to pick up the bits of the friends they had just seen killed and put them in their day sacks. They were scraping up hands and feet – literally. These lads were in their early twenties. On other occasions, I have had soldiers who have had to take DNA swabs from the dead body of their friend, take photographs of it.

It's hard to imagine more horrific circumstances and, for me, the quiet courage of those individuals on that day was something that is very rarely acknowledged, but is worthy of recognition. It wasn't a case of an individual charging an enemy machine-gun. It was just normal blokes doing a normal job – or perhaps it's more accurate to say, doing an extraordinary job in extraordinary circumstances. I think there is a perception in Civvy Street that soldiers are to a certain extent immune from what they see. But nothing is further from the truth. I have had individual RMP guys who have seen and done too much out here and I have had to take them from their jobs and put them in less stressful areas to give them some down-time because of the things they have seen and experienced. These lads are so young and it does affect them. I know it affects them. I certainly wonder in later life what sort of impact the things they have seen and done here will have on them. For me, this quiet heroism, this unsung heroism that never gets talked about, is worthy of note.

There is this kind of approach to life in the military where it is all about machismo – retaining that manly, macho approach to life. But you can see that some of them are hurting through some of the things that they have seen whilst they have been out here. Very often they won't talk to me because I'm their boss. I'm the person who writes their confidential report and any sign of weakness could be seen as just that. But I would never look at an individual and consider them weak in that respect. I would consider them an individual who has seen a little bit too much and they need, probably, a little bit of extra care to make them feel better about themselves. The way they are treated will reflect that. But I have plenty of people around here who are trained to do that and have done it for some of my soldiers. People are different. Some individuals will talk about it quite freely, others will bottle it up. I'm not going to force people to talk about their issues but we're there for them if they need us. And as I say, to date, I have had a number of individuals who are obviously in need of a rest.

It's blatantly obvious, because of a reluctance to go out or the fact they are in some way, shape or form behaving differently from how they were prior to an incident. In that respect I have pulled people off front-line duty and put them back into the police station in order to give them a bit of respite. But they are also very young and, for most people who are in a position of command/responsibility, it is some-thing we're very aware of out here – high stress, you know, a very fast pace of life, a hugely dangerous environment for them to work in. If you're any sort of decent boss you've got to be acutely aware of that and to react on an individual basis when your people have got something that they need, when something is happening in terms of their normal approach, which is not normal any more.

Then you need to give them the care that they require.

7 April 2008 [diary/interview]

Ranger Jordan Armstrong, The Royal Irish Regiment

Ranger Jordan Armstrong, 1 Battalion The Royal Irish Regiment, is twenty. He was born in Omagh, Co. Tyrone. The son of a computer worker, he is the second of five brothers. Armstrong was an Army Cadet until he was seventeen when he decided to pursue a military career. He joined up in May 2007, when he was eighteen. He enlisted because he specifically wanted to go to Afghanistan, which he saw as a great challenge and an opportunity to gain experience of battle. During his time in Afghanistan, he kept a daily diary about his thoughts. Armstrong, who is single, is based at the Royal Irish's barracks at Tern Hill, Shropshire.

I joined up just as our boys were starting to go to Helmand province. I wanted to go and experience the fighting. I knew before signing papers in the careers office that I would go to Afghanistan. I had seen videos of the boys in Afghanistan. It definitely looked mad but I still wanted to try it. I always got a nervous feeling just thinking about it.

We flew to Afghanistan for my first tour on 25 March 2008. I had been abroad once before – to the

South of France for holidays – and that was it. We flew out from [RAF] Brize Norton [in Oxfordshire] to Kandahar. I was thinking: This is it. I'm going to do whatever I have to do and hopefully I'll come back. I had butterflies when we were on the runway at Brize Norton. I thought: I have a long six months ahead of me.

My first impression when I arrived in Afghanistan was of the heat and dust – and how flat it was. It was flat in Camp Bastion. I'm an LMG [light machine-gun] gunner. That is my weapon. I'm trained to fire it. I was in Corporal Harwood's section. There were eight of us in it.

April 7 was a bad day. The ANP [Afghan National Police] came back from a patrol to Sangin DC. We were supposed to go out at the same time that they came back in – around 3 a.m. But the FSG [Fire Support Group] boys were firing off Javelins [anti-tank missiles]. One got fired and instead of going off into the distance it actually landed in the camp [Sangin DC]. But it didn't explode so they cordoned it off. This meant our patrol was delayed. It was good for us because we were then still at the base to deal with a major incident.

An RPG, being carried in a bag by the ANP, went off inside the camp. I think it was dropped by mistake. They had been carrying the RPGs in a bag on their backs. It blew up seven of them. Two of the men were killed, others lost limbs. It had gone off at the back of the base – Sangar Two. It was an ND – negative discharge. I don't know if it was bad drills or bad luck.

We were nearby unloading. I ran over with the others. I saw a lot of boys with their guts hanging out. There was one being carried away with both legs blown off above the knees. He wasn't screaming. He was quiet. We got them [the injured] on stretchers and took them over to the med centre. I had to pick up one of the dead boys. His back was blown out and I had to throw him up in the truck. It sounds a bit rough to throw him in the back of a Land Rover but that was what I was told to do.

I hadn't seen anything like that before [Armstrong was then just nineteen and only two weeks into his first tour]. I was actually all right when I saw them [dead and maimed bodies]. I wasn't sure whether I was going to be sick but, as soon as I saw them, I was all right. I thought I would have been faintish, but I wasn't. We had a good platoon sergeant. He took control and said: 'Get a grip, boys. Just get the job done.' Some boys were sick, though – they couldn't handle it. You don't know how it's going to affect you until you see it.

15 April 2008

McNab: *Some deaths inevitably capture the public's attention more than others. This was one: Senior Aircraftman Gary Thompson, fifty-one, became the oldest serviceman to be killed on operations in Afghanistan and*

Iraq. He died with a comrade, Senior Aircraftman Graham Livingstone, when their Wolf Land Rover was blown up during a patrol outside Kandahar airfield. He left a widow and five daughters, aged from sixteen to twenty-four. His family said that Thompson, who was the ninety-third British serviceman to die in Afghanistan, 'touched the lives of everyone that knew him'. In February 2008, he had told the Rutland and Stanford Mercury, *near his base at RAF Wittering in Cambridgeshire: 'I have five daughters, three of whom are at university. I want women in Afghanistan to be given the same opportunity as my daughters have had.' Thompson and Livingstone served with the Royal Auxiliary Air Force Regiment.*

May 2008

Ranger David McKee, The Royal Irish Regiment

My first contact was when we were out on foot patrol in Musa Qa'leh. It was during an afternoon patrol – from 2 to 4 p.m. – with the ANA. We were six Brits and thirty ANA. We went through this big piece of open ground, then past a graveyard. I was carrying a 51mm mortar plus my LMG. We got up to the graveyard and it came over the net that they [the Taliban] had spotted us. 'Get your men ready, get your guns,' they warned us. So the boss, on hearing this, decided to pull us back and get back into the base, which was about three miles away. We had noticed that on the way in there were people about. There were shops open, kids running around. But now we looked behind and everyone had gone. The place was deserted. At this stage, we knew we were going to get hit. As soon as we reached that open ground again, one single round was fired, followed by this big burst of machine-gun fire hurtling up beside us. We were in open ground, so there was no cover. All you could see was the splashes everywhere. All you could hear was 'Contact rear,' and the boys were just running to find a decent bit of cover.

Before I knew it, most of the other boys were in cover. But I was still running. There was me, my mate [Ranger] Simon Wade, and the boss, Captain [Graham] Rainey. So I jumped behind this small bit of dirt [mound] that was on the floor and Simon and Captain Rainey were in a compound firing out of a hole. At that time, I was shitting myself, proper crapping myself. I could see the rounds bouncing, literally beside my feet. And I could hear the cracks flying over our heads. It was the first time I had ever come under contact. I thought: Oh, fuck, here we go. I had to lie down flat on my stomach because the mound wasn't that big at all. And I knew that if I stuck my head up, I'd have exposed every part of my body, pretty much. So I was down. I was hoping to fire my LMG, but I didn't fire it once. Then the boss came over the radio and said: 'Get the 51 out and start firing it.' I shouted down to the GPMG gunner to give me fire support so I could get the mortar up. He started firing up towards the hill [where the enemy was firing from].

And what we could see was a [Taliban] PKM gunner on the top of the hill plus an AK. The PKM gunner was down on his belly, firing the machine-gun. The other guy was standing firing and moving about down the hill trying to get away from us. So I got the 51 up and I asked Sergeant [Charlie] McKinney what to do – because he is an MFC – a mortar fire controller – and he knows all about this. He came up to give me guidance on the target. First of all he said: 'Go for 250 metres.' So I dropped in the bomb first and fired. It came down but it landed behind the hill. So I decided to drop fifty metres and go for 200 this time. So I threw the mortar down the barrel and I was waiting for the splash to come up, just waiting, and it was bang on target. That PKM gunner would have shot his mouth out after that bomb had landed on top of him. And everyone said later: 'You got him. You definitely hit him.' But because of the dust and all that, I don't know if it landed right on him or slightly beside him. But it shut him up and he didn't fire at us ever again. So he was gone. He was out of the picture then.

The next thing for us to do was extract. There was no fire coming from our front, but we had to worry about our flanks – because we had just come under attack from the flanks. The boys were exposed on the left. We – me, my mate Simon and Captain

Rainey – were right in front of the urban area. We were the ones that were more protected. We decided to give fire out in the flanks so the other boys could extract back through us. But what I forgot to do was to pack the mortar away. I was in a predicament where I had to get people to come down and protect me so I could pack the mortar away, get my weapon – my LMG – and extract. All I could do was to get one of the lads to give me cover. He had a UGL [underslung grenade launcher] and he was firing grenades at them. He was firing away. He said: 'Right, leave your LMG where it is and get the mortar into the hard cover.' I went down, packed the mortar away, put all the bombs in the rucksack and then got my LMG. But I couldn't move yet. I was standing behind a wall with my weapons and the rounds were coming in. But in the end I just grabbed my LMG and everything and did a runner. And that was us [heading], all the way back into base. We were power smoothing: you had two [soldiers] moving down and then another two moving through you and so forth, all the way down. Just to give protection. That was really, really scary, so it was. You hear people talking about it [a contact] and you see it in the movies, when the rounds are landing beside people's feet. But I didn't actually think it happened like that. I always thought: If they're going to start shooting, they're going to hit us. The rounds aren't going to start landing all over the place. But that day, the rounds were landing all over the place. I'd seen it, the fucking dust kicking up by your feet and thinking: Oh, my God!

May 2008

Lance Corporal Daniel Power, The Royal Welsh

I was with the Royal Welsh in a sniper role. We were up on the hill above Now Zad that looks over the old town. We had all the fire-support elements up on there – machine-guns, etc., Javelin anti-tank missiles, etc. We were all sleeping in these man-made bunkers, which were only waist high. We had to crawl in; at best you can sit in them. On a daily basis, we used to get contacted there, mortared, we had rockets fired from there. Now Zad is deserted; most of its residents have been moved out of the town. We were over-watching the old town and there was enemy known to be in that area. We identified where they were hiding out in the Green Zone. We would often push into the town, to draw the enemy out into a contact, then hit them hard. We would normally have a couple of contacts.

We were out on an op one day in May. We surged into the Green Zone on a planned op. We had no reaction, really. A couple of rounds, but there was nothing to sustain it – to fix on the enemy. But on the route back one of the MFCs initiated a victim-operated device – a pressure pad – which exploded into his groin area and he ended up losing half his foot for that. This was Corporal Dan Sheen, who is in his mid-twenties. He was on a foot patrol and he stood on the device and initiated it. This was just after midday, close to Now Zad. I was nearby at the time. I saw him being carried on to the Chinook. You can't really crowd the situation. As much as you want to help you have to leave it to the trained medics. They got on with that. But something like that is always disturbing. We have been quite fortunate as a unit. We have been in quite a few contacts during two tours in Afghanistan and – not to lose anyone – we have been really lucky.

I would say I have been in five big ambushes in Iraq and Afghanistan. I have been in a lot more contacts, but proper ambushes? About five. I count myself quite lucky to be alive from that. The thing with ambushes is that you [the target] are not meant to survive. For the initial part in any contact, you are on auto-pilot: you do what you have been trained to do, like a racing-car driver does, or a boxer. You train that much that your reaction becomes instinctive. With the Taliban, you rarely get to spring ambushes on them; they normally spring them on you for the simple fact that they can blend quite easily into the civilian population – their biggest weapon. And it's hard to keep track of them. The Taliban were fighting long before I ever joined the Army. They have a lot of skilled people, they are well organized. They are always well concealed. If they were wearing uniform, this job [restoring law and order to Helmand province] would be done and dusted by now, I imagine. But the hardest part is identifying your enemy. One thing is certain – when dealing with the Taliban, I will never get complacent.

8 June 2008

McNab: *Another tragic landmark. The number of British servicemen who had died in Afghanistan reached 100 when three paratroopers were killed by a suicide bomber. It happened when an insurgent detonated a large explosive device strapped to his chest as servicemen were on a routine patrol near their base in Helmand province. The three privates who died, two aged nineteen and one aged twenty-two, were from the 2nd Battalion The Parachute Regiment. A fourth was injured. It was the deadliest attack on British forces to date in 2008 and the biggest single loss of life by troops in the country since August 2007. The 100 victims were aged from eighteen to fifty-one. Of those who died, seventy-four were killed in action from enemy fire or explosives and twenty-six died as a result of non-combat-related injuries. Air Chief Marshal Sir Jock Stirrup, the Chief of the Defence Staff, said of the 100 servicemen: 'They laid down their lives for their country and their comrades. Every one of those deaths is a tragedy.'*

June 2008

Ranger David McKee, The Royal Irish Regiment

As part of the OMLT, we worked with the ANA. But that didn't mean we trusted them all. Me and my mates said the only people we trusted in Afghanistan were the Taliban – because we knew they were the ones that were trying to kill us. Some of the ANA were a bit dodgy: we suspected that some of them did support the Taliban or, even, that some of them were members of the Taliban. There were some situations where it got out of hand and weapons were pointed.

I had first-hand experience of that in Musa Qa'leh. We had gone out on a foot patrol in the Green Zone, just to get a bit of ground orientation with the ANA. There were six British and thirty ANA soldiers. It was daylight. It was an early-morning patrol – when we would leave at about 7 a.m. and be back in at 10 a.m. But we weren't back in for ten that day – trust me.

To start with, it all went well. Then, suddenly, bang on right beside us, there were mortars being launched. They were being launched at British forces and PBs [patrol bases]. It was a co-ordinated attack. The mortars were being launched beside us but they were hitting different PBs, including Roshan Tower. When it kicked off, we had been out for about an hour and it was eight o'clock. When you hear the first bang, your initial reaction is to get on the ground, find cover and find out where it is coming from. This was only our second contact of the tour.

When it kicked off we had three different teams of ANA – one with us [the British] and the other two off to the flanks. The ANA commander got on his radio and tried to find out what was going on. He discovered our right flank had come under heavy contact – including RPGs. They were fighting like fuck up there, so they were. And they needed re-inforcements to come up and help them. But as we went up to help them, we came under contact from our left.

So we ran. It was a beast of a run: I'd say we were running at least 800 metres in that heat on uneven ground with boys falling all over the place. It was boiling hot. I was an LMG gunner so I was carrying my LMG, full-scale ammo, a pack of water, water bottle, rations just in case, body armour and helmet. It must have all weighed about eighty pounds. It was absolutely lethal, so it was.

Our first reaction was to get the boss, Captain Rainey: he was the OMLT commander. At this point we got a few rounds off. I managed to get some off. I could see clearly what I was firing at. There were people running across the fields with weapons and they were firing – they were taking pot-shots at us as they were running. They were doing the team drills that the British Army do because obviously they had been watching us out on patrols. So there was one guy firing, there were other guys peeling around him and getting down and firing as well. I would say they were at least 500 metres away from us. Light machine-guns can fire that far and pretty accurately. But it was impossible to say whether I hit anyone.

I was firing at the ones running into the compounds, which were all linked together. Me and the boss were going to go around and flank the compound. But before we could get out in the open, these boys [of the OMLT] had called us back [on the radio] and they sounded pretty scared. Initially we thought one of our boys had been injured. We had run down and the compound door had been kicked in. And we went in and the ANA were beating up a member of the Taliban whom they'd caught as he was trying to run away. They were beating him up with boots and fists. Around that one Taliban I would say there were six or seven of them. So the boss, being aware of the Geneva Convention, ordered the ANA to leave him alone. All we wanted to do was to get the ANA off him, treat the Taliban casualty and extract him so we could gain information from him. He had not been shot but the boss wanted me to patch him up. Through the interpreter, Captain Rainey was shouting at the ANA, telling them to get off him. Most of the ANA stopped and backed off, but our main concern was the ANA sergeant major. He didn't take too kindly to us pretty much offering our help to this Taliban.

He – the sergeant major – was the boss of that group we were with.

So I – the team medic – was patching up the Taliban casualty. He had a gash on his head, blood running from his nose. His one leg was badly swollen: I mean, the whole leg was massive compared to his other leg. We felt around – he was complaining about pains in his side – and there were a couple of ribs knocked out of place. He had also taken a good boot to the head, which had hurt his neck. He was young, early twenties. He was in a bad way. But he wasn't frightened – he was angry. He was slabbering [ranting] like mad, even though he was in pain. When I was down patching him, he was slabbering and spitting. But you have to take that, you know what I mean?

The ANA didn't like us helping him. So, as I was patching him up, one of the ANA came over and he cocked his AK and stuck it in my head. The interpreter said: 'He says he's going to kill you if you don't stop.' So I thought: This is it. This guy is going to kill me. I sort of put my hands up in the air. But then the boss, who was on the radio, and Sergeant McKinney came over and pulled him out of the way and told him to wind his neck in.

At that point, the casualty was still lying there and then, suddenly, we were fired on again from this compound. The boss told me to engage the enemy. I saw this guy who was firing his AK-47 from less than a hundred metres away. He was fiddling about with his weapon behind a tree. I lifted my LMG up to fire, but then I got a dead man's click. It didn't work. It was a stupid moment. I moved into the smallest piece of cover [from a wall]. I was trying to rectify the stoppage. Captain Rainey had asked where he [the Taliban attacker] was and I showed him.

The boss sort of moved around and he looked but he said he couldn't see him. Then you could hear a round: it zipped past his head and hit the wall behind him. The boss then fell at this stage and I thought he had taken a round, a hit. So this was where I started getting a wee bit scared and panicky. I was still fucking around with the weapon, trying to get it fixed. But the boss was all right – he got up, then he said: 'Right, try and get that stoppage rectified and we'll go and flank him [the attacker].' So the boss and Sergeant McKinney went round to flank him. The rest of the team were inside the compound. But this [Taliban] guy, he was persistent in trying to get me. He was firing like mad and the wall kept crumbling. I saw the wall starting to fall apart – the cover was getting small – and I couldn't get the weapon fixed. My only option was to make myself as small as I could. I sort of curled up into a ball. But the longer the boss and Sergeant McKinney took, the more panicky I started to get. I went into a stage of battle shock, so I did. I was calling a mate, Ranger Simon Wade, and he was there with his LMG and I was telling him to fire on him [the enemy], but there was a wall blocking his view.

There was no point bringing him into somewhere where he was going to get endangered. So he was there and trying to calm me down saying: 'Davey, calm down. You'll be all right, you'll be fine.'

But he [the Taliban fighter] was still firing, I shouted to my mate: 'Fuck this here. Listen, I'm taking a chance.'

He said: 'Right, I'll get on the radio to Charlie.' That's Sergeant McKinney.

Sergeant McKinney says: 'Right, on my count-down, I want you to move after five seconds.' He started to count down on the radio: 'Five, four, three, two, one.'

As soon as he got to one I was gone. I was straight past that gap [in the wall where he could be shot]. I could hear the rounds smacking into that wall. And it was just me. As soon as I hit the ground, I sat down to get my breath back and all that. There were loads of things going through my head. I just sat there and my mate came up, gave me his water bottle and a fag and told me to smoke it to calm myself down.

When I had calmed down, I got myself back to the casualty, where I was treating him. But then the worst possible thing happened. The ANA came into the compound and it wasn't one soldier [getting angry] this time. It was the whole lot. As I was treating him, as one got my attention, another one come from behind. It was fucking mayhem, they were trying to get more boots and punches in. It was me and the Taliban casualty. All the ANA soldiers had managed to come into the compound by this time. There were at least twelve and they were all wanting a piece of him. So there's me, in the middle, with loads of ANA soldiers around. My mates were trying to get in, to get them away, but I just got up and I lost my rag. The ANA sergeant major came over and cocked his weapon in my face. But what I did was I jumped up and pushed him. Very violently I pushed him. He lifted his hand as if to backhand me and he swung to hit me. But I moved out of the way. In the end, Sergeant McKinney, he came running in then. He shouted: 'Right, if you want to kill him, you have to get through me first.' They [the ANA] were all scared of Sergeant McKinney – really frightened of him. He was giving me a wee bit of support as well, as if to say: 'Listen, you're not on your own. Don't worry about it.'

One guy [ANA] now came walking into the compound. And when you saw this guy you thought, He's no happy chappy – and he always looked like an angry person. And he came walking in and he saw us with the Taliban and he saw all the ANA shouting and he came over and he cocked his weapon – with his finger on the trigger. He was walking backwards saying something in Pashtu. He was all for pulling the trigger on me with the casualty. But by that stage the ANA officer had come in: the main commander. He had heard and seen what was going on. So he went mad and started slapping his boys about, and throwing them out. Next the [British] QRF [Quick Reaction Force] came in, and everything went mad. They had managed to come down in their vehicles to help us out. I now got away with the casualty. But he was complaining that the splint was annoying him and the ANA said: 'Just take it off. Don't worry about it.' I knew the leg was broken. But they made this guy walk back three miles with a broken leg. It was quite sickening.

But as we were going back to our patrol base – Satellite Station North – we heard on the radio that it had come under RPG attack. So the boys we had left to secure the camp were now having to fucking defend it. It was a mad day! Eventually, all the fighting stopped and we did a body-count. It turned out there were three Taliban killed. When we were coming back from the patrol I was thinking: Fuck. That was crazy. But then you and your mates start joking about it. 'Did you see him falling, back there?' one of them said, pointing at me. Because I had fallen in the river, as I was trying to get up near the boss. I had properly fallen in when we were under fire. Eventually, we got back well after midday. We had been fighting through midday heat, which is about 50°C.

When we got back, I just wanted to get my clothes off. I was soaking wet with sweat. My helmet and body armour needed to come off. I wanted to have a sit down on my own, have a cigarette and think about what had just happened. I was thinking: I was nearly killed. I didn't think I was going to get out of there. I was thinking about my family, about the people back home, [times] when I was happy. All I wanted to do was to think happy thoughts.

But I wasn't happy at all that day with some of the ANA and since then I have been paranoid. After that, I was always watching the ANA more than I was watching what I was doing, if you know what I mean. Because I was always scared of one of them popping off a round and putting one through me. They're the sort of people who will hold grudges and they will try their best to get rid of you if they can. It was the sergeant major and one of the sergeants who didn't like me. We knew the sergeant by his nickname – Medoza. He was a nut, he was crazy.

June 2008 [diary/interview]

Ranger Jordan Armstrong, The Royal Irish Regiment

My first contact was in Wombat Wood, when we stayed in a compound for five days. It's just over a kilometre from Sangin in the Green Zone. We were on foot. There was a base for the Afghan National Army. We were there as a decoy, while others were building a new FOB for the ANA. They were putting their base in the Green Zone, up north. It was Friday, 13 June. We – 7 Platoon – went out on patrol in the morning, around 10 a.m. We went out on foot with the whole platoon – twenty-seven of us – and there were a couple of interpreters and medics. We also had five American snipers out with us as well. We were on a resupply route, and we went out as a section over to the ANA [base]. We had rations for them and we were in a convoy, on foot, from the base. Two days later we left the base. The whole platoon went back on the same supply route that we had come in on.

We left at 1430. We just knew, because we had comms [from intelligence], that something was going to happen that day. We had a feeling we were definitely going to get it – even though we had never been hit before. The terp [interpreter] was acting all nervous too. Our section and the quad [bike] pushed up on the open ground and that was when they [the Taliban] fired the first RPG. It landed about fifty metres from where I was but closer still – about thirty metres – to one of the other boys. They started attacking us with small arms. Then the second RPG came in. I think it was an airburst [calculated to explode before it hit something]. It just happened so fast. As soon as that happened, we started firing in their general direction, but it was very hard to pick them out. We fired for a bit. My gun [a light machine-gun] was ready – all I had to do was pull the trigger. My first reaction was to hold it up by my hip [to fire]. Then I got down on my belt buckle and started firing. I had to crawl forward, because we had got caught in open ground, and let off a couple of rounds.

We got penned down for a wee bit – a good ten seconds. Then we ran to a ditch. All the section were in different places by this stage, taking cover. But it [the contact] was soon over. It lasted about ten minutes. We didn't take any casualties, but one of the snipers was sure he hit one [of the Taliban]. It all happened so quickly. You go through the drills – which meant the fear didn't hit me until it was more or less over and then you can think about it a little bit. I can honestly say I wasn't scared because it all happened so quickly. You just had to do what you had to do and return fire. I thought, once it had calmed down: That was a bit close. But we got through it. It showed our drills definitely worked. I thought: If you listen [to orders and training], you can get through, no problem. So that was our first contact, but I was sure it wouldn't be our last.

17 June 2008

McNab: *Sergeant Sarah Bryant, twenty-six, became the first British woman killed in action in Afghanistan. She died along with three SAS reservists in what was the deadliest attack since hostilities had begun nearly seven years earlier. Their Snatch Land Rover was hit by an explosion near Lashkar Gah. Des Feely, Bryant's father, said: 'It's truly devastating ... an absolute massive* *shock. Ever since she was a schoolgirl she wanted to be a soldier. I cannot believe she will not be coming home.' He added that he and his wife, Maureen, were 'absolutely devastated to have lost the beautiful daughter we adored'. Bryant, who served in the Intelligence Corps, had married a fellow intelligence officer, Corporal Carl Bryant, two years earlier. She had been due to end her tour in Afghanistan the next month. Her husband said: 'Although I am devastated beyond words at the death of my beautiful wife Sarah, I am so incredibly proud of her. She was an awesome soldier who died doing the job she loved.'*

June 2008

Captain Alan 'Barney' Barnwell, 845 Naval Air Squadron

Captain Alan 'Barney' Barnwell, a Sea King helicopter pilot, from the Royal Marines serving with 845 Naval Air Squadron, is forty-nine. He grew up in Portstewart, Northern Ireland, and attended Coleraine Academical Institute until he left school at eighteen. The son of a printer and one of four siblings, Barnwell joined the Royal Marines as a 'grunt' – a standard Marine – in 1978. Serving in Commando units as an assault engineer until 1986, he saw action in Northern Ireland and the Falklands War. In 1986, he became the first ever corporal pilot in the Royal Marines. Barnwell served three three-month tours in Iraq in 2006 and 2007. He

went to Afghanistan in June 2008 to serve his first three-month tour there. Married with two grown-up children, he lives in Montacute, Somerset, and is based at RNAS Yeovilton.

I am loving it [the tour]. Some parts are harder than others, but I enjoy it – or I wouldn't be here after thirty years. My decision to become a pilot was conceived by an incident in 1982. I was in a minefield at night getting 'artilleried' and shot at. I decided I was never ever going to be in another minefield for the rest of my life. The only way of doing that was by being a pilot and you could fly over the top of them. So I went through pilot selection and training with the Army Air Corps at Middle Wallop [Hampshire] and, after many years of flying the Gazelle, here I am now as a Sea King helicopter pilot.

The helicopter is absolutely crucial in a conflict like this. It's the same as in Ireland in the seventies and eighties: nobody ever moved around South Armagh on the road. We are in the same sort of position here, even more so. Every road and track has a proliferation of IEDs, which can be laid quite quickly. The baddie locals, the Taliban, bury the IEDs months in advance sometimes, before they are used [detonated]. So to move anywhere on the ground at all, which is the only way you can dominate an area, is very dangerous. The proliferation of IEDs is such at the moment that there isn't a day goes by when we don't have five or six explosions, and people get hurt and killed. So to use the Sea Kings to carry the troops in makes it much safer for them to move around.

The Sea King is a support helicopter, now some forty years old, which cruises at 120 knots. It normally has a crew of three: an aircraft commander, a pilot [effectively the co-pilot working to the commander] and a crewman. The commander and the pilot sit side by side with the commander in the left-hand seat and his pilot in the right-hand seat. The pilot normally flies the aircraft but the commander takes charge of the situation, doing the map reading, the radios, and he flies it if he wants to. In its original days, the Sea King could lift twenty personnel. It has been updated over the years – including a special update to go to Afghanistan – and it is now Sea King Mark IV Plus. It can carry up to sixteen men – less than before because men now have their body armour and so much kit – and it has less performance in high temperatures. The crewman also acts as door gunner, firing a GPMG.

A military life can be tough on families. Maybe that was why my wife divorced me fifteen years ago – although we got married again. It's hard on her. Being on operations is a bit like having an illness. If you've got the illness you know what's going on and how it feels and how you feel physically. For the person who has got it, it's not so difficult. It's more difficult for those you love. It's certainly the same for us. When we're out here, we know how safe or unsafe we feel. But at least we know. And we can feel it within our own being and we can cope with it. For those at home who love you and miss you, it's a much harder situation because they don't know what's going on. It's difficult to try to explain how you feel about things.

I only joined up for three years. And here I am ten times that later. Anyone who decides on a military career has to expect that the job is going to be different from that of somebody who works in a pub, or on a newspaper or anywhere else. With the job, you have some danger, which for some people is the attraction, even why they joined up in the first place. But for most of us, once you get in the system, the greatest pull is the camaraderie, the friendships you make, the work ethos that you come across and the like-minded people you work with. It's a common enough saying – when we're out there in an aircraft, or on the ground, or making an assault or whatever, we're not really doing it for the Queen, we're not really doing it for the country, but we're doing it for our comrades: the bloke beside you, the guy who joined up, the bloke who's been my mate for the last ten years, the guy you met two minutes ago who seems like a really good bloke. You're doing it for him, whether that involves you doing something a little bit more dangerous than you would normally do, or it goes to the point of some of the extraordinary examples of courage from people out here. You've had people out here storming Taliban positions to save wounded comrades. And the reason they do it is because of the extreme feeling of friendship, camaraderie, brotherhood, whatever you want to call it, for somebody who has a similar life to you.

June 2008

Colour Sergeant Simon Panter, The Royal Anglian Regiment

The initial incident happened back in the summer of 2007. I was on an op and I lost my footing crossing a ditch and did my ankle in. We had been out in the Green Zone for two weeks. To start the op, we had to march from Sangin in the dead of night, eighteen Ks into the Green Zone. There had been quite a few fire-fights on the way with the Taliban. We had taken over some compounds and we were watching the area. Our supplies had run low. We were getting the odd helicopter drop in but there was one time they did not drop in because they got RPGed as they were coming in. So we had to do a march to FOB Inkerman, which was about six Ks away. We left at 1 a.m. We got there about 3 a.m. to do a resupply of food, water and ammo. Then at 5 a.m. we marched back into the Green Zone.

The remainder of the platoon had just got out of

the gate and I was the last man out. I crossed over the 611 [a notoriously dangerous main road], then a ditch, lost my footing and fell over in it. As I lost my footing I thought: Ow, that bloody hurt. It really did. I felt my ankle click three times. I actually thought I'd broken the bloody thing. I was lying on my back wincing and one of the corporals was laughing at me, as you do in the Army. I was like: 'Don't tell anybody. Just give me two minutes and I'll get up.' I started to walk, but the pain was getting worse and worse. At one point I almost wanted to give myself morphine: we always have morphine on us. I got back to the compound – having hobbled six Ks in severe pain – at about 7 a.m.

Because the sergeant major was still in Inkerman, I was acting sergeant major, being the senior platoon sergeant. I was with the OC and he was taking the piss out of me for being weak. But when I got back I took my boot off and got the medic. It was a total mess: my left ankle was all black and blue and swollen. The medic was saying: 'You need to go back to Bastion.'

The helicopters wouldn't come out and get me because they were worried about getting fired at in the Green Zone. I was not an emergency case. And so the CO's rover group came down to pick me up instead. I got the piss taken out of me a hell of a lot because I came out on this makeshift crutch and the RSM thought it would be funny to pick me up and put me on his shoulders and carry me out of the Green Zone. And people were taking photos too. So, of course, I didn't get the piss taken much!

They took me back to Inkerman in a WMIK [armed Land Rover] and then I was casevaced back to Bastion the same day in a Chinook. I got there, had the ankle X-rayed. They said, 'You have got a severely sprained ankle,' and that was that. Then I spent two or three weeks in Bastion trying to get myself back out on the ground with my boys. I didn't want to miss anything so I pleaded with them not to send me back to Britain because I wanted to be at Sangin. The colonel in charge of me in Bastion said: 'You can go back to Sangin as long as you don't go out on the ground.' I went on a routine Chinook flight. Over the next few weeks I sort of cracked on. My ankle really never recovered. I went out on patrol and did it in again.

When I got back to the UK in October, I was still having a lot of problems and I went to rehab. I had an MRI scan and then I had an operation. It wasn't until I had the first operation that I found out the bloody thing was fractured, after all. It was not until they cut me open that they found the fracture. So they repaired it by drilling sixty-two holes in the bone and sorted bits of cartilage and ligaments. But I'm still suffering from it now. I have my own bottle of morphine on tap when I want it. I'm getting an ankle reconstruction next. I hope I'll be able to continue to serve. My surgeon said I might have to think about a career change if the ops don't work. They talk about fusing it, but if that doesn't work, they're even talking about having it lopped off. Hopefully it won't get that far. But it hasn't helped walking around on it for a year not knowing it was fractured.

24 June 2008

McNab: *The Chief of the Defence Staff delivered a tough warning. He said that Britain could not carry on fighting two wars, in Afghanistan and Iraq. Air Chief Marshal Sir Jock Stirrup said that military operations had left the forces 'stretched beyond the capabilities we have' and that Britain could face decades' more involvement in Afghanistan, which he described as a 'medieval state', lacking even basic government structure. He added: 'We are very stretched at the moment. Until we get down to one operation at this scale, we are always going to be stretched.' His warning came at a time when there were 4,000 British servicemen in Iraq and the total of troops in Afghanistan was about to top 8,000. His comments followed the announcement that another British serviceman had been killed in Afghanistan.*

24/25 June 2008 [diary/interview]

*Ranger Jordan Armstrong, The Royal Irish
Regiment*

We knew a couple of days in advance that we were
taking part in a big air assault on the Taliban in the
Upper Sangin Valley. It was a big compound with
200-plus enemy. It was a stronghold. We were
briefed about what we had to do. We knew from the
brief that something was going to kick off and it was
going to be really bad. None of us had done this sort
of op before. It was due to last for two days. We
were up early – at 0100 hours. We were up, fed and
ready to go. The Chinook picked us up at 0230 hours
to be at our target at 0300. The chopper arrived on
time. I was a bit nervous as I knew it was going to
be hard. As you sit in the back of the chopper, from
the way you have been briefed, you think: There is
a strong chance I might not be coming back.

I couldn't see anything while we were in the air
because I was right at the back, sitting down. As
soon as we landed – in the dark – we started taking
incoming and I thought: It's going to be a long two
days. Even as we were getting out of the back of the
chopper, they [the Taliban] fired a massive
Chinese rocket at us. It seemed really close because it
landed next to us and just went 'bang'. It was difficult
to say exactly how close because there was so much
noise from the Chinooks. But it seemed really close –
landing perhaps fifty or sixty metres away.

As soon as we landed, we were on this big, flat airfield. There was no cover whatsoever. We tabbed away and then we started running, taking rounds. I had twenty-four hours of rations, five or six litres of water, an 800 minimi [small machine-gun], med kit, body armour and a helmet. It must have all weighed eighty to a hundred pounds. And we were boiling because it was so hot – even at night it was hot – but later that day it apparently reached 57°C. We kept going in the darkness and then pushed up to the top of a hill, which made things worse because we were sitting targets and they were firing at us from the Green Zone.

Soon it was breaking into first light. Then we were told that our platoon had to give protection for the Paras' FSG [fire support group]. They had Javelins [anti-tank missiles]. But we couldn't give support because we were being fired at. We were pinned down and getting shot at. Then, as we pushed up, the FSG section commander, from 2 Para, got hit in the side. He [Warrant Officer Class 2 Michael Williams] was killed. For a long time, we were just lying flat in the open ground, in the star-shaped position, with bullets whizzing over our heads and cracking with green tracer. After a bit, it went quiet for a few minutes. Then I heard a shot whizzing over my head but couldn't identify the firing point. Seconds later another fired. I quickly got off the high ground. I was snaking away. I went weak at the knees, as the shots were too close. As soon as

I got off the high ground, they stopped firing.

At this point we had roughly over a K and a half until we were where we were supposed to be. It was very slow progress as every time we moved we were shot at. As we moved, they [the Taliban] were able to engage us with RPGs. There was a constant flow of these. We had an airburst right over our heads, which was really close. This continued for at least another two hours as we were still trying to get to our compound. We couldn't really identify the Taliban because it [fire] was just coming from everywhere. Because the Paras were in the Green Zone, it was too dangerous for us to fire. I never fired one round. We couldn't. As much as we got shot at all day, we could not fire a round. That was frustrating.

We went 'firm' behind a compound up on the high ground and we could see the Apache fire its Hellfire. It was amazing and followed with a really loud explosion. The Apache hadn't stopped firing since we landed. It was rattling away with its 30mm cannon at the firing points. You would hear it firing as we were taking rounds – it could identify the firing points from the air. It was a great feeling to hear it opening up.

At this stage, we were just a couple of hundred metres from our compound so we did our best to keep moving forward. We were having difficulty, as there was a sniper about and he had us pinned for a while and made movement very hard and dangerous. Every time we moved, we could see the splashes of the rounds hitting the compounds and the mountains to the left of us. But we moved one section at a time and the FSG from 2 Para was still with us. We all got across [from one compound to another], luckily without getting hit. All we could hear were the crackles of the rounds going past and hitting just beside us. The adrenalin just kept us going and we didn't feel the weight on our back. We got to our [target] compound around nine or ten in the morning. We stayed 'firm' there for a couple of hours. RPGs were still firing overhead and we could see where they were landing. The sniper was still going and so were the small arms. What a sound it made. Exactly as you hear it in the movies. But they [the Apache and friendly forces] still couldn't get the sniper.

It was pushing on after twelve and things were starting to die down bar the sniper. Near 1500 hours, one section had to push on the high ground to secure an HLS. This was for a replen [fresh ammunition and supplies] and to take the body of the 2 Para section commander back. As soon as the Chinook landed, it took a high rate of small arms but was still flyable. We later found out all the aviation stuff had been damaged and put it out for a month until repaired.

We got replenned with water and were told to hold firm in the compound and wait it out. We had all wanted to head back that night but knew we had another day ahead of us and were to push through

the Green Zone, which we knew was very dangerous and we had never been there before. As the
hours went on and it was getting dark, we had still
heard nothing, until 2100. Then we got the news we
wanted to hear: we were bugging out.

Around midnight we prepared to move out. By
this stage there was no firing and the Taliban had
fled. As we couldn't get up the road to the high
ground, we had to go on to the 611. The Green
Zone was directly on the left. That is where
we were getting hit all day and the CO was taking a
big risk by bringing the whole battle group up the
611.

We tabbed as quick as we could but some boys
were hanging back. We made it safely to the desert
and we just about had a K to go to the HLS. The
choppers were inbound for about 2 or 3 a.m. We
were never so glad to get back to Sangin safe and
alive as that was one mad op. We were lucky: none
of the [Royal Irish] boys got hit. That was my worst
day but it was also amazing. In a way, one of the
best [days], one of the scariest. Nearly every bit of
fire-power was used: artillery, fast air, Apache. It
was amazing. And you could hear all the sounds
and the explosions. It was seventeen and a half
hours of battle. Just madness. We were met by our
OC and CSM [company sergeant major] to say 'well
done' and 'welcome back'. Joey [a comrade] had tins
of cold Pepsi laid on, which was great. We went to
bed around 4 a.m. and lay in until the afternoon,

only to find out we were on guard from 1800 to midnight. The boys weren't happy about that as they were still tired from the op.

14 July 2008

Sergeant Hughie Benson, The Royal Irish Regiment

The fighting season didn't really start until all the poppy crops had been harvested and we moved to Musa Qa'leh. We had massive contacts there. It got to a point when you were out on patrol and you were getting hit on patrol or you would hit them, either way, just about every day. Then you would come back and they would hit the base, sometimes with mortars, or indirect fire or Chinese rockets, or whatever they had. Sometimes you would have a small-arms shoot and a couple of times we had full proper co-ordinated attacks on to the PB: Satellite Station North in Musa Qa'leh – it's the most northern patrol base.

The contact that still sticks out most in my mind is when we were caught in a big ambush. It was during the day – early morning, about half past eight. We had been out for about two hours. Bear in mind that it gets light about five o'clock in the summer. We were with sixty ANA: two teams of thirty. And there were twelve OMLT. We were in the Green Zone and at that stage the corn was waist to chest high. The team that was caught by an IED was

ANDY McNAB

on the right flank, close to a canal. We were patrolling
north. The team on the right-hand side had gone
'firm': they had stopped and provided cover for us.
They told us to move forward, past them. We started
pushing up so we were about 200 metres ahead. They
moved off, then went 'firm' again – and then the
ambush began.

It was initiated with an IED attack. They used a
remote control: it had a command wire. They had
the remote about thirty metres off to the flank, so
that went off and then the electric charge went
down the cable into the centre of the IEDs. And the
IEDs were a daisy chain of twelve, which went off at
the same time.

I was about a hundred metres away when they
went off. There were six British blokes and a few
ANA that were hit. The front call sign and the call
sign behind the OMLT were actually on it [the
IEDs]. But to this day I cannot believe how lucky
they were. There was a wee lad, a British guy, who
lost his right leg. His left leg was damaged. He had
flash burns to his face and eyes. He was A Company.
He was one of the team in Satellite Station North. It
was Ranger Andy Allen. He was nineteen. He
received immediate first aid from the guys and we
were lucky because we had a CMT [combat medic
technician] with us, Ranger Kelly. He and Ranger
Fox were the first two there.

I wasn't sure who was caught in the blast. But as
we started moving forward, we were engaged from

two sides with PKM, small-arms fire and RPG. It turned into a large fire-fight.

At one stage, we were lying in a ditch and the corn on the cob was popping above our head. I had an SA80, a rifle. We also had GPMG and UGL [underslung grenade launchers] with us. The ANA had their PKMs, M16 rifles, RPGs. We're talking maybe twenty Taliban. It was pretty hairy and on two sides as well. It was fairly flat but they had occupied compounds and tree-lines, and they were engaging us from there. To begin with, we could see nothing – until we got about and could see where they were coming from. We got eyes on [the enemy]. Regardless of what was going on, the first thing we needed to do was to try and set the conditions to get Ranger Allen extracted. Believe it or not, the ANA were very good. Their company commander straight away launched teams to where he needed them to go, though obviously it was after I had prompted him. Straight away we had sent a contact report on the radio. Then, once we realized someone was injured, we sent a message: '1 x casualty, catastrophic bleeds to the right leg. Amputation.' The team that was in contact were still trying to stabilize him [Ranger Allen]. Bear in mind, we've only got six blokes, and once one of them gets hurt, there are only five left to carry him. So the team commander that was with them and myself were co-ordinating the plan to get him out.

The first thing we had to do was to get him to a

pick-up point for the QRF [quick reaction force] to come and collect him. But we had to sort that out while we were in a contact as well. It felt like it lasted for ages, but maybe the entire contact lasted seven minutes max. The Taliban then ran out of ammunition; they just bugged out back into the compounds. Back into the Green Zone. I didn't personally get rounds off but the boys did. We definitely would have hit people [the Taliban]. During the contact, their closest call sign would have been 100 to 150 metres away at one stage. Once we started returning fire, the gap then increased to maybe 200 metres – because they start retreating. But what they were trying to do was to get closer [to where the IEDs had gone off] and try and disrupt the guys dealing with the casualty. But they had no chance because there were sixty ANA and the rest of the OMLT.

If there had been no casualties, a follow-up would have been carried out. But at that stage the main effort was to get the wee man [Ranger Allen] in. I set the conditions and positioned the ANA where I wanted them to go. We created a kind of corridor for the casualty to get extracted down. He was taken on a stretcher to a pick-up point where we were met by Warriors [mini tanks]. We were very lucky again, the four Warriors had just returned to Musa Qa'leh DC and they were parked outside the gate when they heard the explosion. So they started to move and, by the time all this had finished and we had got to the pick-up point – it was maybe just two minutes before the Warriors rocked in. Ranger Allen survived but, because of injuries to his left leg – due to the infection – he has actually lost that leg as well.

Once Ranger Allen had been extracted, the ANA and ourselves regrouped and pushed north again in order to clear the area we had been ambushed in and to secure the IED location. A number of small engagements occurred on the follow-up but nothing that caused concern.

But it had been a very well-planned ambush. Twelve IEDs going off which were spread at the distance the boys normally patrol at: five to ten metres apart. But fortunately no one else was badly injured. A few of the boys got blasted into the canal. There were a couple of minor cuts and bruises, but there was nothing else. We were unbelievably lucky.

July 2008

Captain Alan 'Barney' Barnwell, 845 Naval Air Squadron

It is quite pathetic to think we were looking forward to coming out here [Afghanistan]. But you do. You get used to doing the job [in Iraq], and it's nice to do a slightly different one. And it has certainly been a new experience here. We managed to get hit within ten days of arriving in theatre. It was getting dusk and we were heading west. I had decided that we would fly low-level rather than high-level. It was my decision, but it was not necessarily the right decision because we got hit. We had just done our third trip into FOB Rob [Forward Operating Base Robinson] and we were heading back out to [Camp] Bastion with six pax [passengers]. I had made distinct efforts to cross over the Green Zone at different locations – two K between them.

The problem was the time of day we were going back. It was obviously knocking-off time for the Taliban, having done their work in the fields. And he [his attacker] had clearly got back to his basher [home] and was sitting outside, having lit the fire, and was having his brandy and cigar, with his AK-47 sat beside him, when he heard the slap-slap-slap of a helicopter zooming back across. So he decided he'd have a quick blast at us as we flew past at around eighty feet, doing 120 knots. I didn't see him on the ground but we saw the first set of tracers coming up from the five o'clock position and he must have fired. We saw five or seven tracers.

So we broke off to the left, with my door gunner trying to get a bead on it. Obviously, his neighbour, about 200 yards up the road, had heard 'Joss Taliban' doing his rounds and he thought: I can't have him doing a few rounds without me having some too. So another position opened up on us as well. But it wasn't particularly accurate this time. One went across the nose – a couple of rounds of green tracer. This time my gunner did manage to get a bead on him and he fired off sixteen rounds back at him from our GPMG.

We continued to do some manoeuvring to get out of the kill-zone. We got over the desert, where there was nobody [no enemy around]. We looked at each other, had a bit of a laugh, then quickly checked out all the instruments to make sure everything was OK in the aircraft. We checked it for vibration and there was nothing wrong. The guys in the back were by now starting to grin and get some colour back in their faces because I think it was the first time they had been shot at in an aircraft as passengers. It was the first time I had been shot at in an aircraft with small arms as well, but never mind. So we then had a fifteen-minute journey back to Bastion, where we checked everything out and had a laugh about it. We gave the gunner a hard time for only getting sixteen rounds off when he had a box of 200. When we landed we got refuelled, went to our parking spot and I said: 'You'd better get the engineers up to have a quick look, just in case.' So they came up and they said: 'Hmm, seems to be a lot of fuel coming out of the bottom of the cab, boss. Oh, yeah, and there's a hole in one of your rotor blades as well.' So we had taken two rounds: one in the fuel tank and one in the rotor blade. I guess it was a narrow escape. All it takes is one bullet in your head and that's it, isn't it? So that was close enough.

July 2008

Major Jonathan Hipkins, Royal Military Police (RMP)

Part and parcel of the job is to look at incidents in which British forces appear to have injured, or even worse killed, a local national – it's called the shooting incident review process. I look with policeman's eyes to see if I feel there is any act of negligence or criminality – in essence to see whether it's prudent to conduct a formal police investigation.

I review, in a sterile environment, documentary evidence: statements written by people who were there on the ground. So, for me, it is possible to divorce myself to a certain extent from what has gone on out there in a particular incident on a particular day. It doesn't mean that I don't find it sad when, as has just happened, a local girl, who was just six years of age, was killed as a result of a number of smoke rounds fired by mortars that were utilized on a hill to screen friendly forces. The [British] soldiers on the ground took all reasonable steps to make sure there were no local nationals in the area, thus limiting collateral damage, which is in accordance with the Rules of Engagement. And it was unfortunate. They just didn't see that there was a girl in the field on top of the hill. She caught a fragment of mortar shell that went into her chest, and she subsequently died from that wound. But she was so young and she was an innocent. War should be about adults fighting adults. It shouldn't be about kids. But at the end of the day there is only so much you can do in order to limit collateral damage. But I can sit here confident in the knowledge that British soldiers, certainly from what I have seen in all the shooting incident reviews that I have done, have taken every possible step to limit collateral damage here in Afghanistan.

July 2008

Lieutenant Colonel Duncan Parkhouse, 16 Medical Regiment

Over the past three years, I have dealt with high-energy wounds and low-energy wounds. A wound caused by a rifle round, a military rifle, will always be serious because the bullet, or the round, is travelling so fast that it has such a lot of energy, or potentially an awful lot of energy, to dump into the body. It is not just the hole that it drills through, but the energy it passes through the body. Even though the round might be only 5mm in diameter, the hole it can produce can be big enough to put your fist through. And that is purely due to the energy transfer because the momentum is mass and velocity. It's the velocity that's important when you're talking about a rifle bullet.

If you're talking about mortar shrapnel, by most standards it's travelling fast, but it's actually travelling quite slowly. But it's a big hunky piece of metal or stone or whatever, so that would cause damage to what it passes through. So with a hole caused by an assault rifle, you will often see a small hole where it hits the body, but the exit wound is huge. If it's in an arm, it can take the limb off effectively.

The wounds we were seeing have changed since Op Herrick 4 in 2006: a lot of those injuries were caused because of gun battles. They were full-on Wild West gun battles so a lot of the injuries we were seeing were gunshot wounds. There was just the odd mortar attack. Whereas the injuries that you see now, in 2008, are much more commonly associated with IEDs, booby-traps, mines, things like that. This is due to the fact that the Taliban have realized they can't win a gun-fight and they are putting their efforts now into IEDs – they're laying hundreds. The wounds now are multiple amputations, traumatic amputations. The new vehicles are saving a lot of lives, but we are finding multiple fractures, spinal injuries – head injuries due to the concussion effect of the explosion.

I am married but no kids. My wife, Helen, is excellent. She's ex-forces so she knows the score. I think for all people, the families, it's harder on those who are left behind. At the end of the day you come out here, you're fed, you're watered, you're looked after. All you have to do is get up in the morning, do your job and go to sleep. You don't have to worry about the bills, you don't have to worry about going to work, servicing the car, paying the tax. All the crap of life is done for you, so it's the people left at home who have the harder time. They have the separation, and the worry about what the other half is doing.

But we have bad days out here too. It's never nice when you lose somebody. I think we tend to take it personally, which is bizarre because we don't know these guys. We don't know them from Adam but we still consider them to be ours. We had this guy with a wound to his body. There was a long extraction [rescuing the patient] because they were TIC [troops in contact] for a long time. Unfortunately, we had to circle for several minutes before our forces were able to secure the landing site. Then, eventually, we had to go down and pick him up. So he had been down a long time and he came in cardiac arrest.

We continued doing our usual bits, securing the airway, opening up his chest both sides, pumping in as much fluid as we could. He was covered in absolute crap because he had clearly been dragged through ditches and whatever to get him out – to be extracted. I knew pretty much that he was unlikely to survive and I just realized that there was another family, in about four or five hours' time, who were going to be destroyed. You know it. Their world in four or five hours' time was going to be shattered. There is nothing you can do, absolutely nothing. And sure enough he died. But you take it personally.

You shouldn't, but if you reach for perfection, now and again you're going to be disappointed.

July 2008

Sergeant Hughie Benson, The Royal Irish Regiment

On one occasion we were conducting a route clearance. It was a road that runs south to north through Musa Qa'leh. There were twelve of us Brits – but there were another hundred Brits clearing the route and providing protection on the west flank in the Green Zone. We were in the urban desert with sixty ANA and twelve of us, broken down into two teams of thirty ANA and six of us. We started about six in the morning and at about midday all was well. The route clearance had gone fine and everyone started extracting. We were the last to extract. And what they [the Taliban] had done was they let us push through inside the urban desert and then infiltrated behind us. I say infiltrated – they never actually had to fucking go anywhere. They had just come out of their compounds, armed themselves and waited for us to come back. So at this stage we were cut off from the patrol base.

When it started, we were about a K and a half – 1,500 metres – away. They [the Taliban] were between us and the PB. So we started moving back. The team that was on the road were engaged with RPG and small arms, and, straight away, we were hit as well from the north. So we started extracting, back towards the enemy behind us. Again, another planned attack on their behalf. We started coming back towards the PB. And then we were hit by those between us and the PB – and we were cut off. At one stage, there were thirty ANA and my team lying on their belt buckles on the floor behind a wall about two foot high. And the walls were just crumbling. PKM, small arms and RPGs were all fired. A couple of RPGs went over the top of us and hit the wall. Then they were airbursting the RPGs above us: deliberately trying to get them to blow up above us so that the stuff [shrapnel] came down on us. We actually got cut off from one of the squads of ANA – about fifteen of them. They were on the other side of the alleyway – they couldn't get across because of the walls. So we RVed [rendezvoused] at a rally point. I managed to get shots back, only because we were trying to get out of there, to be honest.

The ANA in the sangars [at the patrol base] had identified one of the firing points so they started engaging with a Dushka [Soviet-made anti-aircraft machine-gun], the equivalent of our 50-cal. We had a sniper that was at the base and he had pushed up to the top and engaged the enemy. We had people coming to help us but, in the end, we couldn't wait. We had to move.

That was probably the closest I've come to getting shot. We heard the bullets coming in around our feet and they were also hitting the wall we were hiding behind. And the wall was crumbling around us.

July 2008

Major Jonathan Hipkins, Royal Military Police (RMP)

I'm sometimes asked what is the bravest thing I've come across in Afghanistan. I didn't witness this incident but I discovered that a young twenty-year-old from the RMP had been exceedingly gallant when he reacted to help save the life of Lance Corporal Tom Neathway, who was twenty-five when he lost both legs and an arm in a Taliban IED attack. I had to look into exactly what Lance Corporal Chris Loftus had done and ended up having to write his citation. His unpublished citation – which resulted in him being Mentioned in Dispatches – is detailed here:

On Tuesday 22 July 2008 Lance Corporal Loftus was operating as part of a 7 man Section of X Company, 2nd Battalion The Parachute Regiment. Whilst conducting a reassurance patrol to the north of Kajaki, Loftus' sub unit was directed to occupy a local compound in order to provide 'over-watch' to the north of the Area of Operations. A short time after establishing the position and without any warning, an Improvised Explosive Device detonated approximately 10 metres away from Loftus' position. As a result of the explosion, the Royal Military Police Junior Non-Commissioned Officer was blown off his feet and stunned. Whilst picking himself up, Loftus heard one of his comrades screaming for help and, without regard for his own safety and despite suffering from shock, he immediately went to the aid of his wounded colleague. Upon arriving at the location of the explosion, Loftus could see that his comrade had suffered traumatic amputation of both legs and extensive injuries to one of his arms. Despite the horrific scene before him, Loftus remained calm and, together with another member of the Section, carried out first aid treatment; applying four tourniquets in an attempt to save the life of the wounded Parachute Regiment soldier. Shortly after they had started medical treatment, the patrol came under attack from Rocket Propelled Grenades and Small Arms Fire. Despite the threat to his own life, Loftus did not flinch from his duty and courageously remained by the side of the wounded man in order to treat and reassure the casualty until a Medic arrived to take over. Loftus then remained in the open assisting the Medic in lifting the gravely injured soldier onto a stretcher and then onto a waiting quad bike. Once the casualty had been safely evacuated, Loftus returned to the scene of the explosion and whilst still under sporadic harassing fire, coolly reverted to his Royal Military Police role, taking a number of post incident photographs and recovering the casualty's military equipment in order to assist in any future police investigation.

Throughout this incident, Loftus displayed a high measure of physical courage and, despite the very real risk to his own safety, a resolute determination to help his wounded colleague. The fact that the casualty survived is testament to this young Royal Military Policeman's fine performance under the most testing of conditions; a performance made all the more remarkable considering that Loftus has only been a Royal Military Policeman for 18 months and is engaged on his first operational tour. He is strongly recommended for the award of a Mention in Dispatches.

August 2008

Captain Nick Barton, DFC, Army Air Corps

I have never dwelt on how many I have killed [as an Apache pilot]. We debrief everything: you watch it all [recorded film] in slow time on a big video screen. You know if there is any doubt you don't engage. But once you have made the decision to engage, then you need to engage accurately and to kill. There is nothing worse than if you rush it and you can only get twenty rounds off. You want to be in a position where you get the whole hundred rounds in one pass and guarantee that the target is neutralized.

For perhaps 50 per cent of our engagements, you probably don't see anyone [the pilots are firing at buildings or tree-lines]. If it subsequently came out in an int [intelligence] report that five women were killed in a building you had fired on, you would feel absolutely terrible. Fortunately I have not had any of those. We [the British Apache pilots] have probably only had one example of it and he [the pilot] was completely right to do it [to open fire]. They'd had two guys firing a mortar out of one end of the building and, on the other side, inside the building, there had been two women. It was in self-defence under the correct Rules of Engagement and, prior to firing, he had checked the building and not seen any women. It would be difficult to take but I suppose one must console oneself in that he had done everything right at the time. We have good squadron camaraderie and attitude to debriefing. After a mission, we will debrief everything and we will talk about it. This helps with our drills and improving our support to the troops as well as dealing with difficult scenarios.

I have been in a night-time scenario in Nad Ali that, taken out of context, could be seen to be quite damning from our gun footage. Our guys had been contacted. They had been caught in an ambush, which they had pre-seen but could not get the Rules of Engagement to engage on. They were subsequently contacted and they swiftly dropped two 500-pounders from a B1 [bomber] because that was all they had on station. They were pretty sure they got one [Taliban], but they were still tracking another with an ISTAR [intelligence, surveillance, targeting, acquisition and reconnaissance] asset. They tracked him for over a K and a half through the fields. We were on high readiness from Bastion – a ten-minute flight time – and were woken up and launched as soon as the initial contact occurred.

When I arrived on station at approximately three in the morning, I had one guy in the middle of the maize-field. It took quite a while picking him up at night. When I actually saw him, I had no doubt in my mind that this guy was one of the original men from the ambush, still rapidly on the run in the middle of a field using the high crops as cover. I was flying at about 2,000 feet with night-vision goggles on. I had all the Rules of Engagement and fired, and I made sure I did it pretty clinically. That sounds shocking. I fired a burst of twenty [rounds], then re-adjusted and then I fired probably eighty or a hundred rounds at him. Once you have caught him, once he is on the run, you make sure you hit him really hard. You just want to be professional and clinical.

We video everything we do and watch it not only to improve our weaponeering, but also to record every engagement for any Rules of Engagement questions or investigations. Taken out of context, without the background, this footage would be quite shocking in its cold harshness. The fact that we video everything does put the crews under additional pressure in a way that, perhaps, the rest of the Army does not face.

August 2008

Major Jonathan Hipkins, Royal Military Police (RMP)

We have just had an incident whereby a British forces ground call sign conducted an offensive operation up near FOB Inkerman. During that operation, they received intelligence to suggest that a certain compound was being used as a form-up point to launch an attack by enemy forces on them. They pushed a couple of snipers forward to reinforce the evidence they had got through intelligence. And the two snipers saw two individuals on the roof of a particular compound that they believed was being used as a form-up point and they saw the two individuals carrying long-barrelled weapons.

On the basis that they felt an imminent threat from that compound to them, they decided to launch a strike by GMLRS, the multi-launch rocket system. And they basically hit the compound as a pre-emptive strike to neutralize the enemy threat that was contained within that compound. Unfortunately it appears, and there is no way they could ever have known this, there were civilians inside the compound and unfortunately a female was killed. Two of her children were killed as well and two other children were put in hospital along with the owner of the compound's second wife, who subsequently lost a hand. His nine-month-old baby was also hospitalized and went up to Kabul and lost an eye in a subsequent operation.

And part and parcel of my job was to look at whether or not British forces were at fault in the actions that they took that day. So I managed to get hold of the man who owns that compound, the father of the children, the husband of the wife. He was at Kandahar hospital. He was visiting his injured second wife, and his two injured children were there too. I managed to reach him through the International Committee of the Red Cross. So I had this thirty-four-year-old man in my office in tears talking about the incident where he had lost most of his family and the very serious wounds to the rest of his family. And for me, at that one moment in time, and even now just thinking about it, I felt a tingling down the back of my neck. This poor bloke had gone through a hugely traumatic experience and I had to basically try and find out whether he felt British forces were at fault, whether Taliban were present there that day and whether or not there was anything, in fact, that we could do to recompense him for the loss that he had suffered.

It's a very sad example of the nature of the conflict here in Afghanistan. And really it brought it home to me how these guys suffer no end. British forces always try and do what is right in terms of limiting collateral damage. But it doesn't mean that I am not acutely conscious of the fact that a number of individuals out there have died – innocent people have died – at the hands of British forces. Accidents will always happen, but it's still just as sad, still another person's life.

August 2008

Sergeant Hughie Benson, The Royal Irish Regiment

We were at Musa Qa'leh – Satellite Station North – when the base was attacked. The base was all Hesco bastion: metal crates that have a cloth on the inside and you just fill them with mud and whatever you want. The ANA had a small compound to live in inside our PB. We had two huge sangars, which were up on the high ground to the north: the north-east sangar and the north-west sangar. And, from there, you could see the whole of the north to the edge of the Green Zone and the urban desert as well.

The base was regularly attacked: depending on how they [the Taliban] were feeling, they would throw different things at you. In the space of about eight weeks, if you went two days without the base getting hit you were lucky. Some [incidents] were just some hero trying to make a name for himself, coming down on his own with an RPG. And then you had more co-ordinated ones where they were firing SPG9 – like an 82mm rocket that they fire at you. You get the odd mortar round – not very accurate. The closest they got was, after about three days of being mortared every day, a hundred metres away from the PB. That was not very good.

But on one day in August, it got lively. There were only ten Brits in the patrol base at this stage because we took two people back who were being extracted – they had finished their tour. The next day we were getting two more people coming up to us. So there were ten of us in the PB and about a hundred ANA. It must have been about last light. The British sangar, which we manned, was engaged with small arms. The top two big sangars were engaged with RPG. One actually hit the front of the sangar but didn't injure anybody. And then that was followed by a full-bore attack. They wanted to have a go – they wanted to take the PB. One minute we were standing around chatting, and then we had to stand-to beside the sangar and start to engage the firing points. We all stood-to. And then everything slipped into place perfectly.

Due to previous attacks, all firing points and approach routes were marked and recorded for the 81mm mortars to engage. Everyone, including the ANA, was well practised at defending the PB. We are talking easily sixty Taliban attacking us – probably more. They came through the urban desert and the closest they got that day was sixty to seventy metres away. There was no chance of them overrunning us, but they were definitely trying to take the base. Later on, the ANA were telling us that they had heard through their local sources that they wanted to get in [to the base].

I was the PB commander in charge of the base, so I was co-ordinating the defence. But everyone knew what they were doing. In there, we had four GPMGs, a 50-cal machine-gun, a GMG [grenade machine-gun], a 51mm mortar, with 81mm mortar on call, which was used effectively, rifles, UGLs and LMGs. Everything was being fired. We had air [support] as well: an A10 American bomber.

This contact lasted three and a bit hours. The engagement finished just after half past ten [at night] – when our last round was fired. We didn't take any casualties. Unbelievable. They did, though. We got reports that they were collecting casualties. We could see them extracting their casualties through [our] night-vision. All the night-vision gets put on just before last light. We don't know exactly how many Taliban casualties they took. But I know for a fact that we finished fighting at half past ten and at three in the morning they were still trying to get casualties out of the canal. And whenever they were collecting the casualties, the ANA were engaging them.

1 September 2008

*Captain Kate Philp, 17 Corunna Battery, 26
Regiment The Royal Artillery*

I see myself as a front-line fighting soldier out here.
I am two and a half weeks into a six-month tour. My
parents [Donald and Susan] are extremely proud of
me. They think it is a worthwhile career. They think
the people they have met through us [their three
children] are fantastic, sociable, loyal, hard-
working, and have a big emphasis on teamwork.

Nothing has woken me up in a sweat [since arriving in Afghanistan]. I'm a lot happier now that I'm
out here. I think the waiting to go and all the pre-
deployment training is worse because, by the end of
it, you just want to get on and do it. I would be lying
if I said I wasn't nervous about going out and doing
the job. No matter how well trained you are and
how well your team works, going out and doing it
for real for the first time is obviously something you
can't fully prepare for.

We are all keen to do as good a job as possible. We
have been training with the company for the last few
months and obviously we want to be able to support
them as best we can. And so I hope that we can do
what we're trained to do [even] when we're under the
ultimate pressure of being in contact and, perhaps,
being tired and, perhaps, having taken casualties.

A move [from Camp Bastion to a front-line
position] can take from between twelve hours to

two and a half days for various reasons. On one occasion [on our move to the front-line], we had several vehicles break down but we also had a rocket come in and a sniper have a go at us, so we experienced quite a few things just on the move up here. But it was probably a really good thing that happened because you get here in one piece knowing that you got through that. You have to face it again but you've done it now for real and you've got through it.

We hope to push down the Musa Qa'leh valley and drive back the Taliban. Whether we stay in this area or move elsewhere, we're here for now, continuing the job the previous company did before us, trying to dominate the ground, providing that intimate support, certainly to the dismounted troops. The protection and fire-power that these vehicles [Warriors] give us is phenomenal, so we want to make the best use of that. If the call comes to deploy us elsewhere, then we'll do so. It's still a relatively new capability out here. We're only the third company to come out in the Warrior role and obviously we'll be going into a winter tour so we would expect our first couple of months to be busy, and then potentially quieten down again. But who knows? We've got to provide stability here for the country to be able to rebuild itself and get back on its feet. At the end of the day, we've got to help these people lead a better life.

The way we do business is to take every measure

possible to minimize collateral damage and any civilian casualties. But, at the end of the day, we work under [rules of] self-defence here. If we're being engaged from a building and we're being pinned down and the only way we can get out of that fire-fight and save our lives is to drop a bomb on it, then we'll do it. Then again, we'll look at dropping the most suitable bomb possible to minimize that collateral damage. Sadly, collateral damage is a fact of war and, unfortunately sometimes an acceptable risk that has to be taken.

I'm in a company of 130 men. When we go out on the ground on patrol, I'll be the only female. It's very simple, in terms of showering here, for example. On the first night we had shelters strung up with solar showers hanging off them. I went last, when it was dark. I said to the boys next door: 'You might not want to climb up on your Warrior because I'm about to have a shower.' And it's as simple as that. I'm not particularly uneasy about it myself, but I also don't want the guys to be uneasy about it, so I'll forewarn them. Also the guys in the gun troop over there have been very good and said I can go and use theirs [shower], if need be. It's being terribly practical and not making a big issue out of it and just saying: 'Look, we need to do this. How are we going to solve it?' It's a very easy thing to do.

To be perfectly honest, I never think of myself as a female captain in the Royal Artillery – I'm a captain in the Royal Artillery. Physical fitness is obviously pretty important and I aim to keep myself as fit as possible. And there's a good few of them [men] who I can beat, which is not me being competitive, although I am a little bit, but it's just one of those things that you will always [as a woman] be deemed to be less physically capable. So that [a physical challenge] is a big way to prove yourself, if you like.

I honestly don't try and prove myself as a female. I just try and prove myself as an officer alongside my peers and, hopefully, here, working for my guys as much as possible. I expect exactly the same from them as any other officer would. In the first exercise I did with these guys – in pre-deployment training – there was a reference made to: 'A normal FOO [forward observation officer] would do this.' I suppressed a small smile, and a wee bit later on I said: 'Look, I am a normal FOO. I may be female. I may need a bit of privacy every once in a while, to wash for example, purely out of practicality. Everything else is exactly the same. If a FOO normally sleeps out here, that's exactly where I will sleep.'

Being an officer is probably the most daunting and most difficult thing you do. That first appointment as troop commander is a challenge. You can be taught all the technical stuff but you can't really teach anyone how to react when you meet the guys for the first time and you're the boss. Yes, you're the boss, but you have to earn respect at the same time. That just comes with time. I remember being told during training that it's a process of handover really – from your troop sergeant who, in that interim period between the two officers, has been in charge of the troop and has obviously been with them for a long time anyway. Officers come and go, but soldiers stay, so it's a question of you gradually taking the reins. So even though you're the boss from the beginning, I don't think you actually earn that [respect] until you've been with the guys for a bit and shown them that you can do the job, that they can trust you and you've got their interests at heart. I was extremely lucky with mine [troop sergeant], that he was extremely good from day one. He would discuss everything with me and he would give me a lot of guidance as well, as and when I needed it. But he let me make decisions for myself, which was what I needed to do. So I couldn't have asked for better support.

It's important to listen to other people's advice but have the courage and confidence to make your own decisions at the same time. And it's interesting seeing other young officers who have come in just a wee bit before you and see how well they have been accepted. I saw with a couple that those who had been accepted very readily were humble enough to accept advice from their soldiers and not come in with the attitude of 'Right, I'm the officer, I'm the boss,' because that's rubbish. These are the guys with the experience. You've got to be humble enough to take the advice and ask for the advice as well. But at the same time you've got to have the courage of your convictions. It's a difficult one, but it's not rocket science, and I think it's just something that unfortunately comes with experience. You really can't teach it to anybody. You've just got to let people get on with it and make their own mistakes – and not be afraid to make mistakes.

We have to learn from our mistakes. We're good at writing post-operational reports and I know we're all very busy, but a lot of value could be gained from applying those lessons [already] learnt. We all know that the Army is very busy and we ask an awful lot of our people – and we keep delivering because it's what we're trained to do – but we need to be careful not to take advantage of this and recognize that people need a break.

2 September 2008

McNab: *I was in Afghanistan when a force of 5,000 British and Allied troops fought its way across a hundred miles of Taliban territory to deliver a huge turbine that would provide significantly more electricity for up to two million Afghans. The secret mission took almost a week to complete and was described as the most vital route-clearance operation since the Second World War. British commanders estimated that more than twenty Taliban were killed as they tried to prevent a convoy of more than a hundred vehicles transporting the machinery* *from Kandahar to Kajaki. For five days, the force battled its way through as the convoy crawled at just two m.p.h. as it carried the 220-ton turbine, 300 tons of cement, a 90-ton crane and other heavy equipment. I witnessed parts of the fighting. The project was aimed at improving the lives of many people living in Helmand province and winning the hearts and minds of the local Afghans. The task was attempted at the climax of the Taliban's fighting season and in the knowledge that a single enemy bullet could have crippled the delicate machinery and delayed the project by a year. Quite rightly, the mission drew comparisons with the 1944 battle of Arnhem and the relief in 1900 of the siege of Mafeking. I was impressed and relieved that our boys had pulled off their objective.*

September 2008

Ranger David McKee, The Royal Irish Regiment

The mission to move the Kajaki turbine involved a convoy of more than a hundred vehicles and there were over 4,000 troops on the ground. It was pretty cool. The ANA were leading it this time. We [the British] were just there as support. We were seeing how well they would do out on the ground for once. And they were amazing. I would say at this stage they were ready to do anything. As part of the OMLT [Operational Mentor Liaison Team], we had helped train some of them up and it was very rewarding to see just how far they had come in less than six months. We [the Royal Irish] were given two objectives to clear. One was Big Top, which was a mountain. The second was Sentry Compound, a village filled with Taliban. Pretty much anyone who was inside that village was Taliban. We knew the mission was going to take a week.

On the first day, we started moving down to a secure location where we could gather around in our team to talk things over, make plans and get organized. The second day we started moving – on foot. The only vehicle we had with us was a quad [bike] and trailer because of all the kit that we needed for the operation. The kit we needed was horrendous. Even getting it [the quad] over the Green Zone was a nightmare because we hit rivers, and couldn't get the trailer over the river. Then we hit bumps and ditches. So we started moving down to another secure location and still no contact. After the second day, still no contacts. That second night we hid up in a compound and stayed there overnight. Then on the third day we moved a little bit closer to our objective. Again, we stayed in another compound overnight. But still no contact. It came over the net [radio] that we had made such good progress we were going to take our objectives the very next day.

So that whole night we – B Company – were just sitting there thinking: This is it. This is the big one. It's going to go down in history. And if it is going to go down in history, then we hope it doesn't turn out badly. We knew this time it was us doing the attack. The Rules of Engagement had changed at this stage for us to go in and do the attack. What we were told was: seven o'clock in the morning, first move, and the contact will initiate from a GLMRS [guided launch missile rocket system] being launched into the Sentry Compound. So, the next morning, we were all packed up ready to go and the GLMRS were launched – you could hear the vibrations. The bombing went off and we started making our move through a cornfield. But the mortars were still coming down on top of our objective to keep the enemies' heads down so we could get ready to go in and do an advance [attack].

We were all lined up, ready to go in for the assault, and one of the other teams were giving us fire support. So they were now firing on the position we were going into. As they were firing we made our move. Straight in. By that time, we didn't even come under contact. Our other team had been fired upon but they had sorted it out and dealt with whoever was firing back. We went in – the place was just flattened, rubble everywhere. There were loads of different buildings, compounds. We had to blow some of the doors off the hinges with the engineers. Either the Taliban were killed or they had fled. That whole day we killed 250 Taliban in total. But I didn't have to fire, although there was plenty of firing done.

That was an amazing day. Only because the

mortars were commanded to land at 'danger close'. That meant, as we moved in, the mortars were meant to be landing pretty much right beside us. And that was happening. I got an adrenalin rush from this but the ANA were absolutely frightened by it. A lot of them refused to move until the mortars had stopped being fired. But we told them: 'This is the last one [attack] you're going to do. Once this has finished you're going home.' So then they were up for it and they were like: 'Yes, no problem.' So we all went in. This position was clear but the only problem there was that the other two teams were clearing Big Top. And they had come under extreme contacts because the Taliban had all these rat-run tunnels underground and there was loads of bunkers all over the place. All they were doing was running underground, then coming up: they could pop you in your back and you wouldn't even know there was a hole around. But the Taliban came under contact and they had lost everything. They had used all their rocket launchers and near enough all their ammunition.

That was the big battle. In our company, there were less than fifty men and we did that operation and even today we're proud of what we did that day. I feel honoured to have been a part of it.

We extracted back after the main battle was done. We stayed in the compound that we stayed in the previous [third] night. But the compounds were getting hit like crazy. At one stage, I was on the roof with no body armour or helmet on because we thought it was all done. Me and the boss, we were up on the roofs of the compounds taking photos and taking videos. And the next thing you know, you could hear the cracks of machine-gun fire. My initial reaction was: 'I'm getting the hell off this roof.' Usually, you got off using the ladder but I jumped off it and landed on my knees, while the boss lay down on the roof. It was just crazy. From then on, we were getting hit every single night but on the sixth night we decided: 'Right, we're leaving.'

As we were leaving, the Apaches came in, the Black Hawks [US utility helicopters] came in. And they just started firing all over the area so we could move out [to provide cover from a Taliban attack]. It was cluster-fuck trying to get everyone out. From our base, there were at least 450 troops on the ground, and trying to get 450 troops moved back in at once was a nightmare. This was moving back into the big base where the [Kajaki] turbine had been taken to. Then we went back up to the dam and everyone was jumping into the water [with delight]. Everyone was taking a dive off the dam. It was brilliant. It was clear blue, proper clear blue, water. And all the boys wanted to do was to go for a swim – and there were big jumps. This was day seven. This was us getting a breather. A bit of fucking down-time. Enjoying ourselves. Having a laugh. The turbine had arrived and the mission had been accomplished.

7 September 2008

McNab: *I made the news by launching a scathing public attack on the British government's treatment of its troops. My comments came after a poll revealed that two-thirds of the public thought the level of care for servicemen was 'disgraceful'. I had commissioned the ICM poll, which found that three-quarters of the 3,040 adults questioned believed the Ministry of Defence did not support troops once they were discharged. In the first poll of its kind, the survey found that 76 per cent believed the government's commitment to the psychological care of veterans was 'inadequate'. Almost half (49 per cent) of those questioned said they would be willing to pay an extra penny in income tax to help former servicemen with financial difficulties. I said at the time: 'What we have at the moment is a time-bomb of post-traumatic stress disorder that will go off in the next ten to fifteen years in people who have experienced the horrors of the current conflicts. It annoys me that we continually get politicians of all persuasions jumping on the back of military success only for the same politicians not to back them [servicemen] with money when they leave.'*

September 2008

Captain Alan 'Barney' Barnwell, 845 Naval Air Squadron

Early in September my crew was back in Camp Bastion as the Sea King HRF [Helmand Reaction

Force] once again. This is usually an arduous seven-day duty with minimum sleep, and maximum coffee, but everyone likes it as you get interesting and crucial tasks, which give a great sense of satisfaction when completed. Also it has some autonomy, where you can make a certain amount of your own decisions rather than implementing someone else's. It exercises your thinking muscles. The down-side is that throughout the day you are at thirty mins' notice to move and at night sixty mins'. Often we were airborne much quicker, especially when escorting the CH47 MERT [Chinook medical team].

This particular day in question, the second tasking Sea King from Kandahar was unserviceable so we were tasked to pick up some under-slung loads [USL], one from Bastion to Garmsir and then back to Lashkar Gah to pick up another to return to Camp Bastion. The other Sea King would act as escort. Under-slung loads are very useful for carrying over-sized stores and in the past I had carried 105mm light guns, even old Land Rovers. But in Afghanistan the altitude and the high summer temperatures have a debilitating effect on the aircraft's performance so the loads must be carefully weighed and the aircraft performance calculations, which include fuel carried, must be diligently made. The distance to the first drop-off was about forty-five miles, then twenty-five to Lash and then pick up some ammo. We would be really light by then and the twenty miles back to Bastion would be a piece of piss.

I calculated the weights, speed about 60–70 knots with a USL, distances, timings, etc. It would be tight but we could make it. The load, we were told, was support weapons for the FOB, so it was high priority. We briefed as a section with the other aircraft crew as usual and got the latest int update for the areas we were going to: Nad Ali and Marhja were pretty hot again with probable AAA [enemy artillery] nearby. I was not overly concerned as we planned to give them a wide berth even though they were on our direct track. We lifted from the spots and headed to the load park 500 metres away. Usually it is the CH47 [Chinook] which does the USL as they have a much greater capacity, so I was hoping the load team had got the load right.

When we got to the load, they didn't seem to be surprised it was a Sea King, which was a good start. Not so good was this mountain of boxes they had in the net for us to lift! The load was the size of a small caravan. I was a bit concerned: if it was as heavy as it was large we would never get it airborne. It was still only 7 a.m. – not too hot – so we had a bit more power than usual. So we set up to give it a go. The load was hooked up and we gingerly raised the collective. As we reached max power, it slowly lifted up. Petchy, my co-pilot, was flying the smoothest he ever had to coax the lumbering beast into the air. We continued to rise at an infinitesimal

ANDY McNAB

rate, and as we transitioned into wind I realized we did not have enough air speed to turn and therefore would have to fly over the camp. Apart from it being against standing orders, there was the matter of the caravan-type load underneath and its refusal to fly like an aircraft. If it became uncontrollable, I would have to jettison it. Not a great idea when flying over the accommodation tents of a Para battalion. They might not take too kindly to being flattened by some boot-neck who can't fly properly.

The seconds ticked slowly by and we passed over the camp fence on our way south. As we struggled higher, we realized our load was bulky rather than heavy, which has its own problems. As we accelerated, the load started to swing: this made the whole helicopter stutter from side to side. To stop this we had to slow down. I thought: It must be Petchy – he can't fly for toffee! So I took control. Shit! It felt horrible. Every time we went past forty-five knots, it felt like some enormous hand was grabbing us from underneath and pushing us from side to side. We were about a third of the way there. The stores were important, and I didn't want to fail the task. 'No, we won't turn back,' I said to myself. I recalculated time and distance, recalculated fuel. Well, if we went straight over Nad Ali and Marhja, we could still make it. As we approached Nad Ali, an Apache called that he was in contact. I thought: Shit. OK, we need to avoid that area. Try to increase speed. Shit, more oscillations. How bad do I need to drop the load? I can't, important stores. Shit.

Travelling around Helmand province at 2,000 feet above ground at forty-five knots with a caravan-like load underneath was starting to feel like I was walking around Leicester Square naked with a target pinned to my arse saying: 'Kick me!' In short, decidedly uncomfortable. I thought: New plan. Let's get the load to Garmsir. Then we'll have to divert, get some fuel at the Yanks' place and carry on to Lash. OK, we'll be about an hour and a half behind schedule but we'll get the job done as long as we get to Garmsir without being shot down.

Eventually we dropped off the load and headed for the diversion and refuel, landing on at our minimum allowed fuel. We only took on enough to get back to Bastion as we had a load at Lash to pick up. Hope this one isn't a caravan, I thought. We routed to Lash, feeling particularly proud and happy. We had achieved part one and we were now doing 120 knots again. We lined up for our approach into Lash, zooming past the rooftops just feet below at full speed making a tactical arrival. Coming over the fence, I saw the load by the first HLS [helicopter landing site] spot. Phew, that one's not too big and the empty ammo cases should fly well, I thought. We set ourselves in the hover, hooked on, and the marshaller indicated us to lift. We pulled up the collective, and more. We were now at a forty-foot hover, nicely above the protected walls but going nowhere. I thought: More power. We're at maximum.

Try a smidge more. Watch the temperatures. But there wasn't a single movement of the load, not a millimetre. 'Shit! Put her down, Petchy,' I said. The poor Sea King had been wheezing like an asthmatic at the end of a marathon. This load was going nowhere by Sea King: the 'empty' ammo boxes were full! We gave our best sorry expressions, dropped the load hook and made a quick departure. We landed back at Bastion and debriefed the Ops Room on what had happened, then went back to our tent for coffee. It was only 10 a.m.: lots of time left for more fun that day.

Epilogue by Andy McNab

I was working in America in November 2008 when a friend emailed me with some sad news. Captain Kate Philp, whom I had interviewed for this book in Afghanistan a couple of months earlier, had been involved in a tragic incident. The *Sun* had revealed that a large roadside bomb, believed to contain some fifty kilos of explosive, had gone off next to her 25-ton Warrior 'mini tank'. Kate's left foot was blown apart, which meant she became the first woman soldier to lose a limb since the 'war on terror' in Afghanistan had begun in 2001. Furthermore, she is believed to be the first woman in the British Army to become a combat amputee.

There was even worse news for another family. The blast had killed Gurkha Colour Sergeant Krishna Dura, thirty-six, as well as injuring two more soldiers. The patrol had been going to pick up a sniper team when they were attacked near Musa

Qa'leh. The large bomb was the first to penetrate a Warrior in Helmand province.

Kate's company commander told the *Sun*: 'We remain in awe of the courage and selflessness with which she has met this tragic event.' A senior military source added: 'Kate has not complained at all about what has happened to her and does not regret a moment of her military service.' Donald and Susan Philp, her parents, told the newspaper: 'Her morale is extremely high, thanks to her enormous courage and determination, but also thanks to the wonderful care she has received.' In a prepared statement, Kate added: 'My thoughts and condolences go to the family of Colour Sergeant Krishna and to those who were also injured in the attack. And my deepest thanks go to the medical staff and others in Afghanistan and UK who have taken such great care of me.' As Kate was treated in Birmingham's Selly Oak Hospital, her visitors included the Prince of Wales. I was glad to learn recently from her father that Kate is making good progress as she recovers from her serious injuries.

There is promising news, too, about another injured soldier. Ranger Andrew Allen, who lost both his legs after being hit by an improvised explosive device (IED) in July 2008, is continuing his recovery. However, he has also had to have an operation on his eyes. He had lost his sight but, following the surgery, it is coming back slowly. His friend, Sergeant Hughie Benson, told me: 'I recently picked

Ranger Allen up so he could attend the medals parade [at the Tern Hill barracks in Shropshire] and receive his Afghanistan service medal. I picked him up in a hire car. He was in a wheelchair. His eyes were completely closed over then. He couldn't see. I arrived down at Headley Court [rehabilitation centre in Surrey] about six in the morning and he was sitting there with his combats on, finishing his breakfast and ready to go. He asked me why I was late because I was supposed to be there at half five. It was a three-hour drive there and a three-hour drive back. Ranger Allen sat in the front with me. He talked for the first ten minutes, then fell asleep.

'When we arrived, his girlfriend was waiting in the Naafi. I walked him out in his wheelchair at the parade. The regimental colonel presented him with his medal. He paraded with the company after that so he was with all his mates. Then we went up to the Naafi, met up with his girlfriend again. He asked her to marry him and she said yes. He is learning to walk again and his girlfriend, who lives in Belfast, has just had a baby boy – their first child. It's all good. If it was me, I would be in turmoil, but the way he is getting about and conducting himself is unbelievable. He is a brave wee man.'

I will sign off with some more cheery news. In the Queen's New Year's Honours List for 2009, Major Hugh Benson QM, the father of Sergeant Hughie Benson, received an MBE. Sergeant Benson himself later received a Mention in Dispatches (MID) in the operation honours for Operation Herrick 8. The Bensons deserve public recognition for their bravery and service. With Major Benson and his three sons all still serving, this is undoubtedly a family that has done Britain proud.

Glossary

AAA: Anti-aircraft Artillery
A&E: Accident and Emergency
AH: attack helicopter
AK-47: assault rifle
ANA: Afghan National Army
ANP: Afghan National Police
Apache: attack helicopter
A-10: US close-air-support jet
Bastion/Camp Bastion: the main British base in Helmand province
BDA: battle damage assessment
bergen: rucksack
BFBS: British Forces Broadcasting Service
Black Hawk: US utility helicopter
blue on blue: friendly fire
BRF: brigade recce force
B1s/B1Bs: US bomber aircraft
cam: camouflage
CAS: close air support

Chinook: support helicopter

CIMIC: Civil Military Co-operation

Civvy: civilian

Claymore: directional anti-personnel mine

CMT: combat medical technician

comms: communications

contact: fire-fight between rival forces

CO: commanding officer

CP: command post

C/S: call sign

CSE: Combined Services Entertainment

DA: duty aviator

DFC: Distinguished Flying Cross

DPM: disruptive pattern material

DSM: Distinguished Service Medal

Dushka: Soviet-made heavy machine-gun

D&V: diarrhoea and vomiting

FAC: forward air controller

FOB: forward operating base

FOO: forward observation officer

FPM: force provost marshal

Friendlies: troops fighting on the same side

FSG: Fire Support Group

FST: Fire Support Team

GMG: grenade machine-gun

GMLRS: guided multiple launch rocket system

GMPG: general-purpose machine-gun

GPD: general police duties

GPS: global positioning system

Harrier: UK close-air-support aircraft

Hercules: transport aircraft

HLS: helicopter landing site

HQ: headquarters

HRF: Helmand Reaction Force

IDP: internally displaced people

IED: improvised explosive device

ILAW: interim light anti-tank weapon

int: intelligence

IRT: Incident Response Team

ISAF: International Security Assistance Force

ISTAR: intelligence, surveillance, target, acquisition
    and reconnaissance

Javelin: anti-tank missile

JTAC: joint terminal air controller

K: kilometre

LMG: light machine-gun

LOE: limit of exploitation

LS: landing site

MC: Military Cross

MC: multiple commander

MERT: medical emergency response team

MFC: mortar fire controller

MID: Mentioned In Dispatches

mini-gun: six-barrelled Gatling-style gun

minimi: light machine-gun

MoD: Ministry of Defence

MOG: Manoeuvre Outreach Group

MPS: Military Provost Service

M60: machine-gun (US)

NCO: non-commissioned officer

net: radio network

OC: officer commanding

ODP: operating-department practitioner

OMLT: Operational Mentor Liaison Team

op: military operation

OP: observation post

PB: patrol base

Pinzgauer: armoured vehicle

PKM: machine-gun (Russian)

Predator: unmanned aircraft

PsyOps: Psychological Operations

QBO: quick battle order

QGM: Queen's Gallantry Medal

QM: Quartermaster

QRF: Quick Reaction Force

RC: regional command

replen: replenishment

RHA: Royal Horse Artillery

RMP: Royal Military Police

RPG: rocket-propelled grenade

RQMS: Regimental Quartermaster Sergeant

RSM: regimental sergeant major

RSOI: reception, staging and onward integration

RTA: road traffic accident

RV: rendezvous

R&R: rest and recuperation

sangar: small fortified position

Saxon: armoured vehicle

SA80: assault rifle

shura: meeting

GLOSSARY

SF: Special Forces
SIB: Special Investigations Branch
sit rep: situation report
Snatch: lightly armoured Land Rover
TA: Territorial Army
tac: tactical group on the ground
TADS: targeting acquisition designating sight
TIC: troops in contact
TQ: theatre qualification
TSM: troop sergeant major
T1: critically injured casualty
T2: seriously injured casualty
T3: walking wounded casualty
T4: dead casualty
UAV: unmanned aerial vehicle
UGL: under-slung grenade launcher
U/S: unserviceable
USL: under-slung loads
Viking: tracked armoured protected vehicle
wadi: riverbed
Warrior: mini tank
WMIK: armed Land Rover
WO: warrant officer
WRAC: Women's Royal Army Corps
YTS: Youth Training Scheme
2IC: second in command

Nick Stone, ex–SAS trooper, now gun–for–hire working on deniable ops for the British government, is the perfect man for the dirtiest of jobs, doing whatever it takes by whatever means necessary…

REMOTE CONTROL
⊞ Dateline: Washington DC, USA

Stone is drawn into the bloody killing of an ex–SAS officer and his family and soon finds himself on the run with the one survivor who can identify the killer – a nine-year-old girl.

> 'Proceeds with a testosterone surge'
> *Daily Telegraph*

CRISIS FOUR
⊞ Dateline: North Carolina, USA

In the backwoods of the American South, Stone has to keep alive the beautiful young woman who holds the key to unlock a chilling conspiracy that will threaten world peace.

> 'When it comes to thrills, he's Forsyth class'
> *Mail on Sunday*

FIREWALL
⊞ Dateline: Finland

The kidnapping of a Russian Mafia warlord takes Stone into the heart of the global espionage world and into conflict with some of the most dangerous killers around.

> 'Other thriller writers do their research, but McNab has actually been there'
> *Sunday Times*

LAST LIGHT
⊞ **Dateline: Panama**

Stone finds himself at the centre of a lethal conspiracy involving ruthless Colombian mercenaries, the US government and Chinese big business. It's an uncomfortable place to be ...

> 'A heart thumping read'
> *Mail on Sunday*

LIBERATION DAY
⊞ **Dateline: Cannes, France**

Behind its glamorous exterior, the city's seething underworld is the battleground for a very dirty drugs war and Stone must reach deep within himself to fight it on their terms.

> 'McNab's great asset is that the heart of his fiction is non–fiction'
> *Sunday Times*

DARK WINTER
⊞ **Dateline: Malaysia**

A straightforward action on behalf of the War on Terror turns into a race to escape his past for Stone if he is to save himself and those closest to him.

> 'Addictive ... Packed with wild action and revealing tradecraft'
> *Daily Telegraph*

DEEP BLACK
✠ Dateline: Bosnia

All too late Stone realizes that he is being used as bait to lure into the open a man whom the darker forces of the West will stop at nothing to destroy.

> 'One of the UK's top thriller writers'
> *Daily Express*

AGGRESSOR
✠ Dateline: Georgia, former Soviet Union

A longstanding debt of friendship to an SAS comrade takes Stone on a journey where he will have to risk everything to repay what he owes, even his life . . .

> 'A terrific novelist'
> *Mail on Sunday*

RECOIL
✠ Dateline: The Congo, Africa

What starts out as a personal quest for a missing woman quickly becomes a headlong rush from his own past for Stone.

> 'Stunning . . . A first class action thriller'
> *The Sun*

CROSSFIRE
⊞ **Dateline: Kabul**

Nick Stone enters the modern day wild west that is Afghanistan in search of a kidnapped reporter.

> 'Authentic to the core . . .
> McNab at his electrifying best'
> *Daily Express*

BRUTE FORCE
⊞ **Dateline: Tripoli**

An undercover operation is about to have deadly long term consequences...

> 'Violent and gripping, this is classic McNab'
> *News of the World*

EXIT WOUND
⊞ **Dateline: Dubai**

Nick Stone embarks on a quest to track down the killer of two ex-SAS comrades.

> 'Could hardly be more topical...
> all the elements of a McNab novel are here'
> *Mail on Sunday*

DropZone by
ANDY McNAB

**An extreme new series for teens,
packed with action, intrigue – and skydiving!**

Everything changed the day seventeen-year-old
Ethan Blake saw the guy B.A.S.E. jump from the top
of his block of flats.

Now Ethan is part of an elite skydive team, but
there's more going on than meets the eye. The team
is involved in dangerous covert operations. In a life
or death situation – does Ethan have what it takes?

*Sometimes you just have to take a deep breath,
and JUMP . . .*

Doubleday 978 0 38561 710 9

The BOY SOLDIER series by
ANDY McNAB

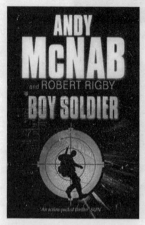

Corgi 978 0 55255 221 9

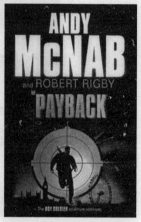

Corgi 978 0 55255 222 6

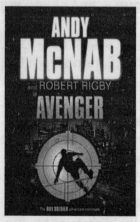

Corgi 978 0 55215 044 6

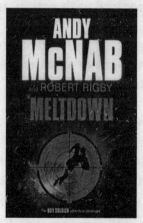

Corgi 978 0 55255 224 0

Packed with breathtaking action, SAS procedures and surveillance and survival techniques, this is a fast-moving, action-packed series for teenagers.